THE ARMY
UNDER FIRE

CONFLICTING WORLDS

New Dimensions of the American Civil War

T. Michael Parrish, Series Editor

THE ARMY UNDER FIRE

THE POLITICS OF ANTIMILITARISM
IN THE CIVIL WAR ERA

CECILY N. ZANDER

LOUISIANA STATE UNIVERSITY PRESS ▐▐ BATON ROUGE

Published by Louisiana State University Press
lsupress.org

Designer: Barbara Neely Bourgoyne
Typeface: Sentinel

Graphs created by the author.

Jacket illustration: "Food for the Tricky 'Statesman,' and Death to
our Honorable Army," *Harper's Weekly*, February 19, 1876.

Library of Congress Cataloging-in-Publication Data
Names: Zander, Cecily N., author.
Title: The Army under fire : the politics of antimilitarism in the Civil
    War era / Cecily N. Zander.
Other titles: Politics of antimilitarism in the Civil War era
Description: Baton Rouge : Louisiana State University Press, 2024. |
    Series: Conflicting worlds: new dimensions of the American Civil War |
    Includes bibliographical references and index.
Identifiers: LCCN 2023031569 (print) | LCCN 2023031570 (ebook) |
    ISBN 978-0-8071-8140-9 (cloth) | ISBN 978-0-8071-8188-1 (pdf) |
    ISBN 978-0-8071-8187-4 (epub)
Subjects: LCSH: United States—Politics and government—1861–1865. |
    United States—Politics and government—1865–1877. | Republican Party
    (U.S. : 1854–)—Influence. | Militarism—United States—History—19th
    century. | United States—History, Military—19th century. | West (U.S.)—
    History, Military—19th century. | United States—History—Civil War,
    1861–1865—Influence. | United States. Army—History.
Classification: LCC E661 .Z36 2024 (print) | LCC E661 (ebook) | DDC
    973.8—dc23/eng/20231103
LC record available at https://lccn.loc.gov/2023031569
LC ebook record available at https://lccn.loc.gov/2023031570

for Mom and Dad

CONTENTS

ACKNOWLEDGMENTS

Lacking any other way to begin these acknowledgments, I will offer an apology for bringing yet another book about the American Civil War era into this world. This apology is mostly for my parents and for my brother, who have helped me move thousands of Civil War books across thousands of miles more than a few times over the past decade. Without them this book would not exist, and for that I am forever grateful. But more on that later.

I'll begin by thanking the team at LSU Press, who welcomed this project and answered every first-time author question I threw at them with tremendous patience. I am grateful to the anonymous reader who pointed out flaws in my argumentation and prompted me to think more clearly about what I really wanted to say. Thanks to Editor in Chief Rand Dotson, for his efficiency and care. And thanks to T. Michael Parrish, who edits the Conflicting Worlds: New Dimensions of the American Civil War series for the press, for his encouragement and his careful reading of the manuscript.

History books cannot exist without archives, and I am grateful to have received support to undertake research for this project across the country. To the efficient and supportive archivists and staff at the Huntington Library, the University of Oklahoma's Western History Collections, the Dolph Briscoe Center for American History at the University of Texas, the Clements Center and the DeGolyer Library at SMU, and the Filson Historical Society: thank you for helping me to find the materials that make up this book. And thank you to the U.S. Army Center of Military History, which helped support nine thousand miles of cross-country travel in 2019 and 2020.

When I graduated from high school in 2012, I turned my back on the American West, leaving behind the towering Rocky Mountains of the Colorado Front Range for the less imposing edifices of Virginia's Blue Ridge Mountains. I did not arrive at the University of Virginia intending to be a history major. In fact, I declared a major in classics, before running in fear from declensions and endless confusion over the ablative. History, it turned out, was more my speed—and the passages from Cicero and Caesar referenced in Nau Hall had already been translated into English. The History Department at UVA became my home away from home—and I like to think that many of the faculty members who tolerated my enthusiasm and overlong office visits have since become good friends. On that score, thank you, especially, to Elizabeth Meyer, J. E. Lendon, and Paul J. E. Kershaw for your steadfast support and your superb teaching. Lingering in Charlottesville and memories of undergraduate days, thanks also to Adrienne V. Ghaly and Lego-master George for your kindnesses, sandwiches, and friendship, and many fond memories of time spent with you all and with Bear.

From Charlottesville I set out for Happy Valley, knowing there were few places as suited to studying the Civil War era as Penn State University. The History Department underwent immense change during my six years in State College and I am grateful to have had the chance to work with so many excellent historians, and to see so many of my graduate school colleagues become amazing teachers, researchers, and writers. Thanks to Kathryn Salzer, Alicia Decker, and Christina Snyder, all of whom offered incisive feedback that helped shape this book and gave generously of their time to read my work. Though I was never fortunate enough to take a class with Carol Reardon, I was honored to spend many happy hours traversing battlefields and talking about tactics, leadership, and strategy with her during my years at Penn State. I will always be thankful for the trail she blazed for women in the field of military history. And while he left PSU early in my time there, I am also grateful to Ari Kelman for the kindness he showed an overeager first-year graduate student, and for his continued support of my work.

Graduate school would not be possible without friends who understand the challenges of archival work, long writing days, and constant revisions. I feel very lucky to have found friends who understood these trials and tribulations at both Penn State and UVA. For his unfailing ability to meet every situation with a smile, thanks to Brian Neumann. For her passion for making wonderful food and ensuring anyone she meets feels at home, thanks to Alice King. For sharing the ups and downs of supporting Arsenal and loving historical minutiae as much as I do, thanks to Clayton Butler. For tolerating history and demonstrating how to try to make the world a little bit better every day, thanks to Shira Lurie. And to Mallory Huard and Carolyn Levy, for always being there when this Duckling has needed a friend, thank you more than I can say. With love, too, for Annabelle, and Sebastian, and Hazel.

I would be hard-pressed to imagine a better place to be a postdoc than the Center for Presidential History at Southern Methodist University. I have been so lucky to have found a community with other recent PhDs—Paul Berringer, Amy Zanoni, Monica Blair, Sarah Nelson, Jonathan Ng, Ashlyn Hand (and Mark!), Augusta Dell'Omo, and Camille Davis—who have read my work, given kind and constructive feedback, and helped me celebrate new accomplishments at every turn. My two years at the CPH have also convinced me that the world needs more people like Brian Franklin, a sterling scholar and better friend, who made Dallas feel like home from the minute I set foot in Texas. The world also needs more women like Ronna Spitz, who accomplishes every task with an efficiency I can only dream of approaching. Finally, and I promise I'm not mentioning him last just to annoy him, thanks to Jeff Engel for taking a chance on a nineteenth-century historian. And thank you for offering us all the space and time to read and write and remember to find joy in doing good history. From my perspective, it is one of the best gifts I've ever been given.

It is a fortunate thing to be a Civil War historian, if only because of the community of scholars who welcome newcomers to the field and champion their work. My work and my passion for studying this era of American history have benefited tremendously from conversations with historians whose work I have long admired. Joan Waugh, Jim Marten, Peter Carmichael, and Carrie Janney have always found time to talk with me about my research or to offer career advice, despite being four of the busiest people in the profession. Chris Mackowski and the kind folks at Emerging Civil War have made me feel welcome in their community of top-notch public historians. Patrick Kelly and Elizabeth Varon agreed to participate in a workshop and provide feedback on this manuscript, and I am deeply grateful for their willingness to help a young scholar hone her work. Steve Cushman has been a steadfast supporter since my Charlottesville days, and I have many fond memories of battlefield hikes and our Huntington chats. Finally, I must thank Andy Graybill for always encouraging me to be myself (dubious advice though it may be), for championing my work, and for being one of the most generous scholars in the business. I count Andy as a true and treasured friend, despite the fact that he roots for the Dallas Cowboys.

I am also fortunate to be able to count two unmatched mentors among the scholars who have pushed me to ask good questions, follow the sources where they lead, and write the answers well. First, Gary Gallagher, who has been stuck with me since January 2013, when I was a first-year undergraduate in his Civil War course at UVA. While I know that Gary is deeply troubled by my now decadelong failure to grasp the function of a comma, he has always proven ready to move mountains on my behalf. And since we agree on what real mountains are, I know how much work he has done to help me get to where I am today. And I hope that he knows how much it has meant to me to have him to fight my corner. Second, Bill Blair at Penn State, who I think knows this book nearly as well as I do. Bill has an incredible ability to articulate why history matters—and always seemed to know what I meant to say, even when I failed to say it well. He offered an endless stream of comments and corrections that improved my argumentation and my writing, though the faults that remain are mine alone. I am grateful that Bill stuck with me through difficult days, and I will always be proud to say that I was his final graduate student.

Last, because alphabetically it is so often the case for my family, I must thank my mom, Joan, my dad, Chuck, and my brother, Derek, for their love and support. Mom and Dad, this book is for you. Without you, I would never have had the life filled with learning and love that provided the foundation for me to write it. In the following pages, I hope you will see how the places you took us, the experiences you gave us, and the encouragement you have always offered us made this book possible. And finally, to Moe the Border Collie—yes, I see the ball, and yes, we can go throw it.

THE ARMY UNDER FIRE

WESTWARD THE COURSE OF EMPIRE

The United States Army's integral role in nineteenth-century American politics has often been marginalized or ignored in histories of the period. This is fair enough, given that military history can often seem inscrutable, so concerned with tactical minutiae that it offers little of substance to historians concerned with society, culture, and ideas. But this is a modern perspective. In the nineteenth-century United States, political and ideological discussions frequently focused on military affairs. Once one looks for the army in Civil War–era politics, it soon becomes evident that conversations about professional soldiers and their work formed the warp and weft of the discourse over national development in the country's most fractious period. There was perhaps no national institution that drew more attention, occasioned more debate, or undertook a wider array of work than the regular army in the Civil War era. But that army was not loved.

The Army under Fire examines a debate that has raged from the era of the nation's founding to the present: What is the role of a professional army in a democratic republic? And to what degree did the United States want to be a militaristic nation?[1] The work focuses on the period between the end of the US–Mexico war and the waning of Reconstruction—an era in which sectional tensions became irreparable and the nation was cleaved in two and then reunited. Meanwhile, Americans gazed westward and wondered how to bring a new, third section under their national banner, how to subjugate, conquer, and control the vast western territories wrested from Indigenous

Westward the Course of Empire Takes Its Way, by Emanuel Leutze, 1862

occupants by decades of brutal conflict and fraught diplomacy, finally linking the great Atlantic Ocean to the wide Pacific shore.[2]

Before proceeding, it is critical to establish definitions for two terms that recur throughout this book: "antimilitarism" and "regular army." "Antimilitarism" serves as shorthand describing an attitude of opposition toward empowering professionally trained soldiers with political or economic support.[3] It is very likely that most nineteenth-century Americans would have expressed uneasiness at the idea of a large standing army, especially one that compelled service from its citizenry, as many European armies did. Antimilitarism, in a nineteenth-century context, extended beyond wariness toward military institutions to political efforts to reduce army funding, keep the number of men in the service as low as possible, and cast doubt on the loyalty of professional officers. Few advocated for the abolition of the army, but the most ardent antimilitarists sought to reduce the institution to its bare skeleton form.

The second term, "regular army," refers to the body of soldiers and officers who undertook military service as their career. Most regular army officers were educated and trained at the national military academy, West

Point. The men who filled out the ranks, meanwhile, varied in their origins but often were recent immigrants who had few other viable opportunities to earn a living as a civilian in their adopted country.[4] The regulars were viewed as "depraved in their habits and character," "destitute of family or friends," and having "no feelings or sympathies in common with the people at large."[5] A nineteenth-century professional American soldier, in other words, would be befuddled by the veneration of military service so prevalent in the post–Cold War United States.[6] The regular army was an army for peacetime, supplemented in times of war with temporary volunteer units composed of citizen-soldiers, who disliked army discipline and despised the authoritarian attitudes of the professional soldiers who commanded them.[7]

The Republican Party stood at the center of the political maelstrom that surrounded military affairs in the Civil War era. Republican legislators emerged on the national stage from the crucible of debates about the expansion of slavery into Kansas and Nebraska. Republicans railed against the political dominance of the so-called Slave Power and claimed that elite slaveholding southerners (most of them Democrats) had controlled national politics for far too long.[8] Republican Party leaders insisted that slaveholders had been enabled in their quest to expand slavery by the work of the nation's professional soldiers, who served in the vanguard of white settlement in the American West. Even in their earliest days, Republicans realized that if they intended to make war against slavery, they also would have to make war against the army.

Republicans deployed their antimilitarism strategically, and at times their Democratic rivals engaged in the same tactics. Republican leaders most often focused their ire on the professional army, singling out officers for their conservatism and suspected proslavery sympathies. But they cast their opposition more broadly when it suited their political needs. After the Civil War, Republicans slashed army budgets and decreased troop numbers in the name of economization. At the same time, they employed professional soldiers in carrying out their program of Reconstruction across the former Confederacy—a decision that bred resentment toward the regulars among opposition Democrats, who balked at martial law in the South.

The Civil War's citizen-soldier volunteers were spared Republican rage, as the party cultivated the political support of Union army veterans in the postwar years. The party's acceptance of one group of soldiers and rejection of another was not as inconsistent as it might seem. In their praise of the volunteers and their arraignment of the regulars, Republicans reflected the dual-army tradition that had defined national military affairs since the founding era. They also garnered thousands of votes, as Union volunteer organizations such as the Grand Army of the Republic became de facto Republican political clubs.[9]

No compromise at the 1787 Constitutional Convention in Philadelphia wreaked more military havoc than the decision to maintain a small regular army to be supplemented with a well-regulated militia in the event of a national war.[10] Militiamen seldom proved to be the boon the Framers imagined for the regulars. In the wake of disastrous militia performances in the War of 1812, the system degraded to the point of irrelevance.[11] In its place, the executive reserved the right to make a national call for volunteers in times of war.[12] These troops would be federalized and placed into military service for a longer period than militias had been, often under the command of regular army officers. Though federal volunteers typically performed far more admirably than earlier militias, there was no love lost between the nation's professional troops and its citizen-soldiers. In the decades after Appomattox, Republicans exacerbated this tension by celebrating the latter while maligning the former.

By recovering and contextualizing the political debate that raged over the role the regular army should play in the American Civil War, Reconstruction, and western expansion, three significant themes emerge. First, Republicans developed a coherent philosophy of antimilitarism, which began as an attack on the antebellum Slave Power. Second, Republican antimilitarism was targeted toward the regulars and did not extend to the volunteer soldiers of the Civil War. Third, Republican antimilitarism, twinned with a zealous pursuit of economic reduction, blinded party leaders to the army's postbellum potential.

There were two consequences attendant to the third theme, which help to join the stories of Reconstruction and western expansion after the Civil War. Republicans preferred to advance their rhetoric of antimilitarism and pursue economization over making efficient use of the army, which meant that thousands of federal troops left the former Confederacy by 1871–1872, compromising the effectiveness of the Republican Reconstruction program. At the same time, Republicans never fully grasped the scale of the challenge confronting the army in the West. As a result, the institution struggled to regain the control it had once exercised in the region. With more territory to protect than ever before and constantly lacking troops to meet every call for aid, army officers dealt with a chaotic landscape of territorial governors spreading rumors of Native uprisings, unregulated and unauthorized militias violently confronting Indigenous peoples, and no time or money to maintain the region's dilapidated forts or to train new troops for the realities of postbellum service.

The point of this analysis is neither to excuse the nation's professional army for its part in the violence that attended the Anglo-American conquest of the West nor to suggest that Republican legislators were ineffective leaders. Rather, it is to recover the rhetoric and ideas that shaped a debate over military affairs in the nineteenth-century United States. It is also to show that Civil War–era Americans thought critically about the role a professional army should play in their changing nation. In a present defined by the military-industrial complex and "forever wars," this analysis also offers a reminder of an era when military appropriations were not taken for granted, the armed forces did not consume the lion's share of national spending, and Americans openly criticized their army everywhere from the columns of local newspapers to the floor of the Senate. It was a debate with high stakes, fought with ferocity—and it indelibly shaped the course of the Civil War era.

. . .

On July 9, 1861, German American painter Emanuel Leutze received a commission to execute a work of art for display in the newly renovated United States Capitol Building. The commissioner was Captain Montgomery C. Meigs, an army officer serving as superintendent of the capital. Over the preceding decade, Meigs had overseen renovations to buildings and infrastructure in and around Washington, DC. The Capitol's renovation was his final project, suddenly threatened by the war clouds that loomed on the banks of the Potomac. As the defeated Union troops of the First Battle of Bull Run convalesced in the hospitals and army camps of the city, Meigs and Leutze agreed that for a fee of $20,000 the forty-five-year-old artist would produce a painting on the theme of "emigration." The twenty-by-thirty-foot fresco would sit atop the western staircase of the Capitol, in the House chamber.

THE ARMY UNDER FIRE

The painting that Leutze produced, *Westward the Course of Empire Takes Its Way,* has since become an iconic depiction of the Anglo-American conquest of the West. Where his contemporaries heralded the work as emblematic of the nation's quest to fulfill its Manifest Destiny, scholars now point to Leutze's work as a defining depiction of settler colonialism. But to Leutze's nineteenth-century audience, content that Manifest Destiny was the path by which their nation must expand, the image captured the pioneer spirit and the taming of the wilderness. In the parlance of the time, Leutze illustrated the transition from "savagery" to "civilization."[13]

And the painter was not shy about celebrating such themes. Writing about the artwork just after the Civil War, Leutze affirmed that he had sought to represent "the grand and peaceful conquest of the American West." The artist mentioned many of the archetypical Americans he used to populate the painting. There were "young men," "a frontiere [sic] farmer" and "his suffering wife with her infant in her arms," "axemen," "an old trapper," and "a young adventurer," alongside "a young vagrant." For the first time in an artwork displayed in the Capitol, there was a Black man depicted (though Leutze called him "a negro boy"). He stood beside "a rough but big-hearted hunter of the border" who lent his assistance to "a lad" wounded "probably in a fight with Indians," as well as "the agriculturalist," "the missionary," and "the hunter." Leutze also noted his efforts to portray Native people, in the typically biased language of the nineteenth century. There were Indigenous Americans in the painting, but they were "sneaking away from the light of knowledge."

Leutze believed the painting to be a comprehensive portrait of western emigration. He did not wish to "date or localize" the work, he explained. It was supposed to represent American expansion as it had looked in the past and as it would look until its completion, which, Leutze explained, would be when the "frame of the Pacific ocean closes our Emigration to the West." As Leutze planned and executed it, *Westward the Course of Empire Takes Its Way* encapsulated American ideas about Manifest Destiny in the mid-nineteenth century.[14]

Scholars now know that the language of Manifest Destiny embraced by Leutze and displayed in his art came freighted with political and cultural weight. Such ideas allowed nineteenth-century Americans to believe that their conquest of the West had been victimless.[15] As Leutze suggested in his description of the painting, Natives vanished from the landscape without resistance or objection. Indigenous peoples, as the painter portrayed them, had little interest in embracing American culture and so they disappeared rather than remain and be forced to abandon their traditional ways of life for those of a conquering society. As scholars such as Jean M. O'Brien and Boyd Cothran have demonstrated, Americans like Leutze crafted powerful ideologies of innocence, of Native peoples vanishing without resistance, and of pristine landscapes, a wilderness that, once tamed, belonged only to them.[16] Works like Leutze's painting or John Gast's *American Progress* etched these ideologies into the national imagination.

In the generations that followed, historians such as Frederick Jackson Turner and Walter Prescott Webb enshrined the same myths as historical truths. In their sweeping treatments of an era not long before their own, they celebrated the struggle to close the mythic frontier, to bring the wilderness under cultivation, and to settle vast western regions that military mapmakers had once labeled uninhabitable. Webb and Turner had known many of the last frontiersmen personally, and they wrote of them with admiration, as well as with a sense that their own generation would likely never have to confront any challenge on the scale that faced the western pioneers—and therefore would never be as consequential in the story of national development.[17]

With historical distance and a healthy need to critique their disciplinary forebears, historians such as William Goetzmann and Robert Utley wrote more dispassionately about western settlement. The pioneers mattered, yes, but the younger historians argued that the central figure in the story of western expansion ought to be the soldier. All that Utley and Goetzmann needed to do to support such a claim was point to the evidence. Much of the firsthand testimony related to western expansion—reports of unexplored territory, sketches of flora and fauna, maps, climate reports, and suggestions for road and railroad networks—was generated by soldiers. To understand the success of the American conquest of the West, Utley wrote in 1967, was to understand that the "US Army played a key, often decisive, role."[18] Utley and Goetzmann withheld judgment on whether the army did such work for good or ill; they only sought to expose the centrality of soldiers to American expansion.

More recently, historians have begun to parse the contested nature of western expansion. Building on a literature founded by Norman Graebner and Frederick Merk, historians have asked when and where Americans with varying political, social, and economic interests questioned the means, method, or goals of the nation's push into the West.[19] Modern scholars such as Patrick J. Kelly, Thomas Richards Jr., and Rachel St. John have strengthened arguments regarding the contingency of American imperialism during the Civil War era, applying borderlands methodologies to demonstrate that for much of this period borders were negotiable, and so too were ideologies regarding expansion.[20] Most recently, Daniel Burge has chronicled the way in which Americans opposed expansionism, by investigating the "collapse of Manifest Destiny" between 1848 and 1872.[21]

Since the era of Utley and Goetzmann, the key development in the historiography of the regular army in the American West has been the willingness of historians to be critical of the means and men involved in the national settler colonial enterprise. Modern historians have not abandoned the soldier as an important player in the narrative; they have merely judged his part with an eye to the violent mechanisms and pernicious consequences of settler colonialism.[22] Even as interpretations concerning the motives and consequences of American expansion change from celebrations of the pioneer spirit to critiques of the outright and implicit violence of Manifest Destiny, soldiers almost always appear.[23] Whether in works of history or in popular culture, the frontier soldier is a major figure in the settling of the American West.[24]

But the soldier did not represent western expansion to Emanuel Leutze—nor in fact to many of his contemporaries, artists or otherwise. Not a single soldier appears in Leutze's six-hundred-square-foot mural. A mural painted amid a civil war that saw 2.5 million men don Union uniforms. A mural composed while federal troops stood just yards away, guarding the building where Leutze worked. A mural that graced a chamber where congressmen daily debated military budgets and army commissions as the painter labored over his art. A mural on the theme of emigration that neglected to include the men of the institution that did more to facilitate white western expansion than any other group. How could Leutze have forgotten such a critical figure as the regular soldier?

The answer to that question lies at the heart of this book, the first study of the Republican Party's anti-army politics in the Civil War era. Historians have dedicated innumerable studies to the historical process of western expansion, but few have analyzed the ideologies and political positions that functioned as impediments to that process, partly because it is difficult to analyze the obstacles to a movement that achieved most of its objectives. It is a historical fact that professional soldiers played a central role in western expansion, so few scholarly works have sought to locate the hinderances to their work. It is also true that the policymakers who were supposed to facilitate white western emigration distrusted and disliked the army. In the wake of the Civil War, then, Republicans underutilized one of their best tools for expanding federal power in both the South and the West.[25]

Leutze's work offers proof of the degree to which mid-nineteenth-century Americans could (and did) ignore the contributions of the professional army in the Civil War era. This is a story that has not yet been told by historians. In the end, the story does not alter the fact that over the course of two centuries professional soldiers helped the federal government to steal and violently seize millions of acres of land from Native peoples, while confining thousands more to ill-managed and often deadly reservations far from their ancestral homes. Rather, the story seeks to show that the ongoing struggle to settle the West shaped the formation of a new political party, gave impetus to the men fighting to save the Union, and intruded on the process of national reunification by demanding its share of national aid after the Civil War.

The questions asked in this study and the sources used to answer them focus on the ideology of the Republican Party, which emerged in the mid-1850s following the crisis in Kansas and assumed majority control of the federal government for more than a decade and a half during the Civil War and Reconstruction. As the party in power, Republicans systematically reduced federal military spending and the size of the national fighting force while publicly criticizing the actions of army leaders. Even as war raged around them, Republican rulers refused to support the nation's professional army. Condemnations of the regulars filled Republican rhetoric in speeches, official reports, and government records.

Like most institutional histories, this study employs a top-down approach. The voices that fill the following pages are principally those of policymakers and army leaders, or of the press that covered their ideas for a mostly white, literate national audience. They are not a diverse set of characters, at least not in their skin color, economic status, or gender. Their ideas regarding the professional army, however, have yet to be systematically presented and analyzed by historians, which is what this work seeks to do. This book lays out the terms of the debate over the army in the Civil War era; others will examine how Americans of all identities, genders, and races responded to that conversation.[26]

Why did Republicans—and the constituents who sent them to Washington—so aggressively oppose the professional army? The simplest answer is that Republican antimilitarism developed in parallel with the party's better-known antislavery agenda. The party's opposition to the standing army was not simply wariness toward professional soldiers, which was shared by (almost) all Americans. Republican feeling went beyond the trepidation expressed by the founding generation in their debates regarding the threat that standing armies posed to republican government. Antimilitarism was a policy that Republicans acted on by stalling legislation supporting the army, cutting military funding, and reducing the size of the institution over a period of almost two decades.

When John Gast set out to paint his masterwork, *American Progress,* in 1872, he too neglected to include a single soldier. Because the Republican Party elected to decrease its military commitments to Reconstruction between 1870 and 1871, 1872 was the first year following the Civil War that troops in the West increased, rather than decreased, in number. As an overall percentage of the federal budget, however, army spending had dropped to just over 12 percent of government expenditures—a significant decline from absorbing more than 20 percent of the antebellum budget. Gast painted his tribute to American imperialism at the army's postbellum nadir and the peak of Republican antimilitarism. In a stroke of irony, numerous works of history and popular culture have subsequently portrayed the 1870s as the period when the regulars were at their most robust. Gast would not have thought so, and he did not assert so in his portrait of Manifest Destiny.

Historian Richard White has argued that Gast left soldiers out of his portrait because of an artistic desire to occlude the truth about the violence involved in the settling of the West. Rather than consider that painters like Gast and Leutze neglected to include soldiers because of successful political

American Progress, by John Gast, 1872

campaigns against the regulars, White suggests that Gast willfully ignored "the realities of expansion during and after the Civil War." As the Civil War wound down and the nation turned its mind to the pursuits of peace, "Congress couldn't wait" and "dispatched troops to conquer Indians."[27] In his own study of Gast's painting, Adam Arenson parsed the image differently, saying it aimed to represent a vision of the West that emphasized sectional reconciliation and reunification, represented by the transcontinental railroad, itself a manifestation of the triumph of the Republican Party's free labor creed.[28]

The latter understanding of Gast's work hews more closely to the conclusions suggested in Republican rhetoric and by the data regarding the army's presence in the postbellum West. If *American Progress* represented a Republican ideology for western expansion, then that ideology did not make space for soldiers. Understanding how Republicans worked against the army during the war and in its aftermath presents a viable alternative explanation for the lack of soldiers in the period's art: Republicans had won their war against the army.

THE CADET

On July 7, 1824, a sixteen-year-old student at Kentucky's Transylvania University sent a brief letter to John C. Calhoun of South Carolina, who was then serving as secretary of war. In his letter the young man accepted an appointment to the national military academy at West Point, where he would soon embark on a course of study in engineering, mathematics, languages, and military science. For his efforts, should he succeed, the president would commission him a second lieutenant in the United States Army and more than likely dispatch him to some obscure frontier fort to while away his mandatory five years of service. It would be a lonely life, with little chance for promotion and sparse contact with civilians, unless a war should come along and offer the chance of advancing through the ranks.[1]

The letter to Calhoun was perfunctory, giving little indication of the soon to be cadet's feelings about leaving his southern home for a barracks on the banks of the Hudson River. It gave no sign at all of what the young man might think of becoming of soldier. Apparently, the young man only agreed to go on the condition that if he disliked the education offered, he could transfer to the University of Virginia after one year. To Calhoun, the cadet stated that he could not reach New York before September, owing to circumstances he assured the secretary he would explain to the academy's superintendent, Sylvanus Thayer.

The reason for the delay in setting off to complete his education was the death of the young man's father on July 4, 1824. He wrote his sister Susannah in early August to lament the passing of their father and to say that he cared "not how soon I may follow."[2] He also said that henceforth his sister

Jefferson Davis as secretary
of war, ca. 1853

could reach him at West Point, State of New York, where he hoped to hear frequently from his family.

Death haunted Jefferson Davis for most of his life. A temporary career as a soldier gave way to one as a statesman and eventually led him to the presidency. Or perhaps it would be more accurate to say that all his political and economic success led him to *a* presidency—of a nation cleaved from the Union and composed of eleven seceded states fighting to preserve slavery. It was also a life that saw him lose his first wife, Sarah Knox Taylor, after just three months of marriage. His second marriage, to Varina Howell, gave Davis six children, though only three survived to adulthood. And while overseeing the Civil War, Davis asked that at least 258,000 southern men give their lives for the Confederate cause—5 percent of the Confederacy's white population and almost 1 in 3 men who served in Confederate armies.[3]

The letter that Davis wrote to Calhoun was the first document selected by editor Dunbar Rowland for inclusion in *Jefferson Davis, Constitutional-*

ist: His Letters, Papers, and Speeches. The ten-volume collection appeared in the 1920s and represented the first concerted effort to create a repository of Davis's writing beyond the volumes he published in defense of the Confederacy in the years following the Civil War. Rowland located only two letters from before 1839 for his collection, both dealing with Davis's West Point appointment. A separate and later effort to collect Davis's papers found dozens of others written before the 1840s, which failed to appear in the 1920s series.[4] Whatever his reason for missing these other writings, Rowland's choice to begin Davis's story at West Point suggested that military affairs would significantly shape the life and work of the future Confederate president.

And military affairs did shape Davis, though Davis did not express a great fondness for the profession thrust upon him. Davis certainly did not enjoy his time at West Point, though he found it tolerable enough that he elected against transferring to the university founded by his namesake, Thomas Jefferson, after his first year (West Point had also been founded by Jefferson, during the Virginian's first presidential term). Davis completed his course of study with mediocre results, ultimately standing twenty-three out of thirty-three in the class of 1828. A significant number of demerits lowered his ranking considerably. West Point did not bring Davis comfort. He did not enjoy having to live and learn with the "Yankee part" of the Corps of Cadets, calling the northern men "pitiful" and telling his brother Joseph they were "not such associates as I would at present select."[5] For all his army experience, Davis never seemed to desire a soldier's life. He left the regulars as soon as he could, so that he could wed the daughter of his commanding officer, Zachary Taylor.[6]

Despite his ambivalence about military life, Davis's contemporaries lauded his military bona fides at the outbreak of the Civil War, especially when comparing him to Abraham Lincoln. Lincoln's military experience prior to 1861 involved serving with a militia company during the Black Hawk War, in which the sixteenth president saw no combat. Davis, by contrast, appeared every inch a commander in chief. His military résumé boasted a West Point degree, regular army service in Florida and Illinois, leadership of a regiment of Mississippi volunteers in the Mexican War, and a term as secretary of war during the presidency of Franklin Pierce.

Davis noted several achievements from his term as secretary in a short autobiographical sketch he composed for *Bedford's Magazine* in 1890. "I proposed the introduction of camels for service on the Western plains," he recalled. "I also introduced an improved system of infantry tactics; effected the substitution of iron for wood in gun carriages; secured rifled muskets and rifles and the adoption of Minié balls; and advocated the increase of the defences of the seacoast, by heavy guns and the use of large grain powder."[7] The remarks focused on technological improvements and practical changes, giving little indication why Davis thought such changes would benefit the service and the country.

Davis's own accounting of his influence left a great deal unsaid. Though he took care to emphasize the improvements he had made to national defense infrastructure, Davis neglected to mention some of the more consequential results of his term as secretary of war. Chief among them was an increase of the regular army by four regiments in 1854. Davis also helped President Pierce uphold a proslavery legislature in Kansas Territory, using five hundred regulars to fire on and disperse the free-state government at Topeka in 1856. Davis combined politics and military knowledge to bend the resources of the federal government to the expansion of slavery—making the professional army an extension of the Slave Power.

Considering recent historiographical trends, the assertion that the slaveholders of the American South sought to expand slavery into the American West (and even abroad) will not seem surprising. Scholars have looked at a range of strategies employed by the advocates of slave expansion, including filibusters, increasing the power of the United States Navy, and developing infrastructure favorable to southern economic interests.[8] Historians have also noted the integration of the slaveholding economy into the burgeoning capitalist enterprises in the free northern states and across the globe.[9] Recent monographs by Matthew Karp and Kevin Waite, respectively, have looked at the role the United States Navy played in expanding slaveholding on a global scale and at the economic and infrastructure programs slaveholders envisioned for carrying slavery into the West.[10] Combined with this study of the army, the new wave of work confirms that southerners made a concerted effort to open western lands to slaveholding and to form diplomatic allegiances with any nations in sympathy with their cause. The Confederate government carried these ambitions forward, investing time and money in continuing this expansionist impulse during the Civil War.[11]

These new works represent a necessary corrective to the older literature concerning western expansion in the antebellum years. Such studies often insisted that proslavery politicians had little interest in moving slavery into the West because slavery was incompatible with the region's geography and climate. A graduate thesis prepared in 1935 at the University of Texas, under the direction of Charles Ramsdell, exemplifies the widespread acceptance of this thinking. While serving as secretary of war, the thesis claimed, Davis "learned of the impossibility of keeping slaves in this territory [the Southwest]." As a result, Davis did not concern himself with expansion, since "slavery would be unprofitable because of the climatic and topographical conditions" of the American West.[12]

A thorough reading of the sources, many of them in Davis's own hand, sufficiently refutes these older but still influential claims. As historians increasingly insist, Jefferson Davis used his political and military power to bolster slaveholding expansion. He made the army an ally of the Slave Power. Most northerners desired western expansion as much as their southern counterparts. Where the two sections diverged was in their view of what to do with conquered western lands once the federal government's representatives extinguished Native title. Americans in the nineteenth century envisaged multiple avenues for fulfilling the country's Manifest Destiny, and their ideas regarding the development of western lands shifted in response to changing political conditions.

Jefferson Davis poured immense energy into the antebellum army. He commanded the War Department with sharp attention to detail, ambition for what its soldiers and officers could achieve, and a steady eye toward advancing the interests of his section and his party. The only antebellum secretary of war who could claim to have influenced the course of the army's development to the same degree as Davis was the man who offered Davis his place at West Point, John C. Calhoun.[13] Had Calhoun lived to witness Davis's zealous administration of the regular army he would have seen an institution reaching the peak of its ability to influence the course of western expansion. The regular army of the 1850s, thanks to Jefferson Davis, was more robust and better supported—with men, money, guns, and yes, even camels—than any iteration that had come before.

THE PROSLAVERY EMPIRE OF JEFFERSON DAVIS, 1852–1856

I know Jeff Davis well. He is as ambitious as Lucifer, and as cold as a lizard.
—Sam Houston, 1861

To establish why the Republican Party so resented professional soldiers, it is worth examining how federal officials, most of them Democrats, managed the army between the Mexican–American War and the Civil War. The 1850s witnessed the culmination of the Slave Power's efforts to control politics at the federal level. Nowhere were proslavery politics clearer than in matters concerning the regular army. From 1852 to 1856, Mississippian Jefferson Davis used his tenure as secretary of war to make slave expansion a national priority.[1] He did so by strategically using military power, deploying the soldiers and officers of the regular army as auxiliaries for slaveholding imperialism. Davis's interventions were evident across the West. By 1860, nearly 60 percent of federal troops congregated below the Mason–Dixon Line, supporting the work of slavery's expansion.

Davis was aided in his efforts by President Franklin Pierce, the Democratic Party's candidate in the election of 1852. In that year's presidential contest, Pierce defeated General Winfield Scott, a career army officer and hero of the war with Mexico, who ran on the Whig ticket but won only four states, for a paltry forty-two electoral college votes. The series of events that transpired between Pierce's election and the next presidential contest, in 1856, saw the dissolution of the Whig Party, further consolidation of national political control by the Democrats, and continued debates over slavery's future, especially in the American West. Because Pierce was a classic example of a nineteenth-century doughface—a northerner with southern principles—Davis encountered little executive interference in employing the army to carry out his proslavery agenda.

Surveying the political landscape in 1852, Davis could safely assume that the Whig Party would take a benign view of his stewardship of the War Department.[2] His political rivals certainly made no effort to hinder the principal legislative achievement of Davis's War Department tenure, a four-regiment increase to the regular army. This measure, which raised the number of troops in the national fighting force for the first time outside of a period of declared war, allowed the secretary to expand federal investment in pushing slavery west.[3] The men of the new regiments undertook work that Davis and his Slave Power colleagues viewed as critical to their expansionist enterprise—including surveying new territory, creating infrastructure for communication and defense, and supporting white emigrants pushing into the Southwest in greater numbers (many bringing enslaved African Americans with them).

On the ground, the members of the new regiments put the federal government's investment to use. In the Southwest, the primary zone of military intervention, soldiers constructed dozens of forts, surveyed and identified potential railroad routes, and bolstered local economies. Their presence encouraged slaveholders to move west in the wake of army wagons and blue-clad troopers. They gave both economic and political power to the designs of the Slave Power. The extent of their accomplishments belies longstanding claims that the antebellum regulars were an anemic and inept body of men who did little work in the West and were ill-prepared for the challenges of the Civil War.

Whether the soldiers and officers embraced the work was moot. They were representatives of the federal government who served regardless of the politics of the party in power. Many of the officers in the new regiments would resign their commissions to join the Confederacy in 1861, while an even greater number remained loyal to—and fought to save—the Union. The army was not proslavery, in and of itself; it was the instrument of a government dominated by slaveholders.

The geographic orientation of the force indicated a disproportionate manpower investment in Texas and the Southwest, while also reflecting a national commitment to facilitating western settlement. The regulars occupied installations from the Eastern Seaboard to the Pacific Coast. In 1860, one-fifth of the army (2,949 troops) occupied posts in Texas and another fifth (3,104 troops) were posted in New Mexico. Oregon and the Territory of Washington claimed 2,236 troops, while the entire Department of the West (everything north of Texas, west of the Mississippi, and east of California, Oregon, and Washington—largely forts in Arkansas, Kansas, and Missouri, and Fort Laramie in Nebraska Territory)—contained 2,808 soldiers and officers. The remaining men were scattered between California (1,218 men) and Utah (828), with only 929 total soldiers east of the Mississippi River (all artillery).[4]

Except for troop increases during declared wars, the number of soldiers in the regular army of the 1850s remained higher than at any previous point in the nation's history. While much of the literature on the army has emphasized a paucity of troops, widening the political context surrounding the army's use and support shows that the army grew in size, rather than shrinking, over the course of the decade prior to the Civil War.[5] Where historians have seen stagnation in the ranks of the regulars, referencing "penurious budgets" and the army's "scattered condition" as reasons for discontent among officers and ill-preparedness for large-scale war, the data reveal nearly constant growth in numbers and geographic assignments for the army.[6]

Budgetary figures also belie the claim that the antebellum army received little support from the federal government. Just as it had done in the aftermath of the Panic of 1837, the federal government raised army budgets following the destructive economic panic of 1857. Of the nearly $1.8 billion aggregate expenditures of the federal government during the pre–Civil War period, $983 million (54.7 percent) was direct military expenditure and another $88 million (4.4 percent) paid for military pensions and other benefits. With congressional and presidential support, the regular army grew to be one of the antebellum federal government's largest institutions (see tables 1 and 2).

Table 1. Army Budgets as a Percentage of the Federal Budget, 1845–1860

Year	Federal budget ($)	Army expenditures ($)	Portion of federal budget (%)	Budget in 2023 dollars ($)
1845	22,937,000	5,753,000	25.1	226,463,817
1846	27,767,000	10,793,000	38.9	419,343,092
1847	57,281,000	38,306,000	66.9	1,397,561,709
1848	45,377,000	25,502,000	56.2	965,751,055
1849	45,052,000	14,853,000	33.0	577,087,274
1850	39,543,000	9,400,000	23.8	360,538,205
1851	47,709,000	11,812,000	24.8	458,934,550
1852	44,195,000	8,225,000	18.6	319,567,954
1853	48,184,000	9,947,000	20.6	386,473,245
1854	58,045,000	11,734,000	20.2	417,911,997
1855	59,743,000	14,774,000	24.7	508,038,802
1856	69,571,000	16,948,000	24.4	596,509,783
1857	67,796,000	19,262,000	28.4	662,369,257
1858	74,185,000	25,485,000	34.4	929,798,469
1859	69,071,000	23,244,000	33.7	837,820,178
1860	63,131,000	16,410,000	26.0	591,491,530

Source: Data compiled from Cambridge University Press, Historical Statistics of the United States, Millennial Edition online, https://hsus.cambridge.org. Accessed May 2023.

Table 2. Total Enlistment in the Regular Army, 1848–1860

Year	Total	Officer	Enlisted	Year	Total	Officer	Enlisted
1845	8,509	826	7,683	1853	10,572	961	9,611
1846	2,7867	2,003	25,864	1854	10,894	956	9,938
1847	44,736	2,863	41,873	1855	15,911	1,042	14,869
1848	47,319	2,865	44,454	1856	15,715	1,072	14,643
1849	10,744	9,45	9,799	1857	15,918	1,097	14,821
1850	10,929	9,48	9,981	1858	17,678	1,099	16,579
1851	10,714	9,44	9,770	1859	17,243	1,070	16,173
1852	11, 376	957	10,419	1860	16,215	1,080	15,135

Source: Data compiled from Cambridge University Press, *Historical Statistics of the United States,* Millennial Edition online, https://hsus.cambridge.org. Accessed May 2023.

INCREASING THE ARMY

In January 1855, newspapers across the United States celebrated a landmark piece of legislation. Congress had voted to increase the regular army by four regiments: two of cavalry, two of infantry. While historians have typically portrayed the antebellum army as a poorly funded and moribund institution, events in 1855 suggested otherwise—as did the popular celebration of the increase in the press. The *Daily National Intelligencer,* a Whig-leaning newspaper in the national capital, claimed that the army increase enjoyed "almost universal concurrence."[7] Meanwhile, the *North American and United States Gazette* raised one of the few complaints lodged over the legislation. From Philadelphia, the editors of the Whig daily lamented that the members of Congress had not undertaken the increase sooner.[8]

No politician was more essential to improving the fortunes of the regular army during the 1850s than Jefferson Davis. As he settled into his new cabinet post in the War Department, Davis intended, according to one historian, "to make the Democratic Party a proslavery instrument" and "wielded federal might to promote a western slaveholding empire." As a veteran of the Mexican War who had received his education at the United States Military Academy at West Point, Davis knew that "southern migration and state-sanctioned violence could make the West safe for slavery."[9] Though his actions to some extent had national appeal—all sections and parties desired a transcontinental railroad, for example—Davis's specific proposals reflected his sectional interests.

Southern Democrats celebrated Davis's appointment to Franklin Pierce's cabinet, confident that the new secretary of war would promote a proslavery agenda within the executive branch. Davis received congratulations from across the South. Mississippian Albert G. Brown, who represented the state as a fire-eating Democrat in the Senate from 1854 until the secession crisis of 1861, declared himself "satisfied fully" by the appointment.[10] Sectionalism, historian Russell F. Weigley later wrote, "had not advanced so far as to make it inappropriate" for the most obvious southern heir to John C. Calhoun to take up a post at the head of the War Department.[11]

Despite his intentions to administer the War Department without partisanship, sectional quarrels characterized Davis's term as secretary of war. Though he assured prominent army officers they would not "be viewed through a political medium," Davis gratified his supporters when he moved immediately to solidify his power and help his Democrat colleagues[12] In one of his first pieces of official correspondence as secretary, Davis complained to Captain Montgomery C. Meigs of the Corps of Engineers, then engaged in constructing an aqueduct in the national capital, that the officer had refused to employ Democrats as laborers for the project. Davis told Meigs that his behavior had been galling enough under the Whig administration of Millard Fillmore, but now, under the Pierce administration, it needed to be rectified.[13]

Though seemingly innocuous, the remodeling of the United States Capitol Building allowed Davis to install proslavery military imagery directly above the head of the federal government. When sculptor Thomas Crawford submitted his designs for *Armed Liberty*, the statue to adorn the Capitol dome, the female figure of Liberty carried a bundle of Roman fasces and wore a liberty cap—a popular nineteenth-century symbol with ties to the national memory of the American Revolution.[14] Davis objected to the liberty cap, telling Meigs that its Ancient Roman origins were "as the badge of a freed slave." Davis did not want to risk the statue suggesting that the country pursue "a recurrence to that origin."[15] Davis abhorred the idea of a symbol of emancipation atop the halls of the federal government. The secretary got his way, using his office to influence the sculptor to opt for a military helmet with a feathered crest. Davis judged the revised headwear "admirable."[16]

When they were not critiquing public art, Davis and Pierce planned more direct interventions to the operations of the nation's armed forces. In 1854, the president and the secretary proposed to increase the size of the army by four thousand men, a decision that invited proclamations of support from proslavery Democrats.[17] While questioning General Winfield Scott, before a House investigative committee, about the propriety of the contemplated increase, Virginia's Charles Faulkner alluded to a variety of concerns that he hoped would justify raising troop levels, saying that more men were needed "in view of our extensive seaboard and foreign frontier; our present and prospective relations with the Indian tribes of the West, and the protection due to our several routes of emigration."[18] Supplying this manpower to Davis and Pierce ensured the consolidation of the gains of Manifest Destiny.

As a preliminary defense against accusations of bias, Davis's fellow Democrats touted his military experience as reason enough to vote in favor of his recommendations. Lewis Cass of Michigan, a former secretary of war himself, affirmed that Davis would minister the War Department impartially. "I have much confidence," Cass explained, "in the gentleman at the head of the War Department. He carried to its administration eminent qualifications . . . the benefits of a military education, much military experience," said the once formidable statesman. "The opinion of such a man ought to have weight, and it has weight with me."[19] Albert Brown echoed the praise of Cass. "If we fail, in a mere spirit of obstinacy," he asked, "to vote the number of men which, we are told by the President and head of the War Department . . . how shall we answer to the country in case of disaster?"[20] Brown's question suggested, in a less than gentle fashion, that his fellow senators should stop assuming they knew better than the secretary of war regarding national military affairs.

Southern Democrats and their allies explicitly proclaimed that an increase in manpower poised the army to secure a continental empire.[21] North Carolina Whig George E. Badger called the United States "a vast empire" and admonished the Senate to realize that "if we will have a nation embracing half a continent; if we will have internal and external frontiers to defend; if we stretch from ocean to ocean; from sea to sea, we must necessarily multiply our military means to meet the emergency we have thus voluntarily assumed." The need to increase the army, in Badger's reckoning, had occurred because of American victory in the Mexican–American War, the Seminole Wars, and the annexation of Oregon and Texas. Badger exclaimed that if the government wanted to incorporate the vast territory of the American West he would vote "for the four regiments." And to drive home his point, he proclaimed, "I would have voted for five [regiments]; I would have voted for six, if they had been asked."[22] When North Carolina passed its ordinance of secession a few years later, Badger pledged his loyalty to the Confederacy.

The Senate overwhelmingly approved the measure, 32–7. Four new regiments, totaling more than 4,900 men, joined the army in February 1855. President Pierce signed the bill into law on March 4. Only seven senators opposed the measure. Six had no affiliation with the Democratic Party: Free-Soilers Lawrence Brainerd of Vermont, Francis Gillette of Connecticut, and Charles Sumner of Massachusetts; and Whigs Salmon P. Chase and Benjamin Wade, both of Ohio, with William H. Seward of New York. The men who voted against the army increase formed the core of the burgeoning Republican Party—and carried their anti-army attitudes into the Civil

War. Seward and Chase joined the presidential cabinet of Abraham Lincoln, while Sumner and Wade became two of the most prominent Radical Republicans of the Civil War era. The votes against the 1854 army increase foreshadowed dozens of speeches, bills, amendments, and newspaper editorials from Republicans and party supporters as they enforced cutbacks to army funding and manpower in the decades following the Civil War.

One Democrat voted against Davis: Sam Houston of Texas. Houston preferred to fund an increase for the militia in Texas rather than for the regulars. The Texan understood that the state he had helped bring into the Union would draw many of the new regular army soldiers into its borders. A savvy politician, Houston figured he might try to get the government to pay him for Texas troops rather than have federal dollars bypass his state entirely. Or perhaps Houston did not believe in Jefferson Davis. When Texas voted to secede from the Union in 1861, Houston was stunned. He cautioned the slaveholding South that they stood little chance of winning a war against the United States, but he died in 1863, before he could witness the truth of his prediction. Every other voting Democrat approved of the measure, regardless of geographic section. Five Whigs joined their ranks from Delaware, Florida, Georgia, Maryland, and Tennessee—all slaveholding states.[23]

THE WORK

Robert E. Lee's military career took a new turn on the day that Franklin Pierce signed the 1854 army increase into law. Lee had just turned forty-eight and ranked as a captain in the United States Army. Until 1855, he served with distinction as one of the army's most capable staff officers. His service during the Mexican–American War received plaudits from the army's commanding general, Winfield Scott, and three brevet promotions to the rank of colonel. In recognition of Lee's administrative capabilities, the army placed him in command of West Point in 1852. Though overseeing the national military academy contented Lee, he could only gain further promotion by returning to active service. The Virginian's new position made him second-in-command in the newly organized Second Cavalry Regiment.

Lee and the men selected to serve in the Second Cavalry carried the hopes of Jefferson Davis and his southern Democratic colleagues on their shoulders. Many served Davis when he became the Confederate commander in chief. Four of the eight full generals in the future Confederate armies—John Bell Hood, Albert Sidney Johnston, Lee, and Edmund Kirby Smith—came from the Second Cavalry, and the unit produced sixteen Civil War generals (eleven of them Confederates) and two Spanish–American War generals.[24] The most prominent officer of the Second to serve the Union was George Thomas, though as a Virginian, he too claimed southern birth. Future Confederate commanders Earl Van Dorn, Fitzhugh Lee, and William J. Hardee also found homes in the regiment.[25]

The Second Cavalry quickly became one of the most active units in the regular army. The regiment's soldiers and officers pursued Indian campaigning, fighting at least twenty more engagements than any other United States military unit between 1849 and 1861. The unit also worked closely with Indian agents and other federal authorities to manage and oversee the systematic deportation of Native nations across Texas and the New Mexico Territory.[26] In addition to these duties, soldiers and officers helped to create and maintain the local economy in West Texas and New Mexico by building new military installations and maintaining existing federal property. All this work helped to advance the national project of settler colonialism and further establish American territorial claims in the Southwest, where southern Democrats envisioned creating multiple future slave states, and where enslaved people would labor in new, regional enterprises, including mining and infrastructure development.

Some of the most substantial extant correspondence produced by Lee in his lifetime appeared during his two assignments to Texas.[27] The letters reflected the wide of array of work Lee oversaw as the second-in-command of the regiment, but like much army correspondence from the period, it gave little indication of Lee's personal opinions about that work. As a soldier in the United States Army, Lee served the politicians in Washington who funded his work and directed his movements, and he did not propose, even his private correspondence, to question that government.[28] Prior to the war with Mexico, for example, Lee had indicated his desire to do all that he could in the service of his country, writing to Joseph G. Totten, the army's chief engineer, "In the event of war with any foreign government I should desire to be brought into active Service in the field with as high a rank in the regular army as I could obtain."[29] Lee desired not only action in the line of duty but also responsibility and a leadership role within the army.

Still, not all military work proved fulfilling, especially campaigning against Native peoples. The frustrations of life away from the comfort of an army barrack became clear to the men of the Second Cavalry after their first major expedition. In June 1856, eight of the ten companies of the regiment pursued Sanaco, a Comanche chief, for six weeks. They showed nothing for the effort. Captain Edmund Kirby Smith suggested the frustration felt by the command when they returned to their post: "As has been the case with all large expeditions against the nomadic tribes on our western prairies, we travelled through the country, broke down our men, killed our horses, and returned as ignorant of the whereabouts of Mr. Sanico [sic] as when we started."[30] Despite Smith's dejection, his letters underscore that the Second Cavalry remained active whether the campaigns succeeded or not, and that most of the troops believed the work contributed to a national mission of expansion.

Smith was not alone in combining feelings of frustration with an appreciation for necessity of the duty the War Department had assigned him. Lee expressed similar sentiments in 1857, despite spending his Fourth of July holiday baking in the Texas sun. Lee had been charged with leading a patrol in search of Comanches who stood accused of raiding white settlements. His men were ill, tired, and dispirited after dozens of miles of riding. They had been out for almost a month and faced two more weeks of scouting. In a letter to his wife, Lee expressed his feelings about the exhausting expedition. He said that after a march of thirty miles he had settled along a branch of the Brazos and sought shade under his blanket, which was elevated on four sticks driven in the ground. "Still," he concluded, "my feelings for my country were as ardent, my faith in her future as true, and my hopes for her advancement as unabated as if felt under more propitious circumstances."[31] The exertions he and his soldiers faced, he claimed, advanced national interests.

Complaining about military life was commonplace among soldiers and officers alike, but complaints did not prevent soldiers from doing all that they could to fulfill their duty as representatives of the federal government. James E. B. Stuart wrote in 1860 that in his command "every body is blue & disgusted" after a 1,404-mile march involved only skirmish with a small body of Kiowas.[32] While serving as a major in the First Cavalry, John Sedgwick wrote to his sister a similarly disconsolate note about the prospect of an impending campaign against the Kiowa nation, saying simply, "I have no desire for it." Given that the duty still needed to be done, however, he admitted he would "do my best to bring it to a successful issue."[33] William Woods Averell, a second lieutenant in the Second Cavalry, recalled in his memoirs that despite all the hardships of life in Texas, the unit's chief characteristic was "devotion to duty—the most rigorous, zealous, and enthusiastic."[34] Even amid frustration, officers affirmed their loyalty to the service.

And their commitment earned plaudits from the settlers they supported. Texas newspapers celebrated "the efforts made by regular officers to conciliate the people and secure their services." The editors singled out Albert Sidney Johnston, the colonel of the Second Cavalry, for fervent praise. Through his attentiveness to the demands of settlers for support, Sidney Johnston had ensured the "harmony and good feeling which ought to exist between the Texans and the United States Army." Texans appreciated the fact that Johnston seemed to share their mutual interest in the country's settlement. The same article concluded "Colonel Johnston, notwithstanding he is an officer of the army, does not forget he is at the same time a citizen of the United States. This is a sentiment, it is to be feared, some officers do not entertain, or cannot sufficiently appreciate."[35]

BUILDING A MILITARY EMPIRE

Soldiers in Texas and New Mexico spent most of their time building and maintaining an array of military installations. In the 1850s, the United States Army engaged in more new construction of military property than at any point in the nation's history. Graph 1 details the total number of posts constructed. Between 1850 and 1859, soldiers platted and constructed eighty-six new posts across the West. In 1860, the army added nine further installations. The army established and occupied ninety-five forts in those years. The number of posts built in the 1860s, 1870s, and after 1880 was seventy-three. In short, the army constructed twenty-two fewer posts in the three decades following the Civil War than soldiers built in the single decade (1850–1860) prior to the conflict. If infrastructure offers any sign of the relative strength of the army across time, the antebellum force outworked the postbellum regulars.

In the construction boom from 1849 to 1859, the Southwest featured the most activity. The need to protect recently acquired territory drove the

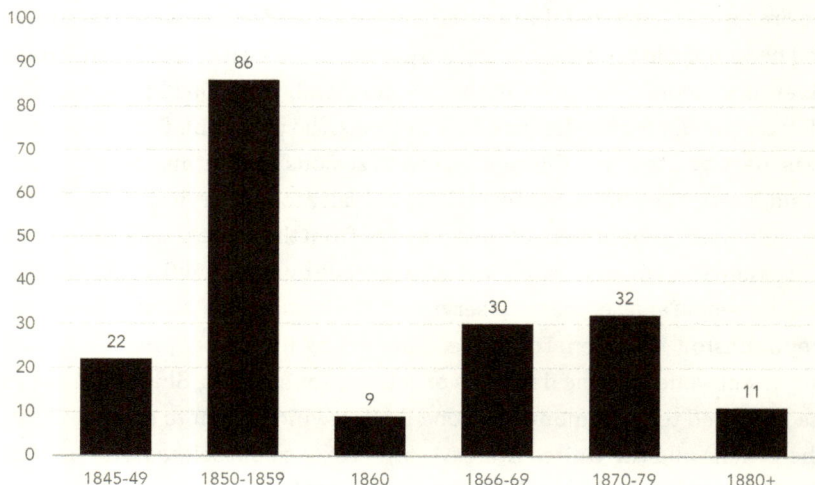

Graph 1. U.S. Army posts constructed, by decade

construction of posts in the wake of the Mexican–American War and the British cession of the Washington Territory. Between 1849 and 1869, the army built twenty-three new posts in Texas, twelve in New Mexico, and five in Arizona. Building projects also occurred in other regions. In Oregon, the regulars helped construct nine new installations, while adding twelve in Washington Territory. Despite this, posts in the Southwest outnumbered those in the Pacific Northwest by nearly 2 to 1.

Building federal infrastructure was necessary for advancing American imperial ambitions. For southerners, these were also efforts to expand slavery. Beginning in 1850, Secretary of War Charles Magill Conrad emphasized, "The most important duty which at present devolves on the department, is the protection of Texas and New Mexico against the Indian tribes in their vicinity."[36] Conrad explained that by building forts and removing the army from cities like San Antonio, Texas, or Santa Fe, New Mexico, "both the economy and efficiency of the service would be promoted."[37] The new installations placed the army in a position to serve as a buffer between white settlers and Native nations. Forts suggested a permanent (or at least semipermanent) intention to occupy a region and attracted civilian communities by promising some economic benefit to nearby settlers.

The soldiers and officers of the army were pleased by the institution's growth. In 1852 and 1853, Colonel Joseph K. F. Mansfield investigated the condition of dozens of military installations in New Mexico and along the Pacific Coast. The War Department tasked the career army officer with assessing existing structures and making recommendations for expanding the army's presence in the West. Officers suggested new posts for their geographic proximity to potential overland travel routes or railroad lines as well as for their usefulness in strategically encouraging white settlement in areas where the federal government could afford military support. Mansfield took a positive view of the present condition and prospects of the regulars. The 1822 West Point graduate proposed few cost-saving measures. In fact, he advocated for greater expenditures and additional appropriations to meet numerous military needs: better food, improved roads, increased frequency of mail delivery, and raises in soldier pay. The reports reflected the ambition of an officer confident in the army's capacity to grow and improve in various pursuits. Across the West, Mansfield found officers of "extraordinary merit" and deemed the "character of the army" to be at the "highest standard."[38]

Determining the best location to situate a new post proved demanding, though the training in engineering that professional officers received at West Point suited most of them to the challenge. Upon his arrival in the Lone Star State, Lee set to work to study the defense system of Texas. The immense task of the Second Cavalry in helping to defend the frontier might have struck the commander as insurmountable. The state had an area of 237,000 square miles, or about 150 million acres. From the Red River to the Rio Grande stretched an irregular "border" line of settlements, with a few white outposts reaching up fertile river valleys still farther west (those of the Colorado and of the Salt, Double Mountain, and Clear Forks of the Brazos). West of the line stood isolated army posts. Lee found a collection of forts in Texas. Forts Croghan, Gates, Graham, Mason, and Worth stood well among the westernmost settlements, as Anglo settlers quickly pushed west after the American annexation of Texas in 1845. West of these older forts were the newer posts of the 1850s—Belknap, Camp Colorado, Camp Cooper, Chadbourne, McKavett, and Phantom Hill.

The Texas system of military defense consisted of two parallel lines of forts built between 1849 and 1857. Fort Inge, established in March 1849, represented the first of the military installations built beyond the line of settlement west of San Antonio. The outer fort line, stretching along the Rio Grande international boundary and across the Trans-Pecos region, had infantry garrisons to watch for anyone moving toward the American settlements from Mexico. Each fort also served as a base for offensive operations against Indigenous peoples, as federal policy in the 1850s shifted from trying to defend settlements against Indigenous raiding activities to the sustained pursuit, capture, and confinement of Native peoples.[39]

Forts also helped to create a local economy. At Fort Duncan, Texas, on the Rio Grande border, monthly upkeep cost the federal government $1,544.90.[40] This was before the post's accountant factored in wages paid to local contractors and extra-duty soldiers. Horses of the First Artillery Regiment and thirty-eight mules consumed 15,882 pounds of corn and 18,067 pounds of hay in November 1860. First Lieutenant Henry W. Clossen noted that he purchased the corn for his post "under contract with L. Colquhoun of Eagle Pass." Clossen, who spent his Civil War service fighting for the Union in various campaigns along the Gulf Coast, recorded that local contractors delivered hay "at post for $15 per ton."[41] Clossen further noted an expenditure of $260 to hire an unnamed worker for repair of a public building "owned by John Twohig."[42] An immigrant from Ireland, Twohig amassed a fortune in land and enslaved people prior to the Civil War. Despite the conflict's devastating economic effects, he remained among the one hundred wealthiest Texans in 1870. The Irishman used the army's presence to increase his personal capital. The quartermaster at Fort Duncan recorded the transaction as a matter of course.

Lee kept his enlisted men employed in building and improving their post at Camp Cooper. For more than twelve months, the Virginian detailed fatigue parties of enlisted men to the woods north of the Clear Fork of the Brazos and to cut logs for fuel and sent others to a nearby quarry for building stone. Others built thirteen structures about the parade ground, in the shape of a large L.[43] A young second lieutenant, John Bell Hood, recalled that Lee took an active interest in the problems of military infrastructure—and exhibited zeal in carrying out Washington's instructions regarding the construction and maintenance of army property. "It was Colonel Lee's custom," Hood recalled, "to ride over the country in search of a suitable location, and to request each day one or more of his officers to accompany him, in order to avail himself of their views in regard to the best point at which to establish this military post."[44] Hood, a Kentuckian, developed a fondness for Texas during his time there prior to the Civil War. When his native state declared neutrality in 1861, Hood offered his services to the Lone Star State instead— and led his famous Texas Brigade at Antietam, Fredericksburg, and Gettysburg, where an artillery shell struck his left arm and rendered it useless for the remainder of his life.[45]

Lieutenant Herman Biggs of the First Infantry made a full report on these improvements to Major D. H. Vinton, quartermaster, on May 24, 1857. The report underscored the immense amount of effort undertaken by the soldiers of the Second Cavalry in improving the post. Biggs provided a detailed list of resources available to maintain the installation, finding "building Material, limestone in the immediate vicinity in abundance," as well as "water—sufficient thus far, of medium quality." Biggs also relayed the cost of goods for sustaining life at the post: "forage—quantity small, quality good, cost (of corn) $2.09 per bushel . . . Beef—quantity sufficient, quality good, cost 5 1/4 cents per pound . . . Hay—quantity limited, quality good, cost $20 per ton." Finally, Biggs noted the post's location relative to other installations and infrastructure, commenting "roads—condition, now good . . . all the above rivers and streams are forded. Water is found on the road at convenient distances. Transportation—by government trains. And Supplies—except those already named received from San Antonio by Government trains, quality good." All of Biggs's commentary affirmed that despite the post's remote location and the relatively sparse settlement of the country, Congress's investment in military infrastructure produced permanent bastions of American authority in Texas.[46]

Military dollars were essential to sustaining the local economies of the West. Of the 1,600 Anglo-Americans who lived in New Mexico in 1850, more than one thousand were members of the United States Army. The presence of soldiers helped the economy of the territory nearly triple over a fifteen-year period. In 1843, goods traveling on the Santa Fe Trail had an estimated worth of $1.5 million. By 1858, after one decade of constant occupation by the regulars, goods worth $3.5 million traveled to Santa Fe. One historian has estimated that by 1860 the trade value reached $10 million. The outposts of New Mexico were expensive to supply but vital for encouraging white settlement in the Southwest. In 1849, the federal government paid twelve cents for one day of ration per soldier stationed on the Atlantic coast, nineteen cents a day for soldiers in Texas, and forty-two cents per day for troops in New Mexico. Supplying the one thousand troops present in 1850 cost the federal treasury $420 per day, or $153,000 per year.[47]

Where the army went, white settlers followed. At Fort Davis in Texas, slaveholding interests dominated the communities that formed near the post, and immigrants brought enslaved people with them. Historian Robert Wooster noted that by 1860 (five years after the post was established), two civilian communities—Wild Rose Pass and Las Limpias—had formed near Fort Davis. Wild Rose Pass, a bustling settlement serving the San Antonio–El Paso Road, had a population of forty-nine. Nineteen of the residents had been born in Mexico, two in Ireland, and one in Saxony. Twenty-three were natives of slave states (including a colony of ten from Arkansas), while only four hailed from states north of the Mason–Dixon line.[48] The governor of Texas, H. R. Runnels, received multiple letters in 1858 informing him that as the army pushed further West, "this country is settling up very fast," with "a large immigration of . . . slave holders."[49] The letter indicated that military installations helped to facilitate slave expansion, putting the army at the forefront of southern expansionist ambitions.

Lee also noted the effect of the military on the development of the West. Writing to his daughter from San Antonio on March 3, 1860, he admitted that the land around the city expressed "a want of trees and cultivation" but noted that the "soil is quick & fertile." Despite the lack of agricultural improvements, Lee said he saw "an improvement in the town." He particularly noticed residences, businesses, and places of worship. Lee regarded "some good residences . . . a few stores of good character, & quite a respectable Hotel." A practicing Episcopalian, he also approvingly explained that "the Presbyterians are also erecting quite a fine church, & the few Episcopalians have congregated together & commenced one." As more settlers moved to West Texas, Lee's letters revealed how institutions representative of white Protestant American life overwhelmed Hispanic and Native institutions.[50]

Slavery did not, however, arrive with the army. In Texas and New Mexico, different forms of coercive labor, debt peonage, and slaveholding met in the borderlands of Mexican, Native, and later, European society.[51] The infrastructure that developed from the army's occupation of the Southwest reflected a particular vision for the development of the region. As then Second

Lieutenant Averell recalled in his memoirs, the army's job was to "maintain the civil government of New Mexico and to keep its communications open with the States." The army helped to provide the authority for the transformation of the region from a Mexican state to a territory in line with the Constitution and American legal and cultural practices. Averell lamented "the despairing struggles" of Native people "forcibly torn away" from their land to accommodate "the wickedness of conscienceless land grabbers."[52] Still, he raised no objection the duty assigned to him.

Despite a deep-seated moral aversion to chattel slavery's expansion to New Mexico, abolitionists rarely advocated banning peonage and captive slavery, the two forms of slavery that had dominated the borderland created by the Spanish Empire, Mexico, and Texas.[53] Indeed, most people "did not view them with the same abhorrence as they did black slavery." New Mexicans, meanwhile, held ambivalent attitudes about chattel slavery but "vehemently defended their right to retain captives and peons."[54] Averell commented that the army did nothing to interfere with Mexican peonage.[55] With few options for westward growth left to them under the Missouri Compromise, the advocates of southwestern expansion needed to establish the conditions for chattel slavery in a borderland where it did not resonate with the local culture. As the agents of the federal government on the ground, the army helped transition the region to American rule, as well as opening the door to the spread of chattel slavery west.

Soldiers seldom encountered geographic spaces as diverse as the American Southwest. For many borderlands residents, representatives of the army served as the first point of contact with Americans, beyond the traders and merchants who plied the Santa Fe trading corridor before the Mexican–American War. The United States' assertion of hegemony in the American Southwest—represented by the army—signaled a moment of transition for borderlands inhabitants. "In the Southwest borderlands," one historian has noted, "officers, soldiers, and the army dependents categorized, assigned meaning and value, and created a social connection to the place facing colonialism—its landscapes, societies, peoples, and events—constructing power and identity for themselves in the process."[56] The army represented the new, exclusive hierarchy expected to control and exploit the people and resources of the region.

Soldiers and officers often deprecated the racial and cultural diversity of the Southwest. Some officers lamented the absence of Anglos because they preferred to rely on white settlers to serve as temporary militias in a military crisis. Officers distrusted the Hispanic population of New Mexico, failing to acknowledge that many Hispanic people considered themselves culturally white. Reflecting the prejudice common among Anglo-Americans, Colonel Joseph K. F. Mansfield wrote in his 1854 report on the conditions of U.S. military installations in the West that "no reliance whatever can be placed on them [the territory's Hispanic residents] as a militia to defend the territory in a war with Mexico." "They are not warlike," Mansfield explained, "and are incapable of defending their property against the Indians as a general thing."[57]

Still, the Treaty of Guadalupe Hidalgo had conferred American citizenship on anyone living in the Mexican Cession, meaning the army had to provide equal protection to both the New Mexico Territory's Hispanic residents and property and its Euro-American white settlers. The casual racial stereotyping deployed by Mansfield against all non-Anglo residents underscored the degree to which most Americans, regardless of their geographic section, believed in and promoted ideas about the superiority of white Americans.

Army officers, meanwhile, contributed to slave expansion in the Mexican Cession by importing enslaved laborers while posted below the Mason–Dixon line. As historian William S. Kiser has documented, "Military officers stationed in New Mexico perpetuated involuntary servitude, either by holding slaves themselves or turning a blind eye to others who held black slaves." The federal government provided army officers with funds to pay servants, between $94 and $398 per year during the 1850s; however, Kiser noted that the lack of involuntary laborers in the Southwest meant army personnel often pocketed the subsidy to increase their pay.[58]

Civil authorities also moved to keep the area open for enslaved labor even as the sectional crisis escalated over this issue. In 1859, New Mexico passed the Act to Provide for the Protection of Property in Slaves. Territorial Governor William Carr Lane (a former army surgeon and Millard Fillmore appointee) and Chief Justice of the New Mexico Supreme Court Grafton Baker (a Mississippi judge) advocated for the act. Both prominent officials held enslaved people. Army soldiers and officers did nothing to prevent the spread of slavery or proslavery attitudes in New Mexico.

EXPLORING AN EMPIRE

The mapmaking expeditions of the army's Corps of Topographical Engineers provided a scientific basis for American colonization efforts. The army's engineers and explorers recorded more of their western experiences than their infantry and cavalry colleagues, as they wrote scientific reports, kept journals of their activities, and described places in the West where white Americans had seldom, if ever, set foot. The extant writings of the corps represents some of the most political prose produced by the institution. Officers making reports knew that their discoveries supported the expansionist policies of the federal government and had the potential to determine the economic interests of entire regions.

Historians have long understood the relationship between scientific knowledge and the empire building facilitated by the regulars. "The Corps of Topographical Engineers was a central institution of Manifest Destiny," as William H. Goetzmann succinctly put it in his landmark study of army exploration. "Under the guise of a scientific expedition, a topographical survey could serve a series of political ends. Under the camouflage of military appropriations, legislators attached internal improvements and various scientific subsidies to the annual army bill." Goetzmann noted, in passing, that the army's explorers served as "pawns" of politicians, but this suggests that army officers were unaware of the larger implications of their work, and the evidence does not support this claim. Officers were collaborators in the government's system of colonization and Manifest Destiny.[59]

Major John Pope typified the career of an army explorer whose scientific efforts were ripe for politicization. Pope experienced almost every conceivable type of military service in his forty-four years with the United States Army. Later, during the Civil War, Pope won a famous victory at Island Number Ten and commanded the Army of Virginia (briefly) until a catastrophic defeat at the Second Battle of Bull Run. He spent much of the Civil War handling the aftermath of the 1862 US–Dakota War. As a senior figure in the postbellum army, Pope became a vocal advocate for military reform while also commanding an array of military departments. His posts included Reconstruction service in Georgia as well as a long tenure overseeing the Department of the Missouri (the second-largest geographic command in the nation) from 1870 to 1883.

Before any of that experience, however, he wandered around the deserts of Texas and New Mexico, from 1857 to 1859, drilling holes in the ground. The assignment given to Pope by Secretary of War John B. Floyd did not contain the potential for winning military fame and glory, but Pope received a $100,000 budget and a detail of one hundred soldiers to locate water sitting deep under the surface of the desert in the driest portion of the Mexican Cession. They did this by drilling for artesian wells. The advocates for a southern transcontinental railroad stood to benefit from Pope's intelligence.[60] Steam engines required a ready supply of water to function, making the Southwest less desirable for the transcontinental route. Proof of accessible water, however, mitigated arguments against the southern line.

Pope's orders directed him to find water and to drill until it overflowed the surface. Once he accomplished this, the captain needed to determine how to store reserves of that water to support travel across the arid southern Plains. West Point graduate R. W. Johnson recalled that the imperial designs of Jefferson Davis and his political allies were clear in Pope's drilling experiment. "To overcome this great drawback to successfully transporting supplies, and with the hope of being able to do something calculated to develop the country," Johnson wrote, "Mr. Davis, then secretary of war, prevailed upon Congress to make an appropriation for the purpose of boring a series of artesian wells."[61] Johnson's observation indicated that army officers understood Davis's plan for the Southwest.

Proslavery politicians relied on army officers such as Pope to provide the data to bolster their case that the southern route of the transnational railroad should prevail over northern alternatives. In 1854, the *Galveston News* printed an exchange of correspondence between Anson Jones and Major H. W. Merrill, commander of Fort Belknap. Jones, the last president of the Republic of Texas and the architect of Texas's annexation to the United States, asked Major Merrill to provide details about the terrain of West Texas, where the projected southern route of a Pacific railroad ran. "In this enterprise, which I deem quite feasible," Jones explained, "I have taken a deep and an active personal interest." Jones told Merrill he believed the major "to be in possession of much valuable and reliable information in regard to the section of the country in question." Merrill's military opinion clearly appealed to Jones, and the major's reply doubtless flattered the former president. "That the line of the 32 parallel is by far the shortest, cheapest and most practicable route for the Atlantic and Pacific railroad is, in my own mind, settled beyond a doubt," Merrill wrote. Merrill emphasized the gentle grade of the land in West Texas, as well as the "tide of emigration" then settling in the state.[62]

Pope spent almost two years fighting broken machinery and unyielding stratigraphy on the Llano Estacado. Some of his wells reached more than one thousand feet below the surface, and many hit water in large underground streams. Pope, however, found no way to force that water to the surface.[63] In lieu of completing his directive, Pope provided critical observations on where future officers might test further wells, including the valley south of Santa Fe, where "the soil is excellent; there are abundant forests of cedar . . . and pine in the mountains." These resources, in addition to gold placers, made the region, for Pope, "a point of much importance to the government."[64] His drilling experiment did not fail entirely if he could at least provide knowledge of resources essential to constructing a transportation network.

Pope's expedition had the potential to provide the last piece in the case for a southern route of the Pacific railroad, which was favored by southern Democrats: readily accessible water to fuel steam engines on their journey to California. By 1854, "the South deemed its railroad extension as of no more worth than the expansion of slavery."[65] A letter from a Texan to his state senate in 1853 underscored the advantages that a southern route offered the South: "The territory of Texas would be occupied by people enough to make four of five new slave states, thus balancing the free North." The same writer believed that the territory north of the Red River was "very poor," and he believed that Davis should prefer the Southwest over the Great Plains.[66] In deploying the army across the country, the federal government apparently agreed with his contention, leaving the Great Plains almost untouched by regular troops.

The Southwest also stood to benefit from a scheme to import camels into New Mexico and Arizona to expedite the transport of military supplies and accelerate land surveys. Davis, while secretary of war, had long championed the idea of using camels to replace traditional American pack animals such as mules and horses as carriers of military supplies in the Southwest. He believed camels were more efficient than other animals because they did not require as much water or rest. John B. Floyd inherited Davis's long-gestating camel experiment when he became secretary of war in 1857. The brief existence of the United States Camel Corps, like Pope's artesian wells, proved slaveholder willingness to invest time and federal resources in efficiently developing transportation networks across Texas and New Mexico, to California. By most accounts the camels adapted to serving in the arid desert regions of the Southwest, but the Civil War sundered the experiment and the War Department later sold many of the camels.[67]

The national embrace of Manifest Destiny in the wake of the Mexican–American War provided a boon for the regular army of the United States. The regulars reached the pinnacle of their work as agents of empire in the 1850s. Amid the vicissitudes of party politics and the splintering of the Union, the soldiers and officers of the regular army contributed to the ceaseless national project of western expansion. Jefferson Davis irrevocably shaped this mission to support the expansion of slavery. As William H. Seward explained in a speech on the dominance of the Slave Power at the end of the secretary's term in office, Davis acted as an "energetic and far-sighted [minister], brought from the slave states, and identified with their policy."[68]

As Seward worked to form a new political party opposed to the expansion of slavery, he often remembered how and where the professional army had traveled on behalf of slave expansion. The election of 1852, which had elevated Franklin Pierce to the presidency and Davis to command of the War Department, was the last in which the Democratic and Whig parties served as the primary antagonists. In 1856, when another Democratic doughface (Pennsylvania's James Buchanan) punched his ticket to the White House, three candidates traded rhetorical blows in a race that saw, for the first time, a Republican presidential hopeful. Though they could not have known it then, the emergence of a true antislavery party augured poorly for the nation's professional soldiers. These new Republicans, it soon became clear, were intent on waging war against the regulars.

THE RUNAWAY

The slaveholding South made its greatest political miscalculation when it attached a reinvigorated Fugitive Slave Law to the omnibus package of legislation that composed the Compromise of 1850. Or so said Frederick Douglass, in an address delivered to a crowd of Boston abolitionists in the winter of 1855. Forcing the citizens of the free states in the North to return escaped men and women to their enslavers, Douglass explained, allowed all Americans to witness the brutality of the Slave Power. The Fugitive Slave Law revealed "the horrible character of slavery toward the slave" and showed "the arrogant and overbearing spirit of the slaves states toward the free states" by making all Americans "parties to the crime" of slavery.[1]

In the summer of 1855, the case of runaway slave Anthony Burns captured national attention. Abolitionists such as Douglass used the story of Burns's escape from his Virginia master, recapture, and subsequent trial in Boston to press their case for emancipation. Newspaper editors filled column after column with detailed reporting of Burns's arrest and trial, ensuring that readers far and wide could follow the case as closely as if they were standing next to Burns in the courtroom. Republican legislators took careful notice of the public furor and began to speak about Burns on the House and Senate floor. Charles Sumner, the Radical Republican senator from Massachusetts, spoke most passionately of them all.

Even careful readers are likely to miss Sumner's disquisition on the Burns case in his "Crime against Kansas" address, which he delivered to the Senate on May 19, 1856. The paragraphs on Burns fell between sharp rebukes of southern Democrats, slaveholders, and President Franklin Pierce, who had all conspired, Sumner exclaimed, to deliver the government of the

Anthony Burns, drawn by Barry from a daguerreotype

Kansas Territory to the Slave Power. Sumner's speech famously summoned the reprobation of Representative Preston Brooks of South Carolina, who stormed the Senate chamber on May 22, 1856, and beat Sumner mercilessly with a metal-tipped cane. Brooks likely thought little about Anthony Burns as he undertook his attack on Sumner, being principally concerned with

Sumner's decision to impugn the honor of Brooks's cousin, Senator Andrew Butler, as he rained blows on Sumner's head.

Though Sumner's remarks about Burns have not rung through history, they nevertheless represented one of the earliest instances of a Republican legislator speaking out against the army on a national stage.[2] Summer pointedly addressed the Slave Power's use of the army for its own political benefit, in describing the army's role in the effort to return Burns to slavery.[3] Sumner expressed indignation over the fact that the federal government would use national resources and federal dollars to uphold slavery. He was incensed by the fact that President Pierce had deployed a contingent of federal troops to force one man, who had reached freedom in Massachusetts, to return to a life of slavery in Virginia and, later, North Carolina.

Sumner's outrage stemmed in part from the fact that Pierce's use of federal force in the Burns case represented an escalation in the tactics employed by slaveholders to maintain control over slavery. When Stephen Douglas and Henry Clay negotiated the Compromise of 1850, they agreed to a stricter Fugitive Slave Law in exchange for the end of the slave trade in the national capital and the admittance of California as a free state.[4] The measure required any federal judicial official in a free or slave state to assist with the capture and return of fugitive slaves.[5] Proslavery politicians did not necessarily mean for the army to be involved in runaway slave cases. Rather, they intended to rely on judges, U.S. Marshals, and ordinary citizens acting under the legal doctrine of *posse comitatus,* which deputized the residents of a locality to act as representatives of the law and capture accused fugitives.

Two batteries of the Fourth United States Artillery Regiment, accompanied by a company of U.S. Marines from Charlestown Navy Yard, marched into Boston in the spring of 1854 because, in the case of Anthony Burns, *posse comitatus* failed. "Our worst fears have been realized," a sixteen-year-old Charlotte Forten wrote on June 2, 1854, when federal troops arrived to take Burns back to the Old Dominion. The scene, witnessed by some 50,000 Bostonians, struck Forten: "With what scorn must that government be regarded which cowardly assembles thousands of soldiers to satisfy the demands of slaveholders." The young abolitionist worried about living in a country where "soldiers are to shoot down American citizens without mercy . . . by express orders of a government which broadly boasts of being the freest in the world."[6]

And Forten was far from alone in her judgments. Abolitionists across the North offered criticism of the army in their responses to the Burns case. Thomas Wentworth Higginson's sermon "Massachusetts in Mourning" declared that the use of the army to capture Burns showed that the Pierce administration intended to make all people in the free North slaves to the ideology of the Slave Power. This was the result, Higginson declared, of "our own military" being made "Slave-catchers."[7] No fan of military force, Henry David Thoreau wondered whether the Burns case was the consequence of maintaining a standing army in a democratic republic. What good were professional soldiers, Thoreau asked, if the federal government trained them "rob Mexico" and "carry back fugitive slaves to their masters?"[8] Richard Henry Dana, who defended Burns in his trial, sarcastically congratulated the federal government on the use of the army. In his closing remarks, Dana noted that "the forts and fleets . . . have been left in great peril, so that this great Republic might add to its glories the trophies of one more captured slave."[9]

Sumner joined the abolitionist chorus. After providing copies of the orders issued by the president directing federal troops to be ready to deploy to Boston, Sumner launched into an attack on President Pierce. "The President was not content with such forces as were then on hand in the neighborhood," he explained, "and the Adjutant General of the Army was directed to repair to the scene, there to superintend the execution of the statute." The reason, according to Sumner, was simple: "All this was done for the sake of Slavery."[10]

And it had been carried out at a reportedly extraordinary cost. When all was said and done and Burns was chained on a ship bound to return him to the slaveholding South, estimates of the cost of his recapture began to appear in sermons, speeches, and editorials. At the low end, some asserted it had cost the federal government $10,000 to return one enslaved man to one enslaver. Others claimed it had cost much more—perhaps as much as $40,000 or $50,000. In 2023 dollars, that meant that the Burns incident cost the federal government at least $345,000 and perhaps as much as $1.7 million. As one Vermont minister explained to his congregation, "This is the law, merciless, and unrighteous, and bloody, whose crushing weight a great and proud nation has just laid on one poor black man, literally enforcing it at the point of a bayonet, the mouth of a cannon."[11] Federal troops and federal weapons, all employed to uphold slavery.

Republicans did not soon forget the Burns case. They turned it into an example of the worst abuses of the Slave Power. Speaking in 1858 on the issue of army appropriations, Ohio's Benjamin Stanton (no relation Abraham Lincoln's secretary of war, Edwin Stanton) made certain his colleagues understood how the regular army had become an instrument of the proslavery faction within the federal government. "For some seven or eight years past," Stanton began, "the president has claimed and exercised the power of using the regular Army as a police." He wondered how long his fellow Republicans would "furnish the president a military force to aid him in establishing slavery." Stanton underscored his belief that any increase to the army, or any show of political support for the regulars, was "essentially a sectional and party measure." The use of the army by President Pierce, and by his successor, President James Buchanan, had "no parallel in the history of this country."[12]

If Stanton's impassioned accusations were any measure of Republican attitudes, the nation's newest political party clearly believed that their Democratic rivals were abusing the powers of government and threatening the rights of free citizens, all in the name of slavery. If the Republicans did not put a stop to these abuses—did not check the power that had been afforded to the regulars—the nation's professional soldiers would soon be seen, in Stanton's words, "shooting down peaceful and inoffensive citizens in the streets as though they were so many dogs." Stanton abhorred the thought of such a future, and he exhorted his Republican colleagues to right the Slave Power's wrongs. The Republican war against the army had begun in earnest.

2

REPUBLICANS VERSUS REGULARS, 1854–1861

The solemnity of the occasion draws over our heads that cloud of disunion which always arises whenever the subject of slavery is agitated. Still debate goes on, more ardently, earnestly, and angrily, than ever before. It employs now not merely logic, reproach, menace, retort, and defiance, but sabers, rifles, and cannon.

    —William Henry Seward, 1856

On April 9, 1856, William Henry Seward of New York rose to deliver a speech to the Senate. "To obtain an empire is easy and common," he began. "To govern it well is difficult and rare indeed."[1] It was a bold opening. The members of the upper chamber had spent most of the first session of the Thirty-Fourth Congress trading blows over Bleeding Kansas. Determining whether that territory should be a free or a slave state threatened to rend the nation in two. The political titans whose oratory and legislative skill had once helped to hold the republic together—Henry Clay, Daniel Webster, and John C. Calhoun—were gone. The age of compromise had ended. And those who would assume their mantle, Seward foremost among them, still struggled to match the eloquence and statecraft of the preceding generation.

Seward faced a significant challenge that early April day. He needed to convince his colleagues that electoral chicanery had gone on long enough in Kansas, but he also strove to articulate how events in a sparsely settled, distant western territory informed his changing political philosophy. "Seward, more than any other Republican," historian Elizabeth R. Varon has written, "assumed the responsibility for weaving events in Kansas into a coherent Republican creed."[2] The senator from New York had spent his political career as a prominent member of the Whig Party, but by 1856 Seward could no longer claim this affiliation. His former party had collapsed under the strain of the crisis in Kansas and its orphaned members had regrouped to form the Republican Party, welcoming Know-Nothings and disaffected Democrats into their fold. The party coalesced around a commitment to stopping the extension of slavery into the West. They were in favor of free labor, free soil, and free men.[3]

Seward gave considerable attention to the non-extension of slavery in his remarks. He also spoke repeatedly of the regular army, a far less obvious subject for a speech about the future of the Kansas Territory. Seward was not alone in his opposition to the army, nor was he singular in describing its soldiers and officers as helpmates to slave expansion. Other members of the emerging Republican caste—among them Lyman Trumbull of Illinois, Henry Wilson and Charles Sumner of Massachusetts, and Joshua Giddings of Iowa—echoed Seward's claims in their own impassioned speeches on the Kansas issue. The nation's newest political party, it soon became clear, had little regard for professional soldiers.

It was in Kansas and Nebraska, in the crucible of the crisis over popular sovereignty known as Bleeding Kansas, that the Republican Party's anti-army philosophy was forged. As their rhetoric coalesced into ideology, it soon became clear that the Republicans differed from their Whig predecessors in vehemently contesting military issues. After 1855, when federal troops turned their weapons on American citizens exercising their constitutional rights in Kansas, the Republican war on the army began in earnest. And it accelerated swiftly. By the eve of the Civil War, only two members of the Republican Party in the House, and none in the Senate, voted in favor of any legislation supporting the army.[4]

The emerging Republican rhetoric of antimilitarism was one piece of the party's effort to define the influence of the Slave Power. While scholars have long understood how antislavery ideology shaped early Republican politics, few have appreciated the sharp attack on the professional army that accompanied the party's assault on slavery, and most influential studies of the collapse of the Whig Party and the rise of the Republican Party have neglected military affairs.[5] Scholars such as Eric Foner and William Gienapp have offered arguments for the centrality of a free labor, antislavery ideology to the Republican political cause.[6] Closer examination of Republican rhetoric reveals that Republicans frequently and explicitly expressed opposition to the army as an extension of their antislavery politics. The army was, to Republican minds, proslavery and anti–free labor.

Republicans, had they set their minds to calculating percentages and fractions, would have found ample evidence for their theories in the history of the House and Senate committees on military affairs. The Senate established its standing committee in 1816, and the House followed suit in 1822. In the Senate, for the period spanning 1816 to 1861, 65 percent of the committee's members hailed from slaveholding states; in the House it was 55 percent. (See table 3 for lists of the members of the military affairs committees in both the House and the Senate. Tables 4 and 5 break down the committee members by their state affiliation.) Republicans in 1860 could have collated the data and concluded that with just 30 percent of the white population of the United States, the slaveholding states controlled significantly more than their share of the military affairs committees.

If the overall membership of the respective committees suggested that the slaveholding states acquired a moderate advantage relative to their population, the data on the men who chaired the committees revealed almost complete domination. In the Senate, men from slaveholding states chaired 86 percent of the committees, while in the House the total was 89 percent. (See graphs 2 and 3 for the state affiliations of the committee chairs.) Thomas Hart Benton of Missouri won the chairmanship of the Senate committee eight times, all prior to the Mexican–American War. Benton also chaired the House committee once, after he turned to opposing slave expansion and the Slave Power, following the Compromise of 1850. When he chaired the committee as a senator, he did so as both a slaveholder and perhaps the country's most ardent expansionist. Jefferson Davis was the only other politician who came close to matching Benton's tenure, with four congresses spent at the helm of the Senate committee.[7]

Democrats met Republican attacks on the army with an anemic defense. With little evidence to suggest that their political opponents had erred in

Table 3. Membership of the Military Affairs Committee, 1849–1861

HOUSE	SENATE
Thirty-First Congress (1849–1851)	
Armistead Burt (D-SC), Chair	Jefferson Davis (D-MS), Chair
Willaim A. Richardson (D-IL)	Solon Borland (D-AK)
James Wilson (W-NH)	Albert C. Greene (W-RI)
George A. Caldwell (D-KY)	James Shields (D-IL)
John A. King (W-NY)	William C. Dawson (W-GA)
Alexander Evans (W-MD)	
David K. Cartter (D-OH)	
Andrew Ewing (D-TN)	
Joseph R. Chandler (W-PA)	
Orasmus B. Matteson (W-NY)	
Thirty-Second Congress (1851–1853)	
Armistead Burt (D-SC), Chair*	James Shields (D-IL), Chair
William H. Bissell (D-IL)	Jeremiah Clemens (D-AL)
Meridith P. Gentry (W-TN)	Solon Borland (D-AK)
Willis A. Gorman (D-IN)	William C. Dawson (W-GA)
Alexander Evans (W-MD)	James C. Jones (W-TN)
Ephraim K. Smart (D-ME)	
Thaddeus Stevens (W-PA)	
John A. Wilcox (U-MS)	
Solmon G. Haven (W-NY)	
Charles J. Faulkner (W-VA)†	
Thirty-Third Congress (1853–1855)	
Thomas H. Benton (D-MO), Chair	James Shields (D-IL), Chair
William H. Bissell (D-IL)	John B. Weller (D-CA)
Charles J. Faulkner (D-VA)	Banjamin Fitzpatrick (D-AL)
Thomas M. Howe (W-PA)	William C. Dawson (W-GA)
William R. Smith (D-AL)	Robert W. Johnson (D-AK)
Nathaniel P. Banks (D-MA)	James C. Jones (W-TN)
James A. McDougall (D-CA)	
Emerson Etheridge (W-TN)	
Joshua Vansant (D-MD)	

Table 3. (*continued*)

HOUSE	SENATE
Thirty-Fourth Congress (1855–1857)	
John A. Quitman (D-MS), Chair	John B. Weller (D-CA), Chair
John Allison (Opp-PA)	Banjamin Fitzpatrick (D-AL)
William R. Sapp (Opp-OH)	Robert W. Johnson (D-AK)
Charles J. Faulkner (D-VA)	James C. Jones (W-TN)
John Williams (D-NY)	Alfred Iverson, Sr. (D-GA)
Benjamin Stanton (Opp-OH)*	Thomas G. Pratt (Opp-MD)
James W. Denver (D-CA)	
James Buffinton (Amcn-MA)	
Cadwaller C. Washburn (Opp-WI)	
Bayard Clarke (Opp-NY)†	
Thirty-Fifth Congress (1857–1859)	
John A. Quitman (D-MS)*, Chair	Jefferson Davis (D-MS), Chair
Charles J. Faulkner (D-VA)‡	Banjamin Fitzpatrick (D-AL)
Humphrey Marshall (Amcn-KY)	Robert W. Johnson (D-AK)
John H. Savage (D-TN)	Alfred Iverson, Sr. (D-GA)*
Benjamin Stanton (R-OH)	David C. Broderick (D-CA)
Milledge L. Bonham (D-SC)	Henry Wilson (R-MA)
Samuel R. Curtis (R-IA)	Preston King (R-NY)
George H. Pendleton (D-OH)	Arthur P. Hayne (D-SC)†
James Buffinton (R-MA)	
John J. McRae (D-MS)†	
Thirty-Sixth Congress (1859–1861)	
Benjamin Stanton (R-OH), Chair	Jefferson Davis (D-MS), Chair
Sameul R. Curtis (R-IA)	Banjamin Fitzpatrick (D-AL)
Milledge L. Bonham (D-SC)*	Robert W. Johnson (D-AK)
James Buffinton (R-MA)	James Chesnut, Jr. (D-SC)
Abram B. Olin (R-NY)	Jospeh Lane (D-OR)
John J. McRae (D-MS)	Henry Wilson (R-MA)
George H. Pendleton (D-OH)	Preston King (R-NY)
Henry C. Longnecker (R-PA)	
Alexander R. Boteler (Opp.-VA)	
George W. Hughes (D-MD)†	

D = Democrat; R = Republican; U = Union; W = Whig; Amcn = American; Opp = Opposition
* Member replaced; † Replacement member; ‡ Elevated to chairman

Table 4. House Military Affairs Committee Members by State, 1822–1861

Congress	South*	Border†	North‡	Total
17th	2	1	4	7
18th	3	1	3	7
19th	3	1	3	7
20th	4	0	3	7
21st	4	1	2	7
22nd	3	2	2	7
23rd	4	1	4	9
24th	5	1	3	9
25th	7	1	1	9
26th	5	1	3	9
27th	4	2	3	9
28th	4	1	4	9
29th	4	0	5	9
30th	4	1	4	9
31st	2	2	5	9
32nd	3	1	5	9
33rd	3	2	4	9
34th	2	0	7	9
35th	4	1	4	9
36th	3	0	6	9
Total	73	20	75	168

* South (AL, AR, FL, GA, LA, MS, NC, SC, TN, TX, VA)
† Border (DE, KY, MD, MO)
‡ North (CA, CT, IA, IL, IN, MI, MA, ME, MN, NH, NJ, NY, OH, OR, PA, RI, VT, WI)

Table 5. Senate Military Affairs Committee Members by State, 1816–1861

Congress	South*	Border†	North‡	Total
14th	3	1	1	5
15th	2	0	3	5
16th	2	0	3	5
17th	2	1	2	5
18th	1	2	2	5
19th	0	2	3	5
20th	1	2	2	5
21st	2	1	2	5
22nd	1	2	2	5
23rd	2	2	1	5
24th	1	2	2	5
25th	1	1	3	5
26th	2	1	2	5
27th	2	2	1	5
28th	2	2	1	5
29th	0	2	3	5
30th	3	2	2	7
31st	4	1	0	5
32nd	3	1	1	5
33rd	4	0	1	5
34th	4	1	1	6
35th	4	0	2	6
36th	4	0	3	7
Total	50	28	43	121

* South (AL, AR, FL, GA, LA, MS, NC, SC, TN, TX, VA)

† Border (DE, KY, MD, MO)

‡ North (CA, CT, IA, IL, IN, MI, MA, ME, MN, NH, NJ, NY, OH, OR, PA, RI, VT, WI)

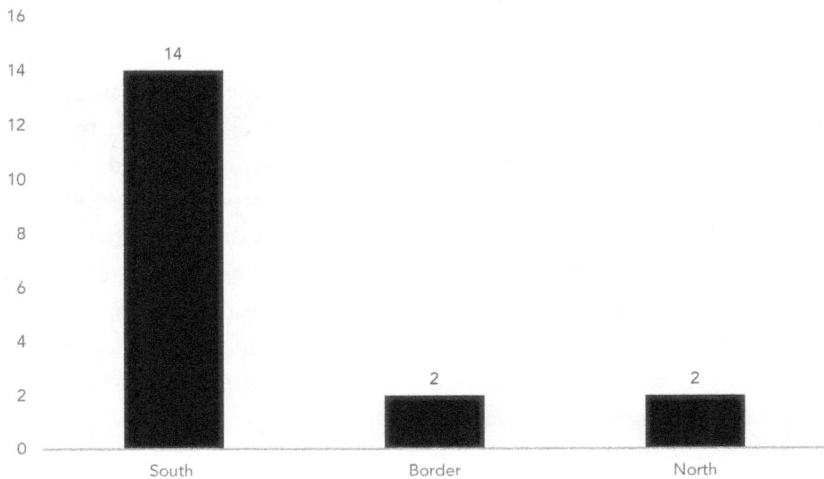

Graph. 2. House Committee on Military Affairs chairs, by region, 1822–1862

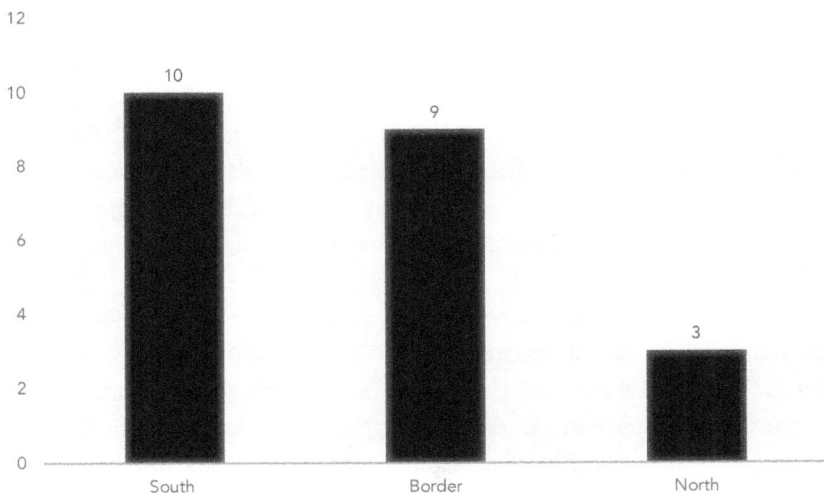

Graph. 3. Senate Committee on Military Affairs chairs, by region, 1816–1861

their descriptions of the army's work, Democrats reached for the rhetoric of civil war. They accused Republicans of attacking national institutions and sowing the seeds of disunion. There was nothing new in this tactic, freely employed by members of all political parties in the decades prior to the Civil War, when they wished to cast their political enemies as threats to national prosperity. That Democrats used it to respond to Republican accusations regarding the misappropriation of military resources represented an admission that the proslavery men had gotten their way. They knew the army was being directed toward supporting slave expansion in Kansas. More critically, they did not wish to see the weapon they freely wielded to spread slavery to the West turned against them. To attack the army, they exclaimed, was to attack the Union itself.

Whether viewed from the Democrat or the Republican perspective, the data told a straightforward story. Throughout the 1850s, the federal government had enabled the expansion of the regular army. Proslavery secretaries of war posted the bulk of American troops to the region legally open to slave expansion: the Southwest. Troops did not spread onto the Great Plains in large numbers, having few federal interests to protect in what contemporaries had labeled the "Great American Desert." Fort Laramie in Nebraska Territory represented the only significant U.S. installation on the Plains before the Civil War. Much of present-day Wyoming, Montana, the Dakotas, and Colorado (save for a slight increase following the gold rush of 1859) saw little military presence. Still, congressional dollars funded dozens of new military installations and helped raise multiple new regiments for service in the West. Southern Democrats used the army as an aggressive instrument of proslavery expansion.

The positive treatment of the army by southern Democrats underscored the dominance of the Slave Power within the federal government.[8] As Robert M. T. Hunter, a Democratic senator from Virginia, declared in the aftermath of the Mexican–American War, "It became all important for [the South] to claim the right to settle and colonize the vacant territory of the United States." This was necessary, Hunter said, for the South to keep parity with the expanding population of the North. The federal government, Hunter believed, owed the South that concession, and he voted at every opportunity to use the army to do that work.[9]

BLEEDING KANSAS

Although President Franklin Pierce claimed to abhor slavery, he supported the constitutional right of southerners to expand slavery into the territories. And he did little to prevent proslavery advocates from making a mockery of the electoral process when it came time for the citizens of Kansas to vote on whether they would allow slavery in their territory. The vote over slavery in Kansas produced two governments, each claiming to represent the will of the territory's citizens. At Lecompton, proslavery men wrote a constitution to govern the territory, while the free-state men convened their conference at Topeka. Pierce favored the government in Lecompton and recognized it as the legitimate territorial legislature.

Writing to Jefferson Davis from Platte City, Missouri, on February 26, 1856, David R. Atchison pressed the secretary to transfer to Kansas army officers who would not interfere with the territory's proslavery element. Atchison, a border ruffian leader, former senator, and prominent slaveholder, demanded from Davis explanations about the army personnel assigned to command in Kansas. When Captain Thomas Lee Brent transferred to the quartermaster post at Fort Riley, Atchison insisted that the officer "confine himself to the duties of his office." Brent should not interfere with the incursions of Missourians along the Kansas border or try to intercede in the violent and ongoing confrontations between the antislavery and proslavery elements in Kansas. Brent, a Virginian who entered West Point in 1830, died in 1858—before the Civil War could reveal his sectional loyalties.[10]

Residents of the territory feared what might come to pass if political contestation over the legitimate government of Kansas continued. One Kansan, writing to Senator Charles Sumner, said he wished for "Pierce to refrain from forcing us in to submission," but he acknowledged that in doing so the president "would be failing to obey his Southern masters." Still, Charles Stearns hoped cooler heads would prevail, saying he did not think the president fanatical enough "to hope of promoting his interests by sending an army to enforce the laws of Uncle Sam's creature the territorial government." In articulating his fears for the future of the territory, Stearns predicted precisely how Pierce would respond to the political challenge posed by the free-state men in Topeka.[11]

The president expressed outrage when antislavery settlers attempted to oust the proslavery government by voting in one of their own. The Topeka men had rankled the administration, and Pierce vowed to treat the abolitionists as traitors, subject to prosecution by the federal government. He bolstered his threats in a way that continued to erode the regular army's reputation among abolitionists, moderate Republicans, and Free-Soilers. Those who opposed the Democratic Party and its relationship to slavery balked at what they considered an abuse of executive power by the president. In late June, under instructions from Pierce, Colonel Edwin Vose Sumner accompanied two companies of the First Cavalry to Topeka to prevent the scheduled free-state meeting at Topeka on July 4. The orders all but guaranteed fireworks in Kansas on the nation's eightieth birthday.

Despite the half-regiment of regular troops on their doorstep, the free-state legislature proceeded with its meeting. Once the men tried to convene, Sumner felt obliged, as he explained to the War Department, "to march my command into the town, and draw it up in front of the building in which the Legislature was to meet."[12] When the legislature persisted, Sumner entered the House chamber, where a member asked the officer whether he was correct in understanding that "the legislature is dispersed at bayonet point?" Sumner could only reply that he would "use all the forces of my command to carry out my orders." When the colonel moved to the Senate chamber, a territorial senator admitted, "We are no condition to resist the U.S. troops; and if you order us to disperse, of course we must disperse."[13]

As Sumner rode away from the building, a reporter for Horace Greeley's *New York Tribune* waved the officer over. "Colonel," the newspaperman said, "you have robbed Oliver Cromwell of his laurels."[14] The accusation stunned Sumner. As far as he was concerned, he had only followed orders. As a military officer, he could do no more or less than the administration asked of him, and he had said as much to the men assembled in Topeka's Constitution Hall. While the legislators were engaged in politics, Sumner stressed that his profession demanded neutrality. Whatever his personal sympathies, "I am called upon to perform the painful duty of my life. Under the authority of the President, I am here to dissolve the Legislature. In accordance with my orders, I command you to disperse." Sumner insisted that politics had little to do with his actions: "God knows I have no party feeling in the matter, and I will have none while I hold my present position in Kansas."[15] He had nothing more than a direct order from his commander in chief, and he pleaded with the free-state men to disperse peaceably.

Sumner did not have long to hold his position in Kansas. Davis reassigned the lifelong soldier to patrol the Oregon Trail west of the territory, where his regiment would search for threats to the settlers traveling the trail to the Willamette Valley. At least one Republican newspaper, sympathetic to Sumner's hesitation over dispersing the free-state men, asserted that Jefferson Davis had dismissed the officer from his duty at Fort Leavenworth "for being an abolitionist."[16]

Sumner's actions provided ample fodder for the nation's press. As the country looked toward the presidential election that fall, newspapers from both parties used the Kansas incident to cast doubts on their opposition. The *Chicago Democratic Press,* a newspaper clinging to its Jacksonian roots and backing John C. Frémont in 1856, exclaimed that Franklin Pierce had perpetrated "the crowning act of outrage on free institutions." Vermont's *Burlington Free Press,* an old Whig sheet, subtly declared the action to be "one of the most grievous outrages recorded in our history." A correspondent to the *Hillsdale Standard,* a Republican paper in Michigan, described Sumner as executing his orders "unwillingly," and the reporter believed the army officer regretted his "odious" actions.[17]

Abolitionists also paid close attention to the increasing willingness of the Pierce government to deploy federal troops to support proslavery politics. Kansas in 1856 was the next act in a drama that had begun two years earlier in Boston, during the arrest and trial of the escaped slave Anthony Burns. Wendell Phillips took a harsh view of Edwin Sumner in a speech following the dispersal of the Topeka legislature. Speaking of the army officer in relation to his cousin, Senator Sumner, Phillips figured "nature took all the brains designed for the name and gave it to Charles and left the others nothing but limbs." Jefferson Davis, Phillips claimed, had "scooped out [Colonel Sumner's] brain and sent him to there to Kansas like a broomstick, with his message written upon it"—the message being that Kansas would submit to the rule of slavery.[18] If Davis had performed such an operation, rumor held, the task would have been formidable. Sumner had a notably thick skull, according to his contemporaries. During the Mexican–American War, at the Battle of Cerro Gordo, a musket ball purportedly struck Sumner in the skull and bounced off the officer's pate, earning him the nickname Bull Sumner.

Democratic papers, meanwhile, applauded Colonel Sumner's actions. Editors and reporters fueled the ire of the Republican Party by insisting on a link between the proslavery Pierce administration and the regulars. The *Carolina Spartan* cheered Sumner for obeying Pierce's instructions in "dispersing the bogus legislature of Kansas traitors." The Philadelphia *North American* took an acerbic view of the free-state legislature. The editors lauded the army officer for dispersing "one of the most treasonable bodies ever assembled in this or any other country." Sumner, the paper explained, had reversed "the degrading result of the efforts of the Aid Society and the 'Free State Movement.'"[19]

As the conversation surrounding Sumner grew increasingly heated, descriptions of the army in both the press and in the halls of Congress underwent a rhetorical shift. Careful editors and orators still clarified that Sumner had acted at the behest of Pierce and Davis, stressing that under federal law Sumner had no authority to act without approval from his commander in chief. Sloppier observers, meanwhile, eroded this distinction. Rather than emphasizing that the men of the army and the officers who led them served under the direction of the Pierce government, they asserted that soldiers and officers acted against the free-state legislature because they concurred with the view of the administration. Republicans intent on condemning the reach of the Slave Power brushed aside legal niceties and asserted that professional soldiers were Democratic drones, card-carrying proslavery conservatives who had no interest in a free labor West.

For the five years prior to the Civil War, the leaders of the rising Republican Party honed rhetoric that cast professional soldiers as Democrats of a conservative, proslavery bent. The *Buffalo Morning Express* provided an early example. Just a few days after the Sumner incident, the newspaper described to its readers the ongoing furor in Kansas. "The United States troops make no effort to stop this pillage," the paper wrote, regarding proslavery men entering the territory from Missouri. The men of the army, the reporter claimed, "never pretend to interfere with the pro-slavery ruffians." Sumner had disbanded the free-state legislature and then his men had allowed more proslavery men to enter the state unimpeded, or so the *Morning Express* believed. It was not the wish of the Piece administration. It was not under orders from Secretary of War Davis. The army, the paper claimed, and the men who served in it, were outright allies of the proslavery cause.

In the wake of Sumner's actions, Congress demanded an explanation from the Pierce administration. The Senate asked the president to provide information relative to any instructions "issued to any military officer in command in Kansas to disperse any unarmed meeting of the people of that Territory, or to prevent by military power, any assemblage of the people of that territory."[20] Davis and Pierce insisted they had granted no explicit approval for violence against civilians in Kansas. Davis forwarded correspondence he believed was relevant to the Senate's request. A February 15 letter stressed the use of proper civilian authority prior to any army involvement. If resistance to civilian authority occurred—and only *after* it occurred—then the territorial governor could call upon the military to aid in the law's execution or to suppress insurrectionary combinations. A March 26 letter echoed earlier guidance that "only when armed resistance is offered" could the government call on federal troops.[21]

To escape from Republican criticism, Davis publicly placed the blame for the dispersal of the free-state legislature in Kansas entirely on Sumner, claiming that the longtime army officer had acted outside the limits of his orders. Historian David Potter observed that Davis calculated the timing of this blame shifting to mollify northern critics who had refused to pass the army appropriations bill.[22] The tactic worked, but it further stunned Sumner, who was at a loss to identify when and where he had erred in his conduct. After Davis met several of Sumner's letters with obfuscation about what the orders had expected of the officer, Sumner dropped the matter and turned his attention back to his work.[23] When Davis left the War Department in March 1857, Sumner did not appear on the secretary's final list of recommendations for brevet promotions, despite his otherwise meritorious service record.[24] Born in 1797, Sumner went on to become the oldest field commander to serve in the Civil War—on the Peninsula, at Antietam, and at Fredericksburg—before dying of fever in March of 1863.

The presidential response failed to mollify Pierce's critics. The *Chicago Journal* called the report "miserable pettifogging." The *New York Herald,* a sheet claiming no party sympathies, deemed the action and the subsequent justification the worst federal military blunder since the Greytown affair, an 1854 incident in which an American naval vessel, the USS *Cyane,* bombarded the village of Greytown along the Mosquito Coast of Nicaragua, then under British protection.[25] In the Greytown case, Pierce had refused to admit he had sanctioned the action in response to taxes being levied by the British on American ships using Cornelius Vanderbilt's Nicaragua route to reach California. When Davis and Pierce again refused to clarify whether they had given Sumner explicit orders to disperse the free-state government by force, the action suggested a pattern to the *Herald* editors. The president and his proslavery allies failed to be transparent about their use of federal resources to achieve administration aims, such as expanding slavery, both in the American interior and across the globe.

THE ARMY BILL OF 1856

Dissatisfied by the administration's continual obfuscation, Republicans in the House responded to Davis's vagaries by refusing to pass an army appropriations bill in late July. The tactic aimed to withhold funds from the regulars to check the perceived overreach of executive power by Pierce. Instead, Republicans in the House proposed a funding bill with an amendment that required Pierce to remove all troops from Kansas in exchange for continued fiduciary support of the army. The legislators also took time to instruct the commander in chief on how he should deploy the army: "No part of the military of the United States shall be employed in aid of enforcing territorial laws not affirmed by Congress."[26] The amended bill received the approval of the majority-Republican House.

The amendment made it clear that Republicans considered Pierce's use of the army to enforce the laws unprecedented and undemocratic. Indiana Republican Lucien Barbour explained, "My amendment prevents [the president] from using the armed force of the United States to arrest individuals alleged to have violated sham laws of a usurping legislature." Alexander Stephens of Georgia captured the view of southern Democrats as he took issue with the Republican directive. "The president is the commander in chief of the army," Stephens reminded his fellow representatives, and he noted, "We can withhold supplies, it is true, but we cannot grant supplies up on the condition that he will use the force as we please. This would make Congress, in effect, the commander in chief." Republicans shouted the future Confederate vice president down, and Ohioan Joshua Giddings asserted that the army's actions in Kansas represented "a despotism such as was never known in this country until the present year, and such, I think, as will never be known again." The Kansas Territory's nonvoting delegate, John W. Whitfield, assured the chamber that the people of Kansas also desired the withdrawal of U.S. troops. "They are ready to appeal to the ballot box," he promised, "instead of to the cartridge box." Whitfield then stated simply, "We desire the territory of Kansas to be let alone."[27]

Giddings accused the Slave Power of a far greater conspiracy than trying to install a proslavery government in Kansas. The tactic was nothing new for the Ohioan, whom Congress censured for violating the gag rule in 1841 when he spoke about the infamous *Creole* incident, asserting that enslaved people who had revolted aboard the ship and claimed their freedom by landing in the Bahamas—a British colony that had outlawed slavery—should gain their freedom. In 1856, he suggested that money from the annual army appropriation would indicate not only that the legislative branch approved of what Pierce had already done with the army in Kansas but also that it would offer the president the opportunity to "bring other troops" to the territory. Passing the army bill would allow the leading men of the proslavery movement "to vie with Nero or Nicholas in tyranny." Giddings used historical examples to drive home his objections to the use of the army in Kansas. The Slave Power, he warned, would be content to accept the funding bill as a rubber stamp for further transgressions against the free-soil advocates in Kansas. They "will use the sword and the bayonet," Giddings predicted of Pierce and his allies, and "drive freedom from Kansas and plant gaunt slavery upon the soil so long consecrated to liberty."[28]

Democrat Lawrence M. Keitt argued against the Republican amendment in the House. South Carolina's fire-eating representative asserted that his party had done more than the Republicans or their Whig predecessors to shape the development of the country. Keitt, who had assisted Preston Brooks in his attack on Charles Sumner in 1854, credited his party with rearing the federal government "through toil and travail, through blood and sacrifice." He then admitted to every accusation Republicans had levied at the Democrats regarding their supposed domination of federal resources. Democrats had, Keitt explained, "invested it [the federal government] with authority, have enriched it with treasuries, and fleets, and armies, and have endowed it with Senates, and courts, and judges." Should the Republicans get their wish in forcing Pierce to run the army according to their will, he said, the government would be "the puppet of Abolitionism." To the South it would be "a *foreign Government.*" And the representative vowed that should his prediction come to pass, "the South will tear it down from the turret to the foundation stone."[29]

When the bill arrived in the Senate, the Democrat-dominated upper chamber only proposed one amendment, striking out the House proviso that required President Pierce to withdraw the army from Kansas. Only two Republicans voted for the Senate version of the bill, which passed with the support of twenty-four Democrats to eight opposition votes from the Republicans. When the bill returned to the House for its concurrence, the body refused to agree to the Senate's changes, and after three conference committee meetings, the army appropriations bill failed to pass before the end of the legislative session. Just as it had done in the House, the Senate debate over the bill proved contentious and was filled with invective.

Lyman Trumbull, the junior senator from Illinois, used a portion of his first speech before the Senate to stake out his position on military affairs. Trumbull's subsequent political career carried him from the high of helping to draft the Thirteenth Amendment and thus playing a part in ending slavery in the United States to the low of being one of ten Republicans who voted to acquit Andrew Johnson in the seventeenth president's impeachment trial. One twentieth-century biographer aptly labeled him a "Conservative Radical."[30] In 1856, just one year into his legislative term, he could already articulate a critique of the Slave Power that focused on the army—and the deployment of troops in Kansas. Trumbull expressed his wish that the nation would "never see United States soldiers engaged in forcing submission to the barbarous and inhuman acts of that spurious legislature which was forced upon the people of Kansas by violence and against their will."[31] For his first effort, Trumbull received warm congratulations from than no less than party leaders Charles Sumner and Salmon P. Chase.[32]

William Seward captured the mood of his fellow Republicans in a speech that defined his party's developing view of the army. "I will grant," Seward began, "for the sake of argument, that with Federal battalions you can carry slavery into Kansas and maintain it there." But he queried his Democratic rivals: "Are you quite confident that this republican form of government can then be upheld and preserved?" Drawing on an infamous historical example, Seward offered a word of caution to the proslavery Democrats of the chamber. "You will then yourselves have introduced the Trojan horse. No republican government ever has endured, with standing armies maintained in its bosom to enforce submission to its laws." Then, introducing a favorite argument of abolitionists—that slavery for any man meant slavery for all men—Seward concluded with a flourish. "A people who have once learned to relinquish their rights under compulsion," he explained, "will not be long in forgetting they ever had any. In extending slavery into Kansas, therefore, by arms, you will subvert the liberties of the people."[33]

Seward had both history and antislavery zeal in his corner. The future secretary of state adapted his comments from the critiques of the Constitution made by the Anti-Federalists, who shared the conviction that standing armies undermined the legitimacy of freely elected governments. Like his Revolutionary-era counterparts, Seward could point to numerous examples as proof of his assertions of the incompatibility of large armies and democracies. Two examples proved favorites of critics of the army: the overthrow of the Roman Republic by Julius Caesar and the dissolution of England's Parliament at the hands of Oliver Cromwell.

Alabama's Clement Clay rebuked Seward for his speech, claiming that all the New Yorker had done was sow the seeds of disunion. Henry Clay's third cousin expressed frustration with Seward's remarks but could muster no defense of his party's reliance on the army to achieve its proslavery aims. Instead, the Alabamian opted for inflammatory rhetoric. Seward, Clay claimed, loved to "minister profanely in this temple of the Union." Northern men, "even now," were "industriously heaping fuel on the flame they have kindled." The reason that Seward and the Republicans had failed to defeat the proslavery partisans in Kansas, Clay claimed, was because the territory had voted in favor of slavery. Still, Clay had no defense against the substance of Seward's remarks, nor did he deny that the army formed an integral part of the effort to expand slavery into the West.

Clay furthered his argument by asserting that men who had no military experience ought not assume to direct the actions of the army. Clay mocked the arguments of Henry Wilson, the Massachusetts senator who would go on to chair the Committee on Military Affairs for more than a decade during the Civil War and Reconstruction (1861–1872). Prior to Clay's address, Wilson had offered negative remarks concerning Jefferson Davis's term as secretary of war and had urged his fellow senators to stand up to the secretary by rejecting the army appropriations bill. In reply, Clay reminded the Senate that Davis had been a military hero, displaying "patriotism and courage . . . on the heights of Monterey and plains of Buena Vista." Of Wilson, who had grown up in poverty and indentured servitude before training as a cobbler, Clay said, "When one who has displayed neither of those virtues makes such a charge against such a man, he should be regarded rather with the pity with which we look upon an idiot, who cannot appreciate an emotion he was never experienced."[34]

Andrew Butler of South Carolina, a leading Senate Democrat, spoke fervently against the House amendment demanding the removal of the troops from Kansas. Butler, who had coauthored the Kansas–Nebraska Act and bore significant responsibility for the events fueling the appropriation debate, made a persuasive observation: there was no surer way to inspire a military coup against the government than to stop paying soldiers. After all, he reminded his colleagues, the first man to lose his head to the guillotine had been the one who invented it. Failing to fund the army, Butler declared, represented "no better occasion" for the president to rally the troops "and establish a military despotism."[35] The response was calculated, turning the very fears of military rule so frequently expressed by Republicans on the Senate floor to a tangible threat, for which they would bear ultimate responsibility.

Failing to appropriate funds for the army was unprecedented. President Pierce called Congress back for a special session to rectify the situation, forcing both chambers to agree to a bill that did not mandate removal of the troops from Kansas. Ultimately, the Democrats triumphed because they controlled the executive branch and Republicans did not yet have the strength in the legislature to overcome their opponents. In early September, the New York Times succinctly captured the results of the political fight over Pierce's misuse of the army. In a short editorial, the Times previewed the sentiments of Republicans in the Civil War and Reconstruction eras, clearly associating the army with the proslavery policies of the southern Democrats: "The Pro-Slavery party has again triumphed. The President and Senate have carried their point, and the federal army may still be employed—at the expense of the federal Government—in dragooning the inhabitants of Kansas into obedience to the infamous laws of the sham Legislature."[36]

Newspapers across the North equated Pierce's use of the military to support the proslavery government of Kansas with the despotism of Oliver

Cromwell during the English Civil War.[37] The Washington, DC–based abolitionist newspaper the *National Era* argued that Pierce had no constitutional
authority to order troops to uphold a proslavery territorial government. No
military decisions could be made, the editors explained, without "legislative
assent." For the president to use the army to "interpose an armed arbiter
in political controversies," the paper noted, "swallows up and overrides all
other powers."[38] In short, the editors argued, Pierce had used the army in a
manner incompatible with the Constitution, confirming Republican arguments that the army represented a threat to democracy. Frederick Douglass
lamented that when free-soilers had been under threat by so-called border
ruffians, "Fort Leavenworth was silent." But "as soon as one Border Ruffian
is shot down, troops leap forth . . . at the call of the President."[39]

The controversy over the Republican amendment elicited widespread
commentary. The politically idiosyncratic *New York Herald* adopted a Republican perspective and decried "the attempt to dragoon the House into
this policy of securing slavery in Kansas by the forcible expulsion of the
antislavery settlers by the United States army and the border ruffians." The
editors urged their readers to remember Pierce's actions when the November election arrived. "The military despotism, the military *coup d'état* which
the little man, Mr. Pierce, is thus attempting in behalf of Mr. Buchanan in the
South, should be resisted by the House," the paper urged, declaring it "better have no army than to permit the Executive, with the army, to override
the constitution and the laws." The *New York Tribune,* a firmly Republican
sheet, meanwhile, wondered whether an army was necessary at all: "For, if
the army should once to go to pieces," the editors claimed, "it is altogether
likely that the people might find out that they could do uncommonly well
without one."[40]

Democratic newspapers responded with equally vehement attacks on
the Republican position. The *Western Democrat* in North Carolina clothed
its response in patriotism. The editors lamented the treatment "our gallant
little army" had received in Congress. The paper adopted a distinctly sar-
castic tone, proclaiming, "We could do remarkably well without our army,
of course—none should bear arms but Black 'Republicans' and they must
carry nothing but Sharpe's rifles." The reference to John Brown's choice
of weapon at Pottawatomie Creek would not have been lost on the paper's
readers. The editors then invoked disunion to bring their case home to

readers: "Yes, these Black 'Republicans' will destroy the Army, destroy the Navy, destroy the Constitution, destroy the Union, destroy our liberties, destroy everything we cherish and revere." "Destroy the army by all means," the *Democrat* exclaimed, "and 'let the Union slide.'"[41] The article contained every rhetorical flourish expected in an editorial on a sectional issue and indicated the agitation both parties felt over the chaos in Kansas.[42]

One Charleston newspaper charged the Republicans with attempting to dissolve the Union by failing to support the regulars. "The Constitution makes it the duty of Congress to provide for the common defense," the *Standard* explained, "but Black Republicans violate and refuse to fulfill the requirements of the Constitution." The editors firmly believed that the Republicans intended to make the army an instrument of their political will and deny the South the support of regular troops. The newspaper explained that should the Republicans deny Pierce the use of the army, he could call upon the civilians of the South to defend Democratic interests, claiming "the South has a standing army independent of the will of an abolition Congress. One Southerner is equal to a dozen white livered cowardly abolitionists." Convinced that the Republicans were intent on dissolving the army altogether, the editors finally exclaimed, "If the North can get along without a standing army," the article concluded, "the South can."[43]

The importance of the 1856 debate, however, lay in the Republican Party's growing concern over how Democrats abused the deployment of the regular army. After 1856, Republicans increasingly linked the regular army to the political philosophy and goals of the Democratic Party, a trend that continued into the Civil War. Another trend that emerged from the 1856 debate was the Republican strategy of using their congressional authority over military affairs to challenge the executive's use of the army. Because the Constitution divided authority over the army between two branches of the federal government—the president as commander in chief and Congress in charge of manpower and appropriations—the two bodies operated within the system of checks and balances envisioned by the Framers. Party members issued similar checks in trying to force emancipation during the Civil War and in fighting for military protection of African Americans during Reconstruction.

Republican attitudes toward the army continued to coalesce during the administration of Pennsylvania Democrat (and doughface) James Buchanan, crystalized by the Mormon War of 1857 (the Utah War). At the height of Buchanan's presidency, the Republican opposition united against using the military for what increasingly seemed to be southern policies. The annual army appropriations bill in 1859 passed with 108 Democrats favoring the measure and only three against, but with only two Republicans backing the bill as eighty-one attempted to vote it down. In the equivalent vote in the Senate, no Republicans approved of the measure, which passed with the votes of twenty-one Democrats.[44] Notably, the Democratic voting block remained solid for military expenditures even as the party moved toward its 1860 split.

Following Buchanan's 1856 election, Jefferson Davis left the War Department in the hands of John B. Floyd. Floyd, a Virginian and a slaveholder, would eventually provide Ulysses S. Grant with one of his first Civil War victories when he surrendered Fort Donelson on the Mississippi River in 1862. In 1856, however, he represented continuity in the War Department, which spent the 1850s entirely in the hands of slaveholders. Southern Democrats viewed control of the War Department as a critical bulwark against the rising Republican Party, which continued to probe military affairs for evidence of the Slave Power conspiracy. In November 1856, a correspondent identifying himself as "Senex" wrote to Jefferson Davis to ask that the outgoing secretary ensure that in the new administration, the "Departments of the Treasury and War, and even of the Navy, are retained in Southern hands."[45]

Senex emphasized the importance of retaining southern control over specific cabinet posts because he believed it would guard against Black Republicans seizing control of the government, even if they won the election of 1860. If the Republican Party triumphed at the next presidential hustings, the mysterious writer declared, "a Napoleonic demonstration would ... be called for." To fight for slavery's survival, he predicted that "grab game" would be the policy. If southerners controlled the government's money, soldiers, and sailors, it would be much easier to seize the resources needed to provide the basis for a war of southern independence. Predicting the Lost Cause rhetoric of a Confederate loss in the face of overwhelming Union resources, Senex told Davis that the outgoing secretary would likely have to act as "the Leonidas of the South" in the coming "Thermopylae ordeal."[46]

Military attention shifted from Kansas to Utah in early months of the Buchanan administration, as the new president confronted the prospect of a war against the leaders of the Mormon Church. The army expedition to Utah was mustered to support Buchanan's decision to nominate a new governor

THE ARMY UNDER FIRE

for the territory in place of Mormon leader Brigham Young. As early as 1851, reports began arriving in Washington of Young's choice to ignore the U.S. Constitution and to flaunt federal laws—installing Mormon judges, harassing federal officials, and causing serious trouble with the Native nations in the territory. Historian Norman Furniss has written that most federal reports from Utah to Washington "left unclear whether the people [Mormons] habitually kicked their dogs; otherwise their calendar of infamy in Utah was complete."[47]

As the expedition mobilized, opponents of the Buchanan administration took notice of the president's activities, with some speculating that Utah presented an opportunity for the new executive to take the country's attention away from events in Kansas. In an anonymous book-length poem entitled *Mormoniad,* one writer took the epic of Homer as the basis for a critique of Buchanan ("he who would not wed"), declaring:

And—when the Kansas war was done,
And freemen were no longer slaves—
His legions toward the setting sun
Drew off, to fill more glorious graves.

Later, in verses depicting the congressional response to Buchanan's request for troops to invade Utah, the poem's author noted that the leaders of the legislative branch "all hipped and all hurrahed." The only men who did not join the chorus of approbation for the army were "a few Republicans, who wept."[48]

The author of the poem imagined the Utah War as a quid pro quo by the president: defeat Mormonism by sending the regular army to Utah, thus also removing troops from the ongoing struggle over Kansas. If Buchanan were to address the Mormon problem, he needed Kansas out of the way. "Admit, I say Lecompton," the poet wrote, imagining Buchanan as his speaker, "and, sirs, I'll draw my army out of Kansas, and with it—what is needed most—Make Mormon Young 'give up the ghost'!"[49] An anti-Buchanan, antislavery newspaper in Emporia, Kansas, put the matter more simply than the balladeer: Buchanan had tried to distract the nation with a Mormon War while working to "plant" slavery in Kansas. "A day of reckoning is coming," the editors predicted. "The year 1860 is not far off, and the people will remember the follies of this Utah business, as well as the villainies practised in Kanzas."[50]

In Congress, Republicans expressed less consternation about James Buchanan's deployment of the army to Utah territory than they had about the use of the regulars in Kansas. Still, Republican leaders questioned yet another presidential ploy to expand the army. Simon Cameron of Pennsylvania suggested that the blame and responsibility for the expedition fell on Buchanan. Cameron, who would soon find himself in the seat of the secretary of war in the Lincoln administration, railed against the cost of sending 2,500 federal troops into Utah. The senator critiqued his fellow Pennsylvanian and said it would have made greater fiscal sense to call out a territorial militia than to spend further military resources. "This war is a war of the Administration," Cameron explained, "and I desire that the responsibility of it shall be on the Administration. I have no faith in their ability to conduct it; and I believe that before a year has passed over it will be evident to every citizen of the country that they have committed a great blunder." Cameron's speech represented another Republican probe into the misuse of the army by the executive, in the aftermath of Kansas and Nebraska.[51]

Schuyler Colfax, the Republican senator from Indiana, pointed out that if his colleagues were to examine the use of the army in Kansas versus its use in Utah, they would find grave inconsistences. Because proslavery southern Democrats had relied on the army to ensure the victory of the proslavery government in Kansas by dispersing the free-state legislature, Utah had every right to enter the Union under the same logic, so long as the people of the territory wished to be governed by the leaders of the Mormon Church. As much as Democrats disliked the idea, Utah represented, according to Colfax "the first fruits of your Lecompton doctrine."[52] That the Buchanan administration would again use the army to dislodge a territorial government that did not meet with the approval of the Democratic Party represented another mark in the record of the abuses of the Slave Power.

From 1856 to 1860, as federal troops marched across Kansas enforcing the will of the Franklin Pierce administration, and to Utah at the behest of James Buchanan, Republicans in Washington articulated a political philosophy of antimilitarism. Though Kansas faded from view, the contestation over the territory had allowed the nation's newest political party to make an issue of the army. The new Republican doctrine spurred James Buffington of Massachusetts to remind his colleagues in the House of Representatives that America had won its independence through the efforts of volunteers, not professional soldiers. The dedication "of any large portion of the community to the exclusive business of bearing arms," he explained, "is as adverse to the rights and interests of the Republic as it is hostile to our common institutions and our common safety." Events in Kansas offered incontrovertible proof of the axiom, he explained. "Military interference," in national affairs, he lamented, "is becoming supreme." He urged the House and the American people to fight against the supremacy of the professional soldier, saying that the country could not allow the regulars "to desecrate the parchment on which the Declaration of Independence in written, by permitting it to be taken for a drum head."[53]

Nearly six years to the day after Buffington's remarks, secessionists in Charleston Harbor turned formerly federal cannons on two batteries of the First United States Artillery regiment inside of Fort Sumter. Under the direction of Pierre G. T. Beauregard, an 1838 West Point graduate, rebel volunteers fired the opening salvo of the American Civil War. By the time Robert E. Lee surrendered to Ulysses S. Grant at Appomattox Court House in 1865, more than 2 million men would don blue army uniforms to fight for the Union. Nearly 1 million more would choose Confederate gray. Save for the twenty-five authorized regiments of regular troops, which were kept in units segregated from the volunteer forces, each man who picked up a musket did so as a citizen-soldier. Buffington and his Republican colleagues could justify a war fought by volunteers and celebrate their contributions to the Union war effort. While doing so, they also found ample opportunity to heap further criticism on the nation's professional troops. The Civil War allowed Republican antimilitarism to reach its peak.

INTERLUDE
THE SENATOR

On December 23, 1861, fifty-two men gathered in the Senate for the last day of debate before the Christmas recess. They could spread out more than usual. Sixteen of their former colleagues had decided over the previous year that they would cast their lot with the Confederacy. Led out in a dramatic procession by Mississippi's Jefferson Davis, they vacated the upper chamber of the Capitol Building for a city just over one hundred miles to the south. These southerners believed, as Davis put it in his final address before the national legislature, that they were "about to be deprived in the Union of the rights which our fathers bequeathed to us."[1] Driven by this fear and committed to maintaining the institution of Black chattel slavery, they swapped the banks of the Potomac for the banks of the James and planned to govern their new nation from Richmond, Virginia.

As it came to its close, 1861 had been, to put it mildly, a monumental year in the still young nation's history. In the wake of Abraham Lincoln's election as the first Republican president, on November 6, 1860, eleven states voted to secede from the federal Union. Lincoln's election proved a powerful threat to the slaveholding South. Though the new president promised not to interfere with slavery where it existed, many in the South believed the Kentucky-born Lincoln would join with the Radical members of his party and pursue slavery's abolition. In one of the great strokes of irony in American history, the act of secession made abolition far more likely than if the South had simply taken Lincoln at his word.

In secession's wake, both the United States and the Confederacy began raising armies filled with thousands of eager volunteers. Young men set off for recruiting depots and army camps like the youth in Stephen Crane's

THE ARMY UNDER FIRE

The Honorable John Sherman, Ohio

Red Badge of Courage, who had "long despaired of witnessing a Greeklike struggle" and "burned to enlist."[2] In the United States, their steps resounded to the call of President Lincoln for 75,000 troops to subdue the rebellion. They were citizen-soldiers in the mold of Cincinnatus and his American cousin George Washington. They would be soldiers for as long as their nation needed them to take up arms and defend its values on battlefields thousands of miles from their homes. They fought for the goal of saving the Union. As soon as that job was done, and the political future of the country was settled, they demanded to return home, to trade swords for plowshares and to become citizens once again.[3]

The Civil War's citizen volunteers consciously set themselves apart from the small class of professional soldiers who fought alongside them. During the war, these temporary troops contrasted their values sharply with those of the West Point–trained officers who often commanded them in the field. They, like the founding generation, held the professional army to be politically suspect, even antithetical to the values of their democratic republic. That 313 commissioned officers of that professional army had resigned their positions and joined the Confederacy did little to help the reputation of the regulars in the eyes of the average American.[4]

Statistics on the antebellum officer corps' "secession winter" somewhat justified Republican concerns. The group that left for the Confederacy accounted for 24 percent of the officers in the old army, a slight overrepresentation in terms of the nation's overall population; 20 percent of all white Americans lived in states that joined the Confederacy.[5] Zeroing in on West Point–trained officers, the bane of the wartime Republican Party, only 67 percent of all academy graduates hailing from Confederate states joined Confederate armies, while 20 percent remained loyal and 12 percent chose not to fight. The military academy had more of a "nationalizing influence," as historian Wayne Wei-siang Hsieh has described it, than Republicans acknowledged. Instead, they claimed that even the academy graduates who remained to fight for the Union were politically unreliable.[6]

The departures certainly did little to raise the esteem of the Senate, which, on that chilly December day, found its members debating an army appropriations bill. Because of the defections of their southern colleagues, the Senate chamber was dominated by the new Republican Party. It was well known that the political coalition founded after the crisis in Kansas and the shattering of the Second Party System opposed the expansion of slavery. Some of its most Radical members desired to see slavery abolished and Black men enfranchised. But that debate was still to come.

As war consumed the energy of the nation, it soon became clear that the new party in power also nursed a powerful loathing for the nation's professional army. And late on the afternoon of December 23, Republican senator

John Sherman of Ohio gained the floor. Sherman was serving his first term in the Senate, elected by special ballot when his fellow Ohioan, Salmon P. Chase, vacated his seat to serve as Lincoln's treasury secretary. But he was not without experience—terms in the House throughout the 1850s, where he had shown opposition to the Kansas-Nebraska Act and had chaired the Ways and Means Committee, meant he understood the process of appropriations particularly well.

In fact, the December 1861 speech was not the first time Sherman spoke on military appropriations. When he was a junior member of the Thirty-Fourth Congress, in 1856, his peers selected Sherman to travel to Kansas and observe the conditions there relative to the ongoing struggle over popular sovereignty in the territory. Sherman's 1,188-page report, which described violence throughout Kansas, seems to have significantly affected the then thirty-three-year-old's political views. Upon his return from Kansas, he proposed an amendment to the annual army appropriations bill that would bar the use of federal troops to enforce the laws passed by the questionably legitimate, certainly proslavery, Kansas territorial legislature. The amendment passed the House but not the Senate, and the work of the army went on, unimpeded by Congress. Still, like many future Republicans, one of the key lessons Sherman derived from the crisis in Kansas was to put no faith in the professional army.[7]

Late in 1861, Sherman maintained strong reservations about passing an expanded army appropriations bill. Even in a time of war, he exclaimed, he could not find any cause to raise the army appropriation. His reasoning? Professional soldiers held no enthusiasm for the war or devotion to the Union. These men had spent more than a decade working under a War Department managed by slaveholders. "For the last eight or ten years," Sherman told the assembly, "the intercourse of the officers in the army has been such, the influences that have been brought over them have been such, as to impair their efficiency and their usefulness."[8] Regular troops were no better than the Democrats who had pushed the nation to the brink of crisis and the slaveholding republic that was attempting to bring the Union to ruin.[9]

While Sherman held forth on the floor—and his fellow Republicans likely nodded their assent to his tirade against the army—a forty-one-year-old brigadier general convalesced at home, attempting to recover from the strain brought on by assuming command of the Union forces in Lexington,

Kentucky, earlier that year. He had graduated from West Point sixth in the class of 1840, and at the war's outset he had served as the president of a small military academy in Louisiana, teaching young southern men the art of war. He retired from this post upon Louisiana's secession declaration and returned North, where he was rewarded with the colonelcy of the new Thirteenth U.S. Infantry regiment. He saw action at the First Battle of Bull Run and gained swift promotion to brigadier general, followed by an assignment to Lexington and orders to take command of troops of his own.

Despite this collapse of self-confidence late in the war's first year, the soldier in question would ultimately play an integral role in securing victory over the Confederacy. He would go on to accept the surrender of the largest Confederate army at the war's end, and in April 1865 he would stand as one of the three most important people in the nation. He assumed overall command of the army in 1868 and tirelessly advocated for professionalization and reform in the institution that had educated him and then employed him for most of his adult life. He was a professional soldier named William Tecumseh Sherman, and his younger brother John disdained everything he stood for. The Sherman boys, it seemed, were fighting a brothers' war of a different kind.[10]

3

THE REPUBLICAN WAR WITHIN THE WAR, 1861–1865

There is no peace to the wicked, saith my God; there is no peace to these rebels and traitors, who have raised their hands against the Government. We will carry on this war; the people will carry it on; the citizen soldier will fight this battle. He is impatient to do it now; but we do not want—certainly not now—to increase the regular army.

—Owen Lovejoy, 1861

In the early days of July 1861, the Republican Party confronted a vexing question. There remained no doubt that a war was upon them—and they needed to decide who should fight it. They had about 16,000 professional soldiers to call on, less the three-hundred-odd officers who had resigned their commissions to fight for the Confederacy. On April 15 of that year, President Abraham Lincoln had called for 75,000 three-month militiamen to suppress the rebellion, and on May 3 he added a call for 42,034 men to join the United States Volunteers for a period of three years. Like the militias of old, these volunteers were to be drawn from the states in proportion to their population and to serve in units so designated—the Fifty-Fourth Massachusetts, the 148th Pennsylvania, the First Minnesota—but these units would be "federalized" and would operate under the direction of the War Department in Washington.[1] These federal volunteers were not intended to become professional troops but rather to serve as citizen-soldiers—"citizen" being the operative word.

Lincoln also announced, in his May 3 proclamation, that he was increasing the regular army by eight regiments of infantry and one regiment each of cavalry and artillery. Republicans in Congress protested this portion of Lincoln's declaration, saying that the president was well within his constitutional authority to call out the militia (now, volunteers) but that the power to raise troops for the professional army lay with Congress and Congress alone. And so both the House and Senate chambers carried on a fierce debate. Back and forth the Republicans went, insisting that they needed more time to determine the mixture of troops that would be capable of winning a war to save the Union. But they had little time left, as Confederate troops under Generals Pierre Gustave Toutant Beauregard and Joseph Eggleston Johnston maneuvered toward Manassas Junction, just twenty miles from Washington.

From the conflict's earliest days, Republicans questioned whether professional troops could be trusted to fight and win the Civil War. "I am entirely willing that any expropriation shall be made that is necessary to suppressing the insurrection," Illinois's Owen Lovejoy explained on July 11, 1861. And then, despite his foregoing assertion, he continued, "If we need to increase the standing army at all, now is not the time to do it." Lovejoy, whose brother Elijah became a martyr to the abolitionist cause when he was murdered by a proslavery mob in 1837, felt certain that "the people" would "give the last cent that they have, the last drop of their blood" to save the Union. And so long as that was the case, the country need not take the risk of increasing the standing army when its citizens were willing "to fight their own battles."[2]

The handful of Democrats left in the Capitol Building agreed with their Republican rivals. John Alexander McClernand pointed out that the nation's professional army was ill-prepared for the coming war. To determine why, his colleagues simply needed to consult the nearest map. "The regular Army has been dispersed all over the country in small bodies," he explained, adding that "if the purpose had been to place them out of the way, so as to enable premeditated rebellion to make head against the Government, it could not have been more effectually accomplished."[3]

What McClernand proposed was a novel conspiracy theory, but the Illinoisian failed to fully connect the dots. The leaders of his own party, the

Democrats of the 1850s, were the ones who had dispersed the army "all over the country." The War Department might have profitably taken note of McClernand's half-baked military sensibilities. He resigned his seat in the House in for a brigadier generalship in the Union Army in October 1861 and spent most of his time in uniform talking to the press about his military achievements while trying to undermine the authority of his commanding officer, Ulysses S. Grant. Grant relived McClernand from command in 1863, ordering him to go from Vicksburg, Mississippi, to any place he liked in Illinois, so long as it was not near Grant or his army.[4]

And so the Republicans and the War Democrats agreed that whatever means the country chose for waging the Civil War, more regular troops were the least desirable option. Their arguments were both political and practical, as well as successful. Objections were raised to professional troops on economic grounds. Funding the regular army was not economical in a time of war. It would be more practical to fund the immediate needs of volunteers rather than to admit more students to West Point or recruit more troops to serve in regular units. As a result, the size of the regular army increased by a mere 10,000 troops (ten regiments) during the war, from 15,000 in 1860 to 25,000 in January 1863.[5] On January 1, 1863, when the combined strength of Union armies stood at 918,191 men, regulars made up 2.7 percent of the total.

Between 1861 and 1865, Republican congressmen revealed their disdain for the professional army in speeches and policies concerning the conduct of the Civil War. Republicans first crafted a damning case against the regulars as part of a Democratic cabal. The army was an element of the nefarious Slave Power that party leaders such as William Seward and Radicals such as Benjamin Wade had long depicted as the enemy of free labor. Republicans associated professional soldiers with political conservatism and resistance to emancipation, even as a war measure. The sharpest rebukes of the professional army originated in the party's Radical wing, but disdain for regular troops became a mainstream party position throughout the early years of the conflict. Though a minority within the party, Radicals pushed their anti-army stance from the party's fringes to the center of national political discourse.

While keeping the number of regular troops low, Republicans willingly allocated money to recruit volunteer soldiers. Their efforts put more than 1 million men in uniform by the war's midpoint and nearly 2.5 million by the war's end. Money seemed to be no object when it came to these temporary troops. The federal government authorized more than $300 million in bounties, paid to induce men to enlist in volunteer units.[6] Historians estimate that 1.7 million volunteers received at least some of this money.[7] Economization did not matter where citizen-soldiers were concerned. Politics, rather than saving costs, drove Republican military policies. Republican legislators preferred amateurs, who were more costly to train and outfit, over ready and willing professional troops. In this way, Republicans revealed their growing distrust of the regulars, linking the army's officer corps to proslavery ideology and anti-administration sentiment. The party showed that its members cared deeply for the well-being and care of the volunteers but little for the health of the professional army.

Not content to hurl invectives from the Capitol Building, Republicans also used the war to assert their authority over the nation's military professionals—by investigating and judging their actions though the Joint Committee on the Conduct of the War, which brought Radical leaders together with sympathetic Democrats. Ostensibly meant to investigate military disasters, the committee membership hounded army officers who were either proven or assumed to be "conservative." This word, which signified a general's tendency to be too cautious or to avoid taking the offensive, also strongly suggested that an officer had an affiliation with the Democratic Party.[8] From its inception the committee offered unsolicited advice to President Lincoln and his advisers to push the moderate president toward prosecuting the war with aggression.[9] Wartime Republicans took special care to refine their anti-militarism, creating a war within the war through their war against the army.

CONGRESS AND THE REGULAR ARMY

Republican senator James W. Grimes of Iowa took a moment in 1862 to reflect on the decade prior to the Civil War. As he did, he felt some foreboding about the role that professional soldiers were to play in the ongoing Union war effort. Even those regular army officers who had remained loyal to the Union, Grimes felt, should not be trusted to help save the nation. As internecine conflict raged around them and the Lincoln government sought officers who could lead Union troops to victory, Republicans in Congress continued to refine their case against the conservatism of the professional army. That a host of professional officers had joined the ranks of Confederate armies provided proof that the regulars ought not be trusted. It mattered little that most antebellum officers, nearly 73 percent, remained loyal to the Union. They too, were suspect by association with their former comrades in arms.[10]

The year 1862 brought major battles at Antietam, Bull Run, Fredericksburg, and Shiloh, and the Seven Days, as well as frequent congressional criticism aimed at professional soldiers. The Union needed victories, but few in Congress trusted their leading officers to achieve positive results, and few Union triumphs materialized to satisfy such a desire.[11] The regulars, according to Republicans such as Grimes, could not win the war. Southern Democrats had exposed professional troops to their political conservatism for too long for regular soldiers to have any devotion to the nation. According to Grimes, Jefferson Davis had been "sedulous" in his efforts "to impress on the minds of officers that the only way in which they could secure promotion was to show that they were fully imbued with the State-rights, disunion, nullification, rebellious sentiment."[12] A good soldier, Grimes suggested, was hard to find.

Beyond the battlefields of Virginia, Tennessee, and even New Mexico, 1862 also brought congressional Republicans an unprecedented opportunity to transform the American West. Free to pursue long-contemplated legislative programs for western expansion, the two Republican-dominated chambers enacted transformative political and social change across the region. Historians have written extensively about the slate of western legislation that included the Morrill Act, the Homestead Act, and the Pacific Railway Act.[13] Army officers, constantly buffeted by congressional criticism, might have been excused for hoping that they would finally receive some commendation from the national legislature as it debated the future of the West. The so-called frontier, after all, had always been the domain of the professional soldier. But they would have hoped in vain. Even as they envisioned a radically different future for more than half the country, and one which would require untold violence to achieve, Republicans continued their attacks on the regulars.[14]

The ideology of the Republican Party—especially as it related to labor, economic progress, and the future of the American West—"focused on turning the West into an agrarian society of free white farmers."[15] To motivate men to embrace the power of their labor, Republicans believed in "the protection of property and the right of every man to accumulate as much as he could."[16] Protecting free labor in the West also helped congressional Republicans advance their case against the expansion of slavery. Republicans strongly believed that "free-soil settlers provided a better guarantee than congressional prohibitions that the territories would be free from slavery."[17] Their wartime legislation relating to the West made that vision a reality.[18]

The Homestead Act encapsulated Republican efforts to empower individual citizens to earn a free labor living and to advance the interests of the nation as they did so. As House Speaker Galusha Grow put it, the act allowed citizens to "contribute to the greatness and glory of the Republic" as they "develop the elements of a higher and better civilization."[19] Senator William H. Seward embraced a similar vision and argued that "popular government follows in the track of the steam engine and the telegraph."[20] When Congress passed the Pacific Railway Act, Horace Greeley's *New York Tribune* trumpeted, "The clouds that have long darkened our National prospects are breaking way, and the sunshine of Peace, Prosperity, and Progress will ere long irradiate the land."[21]

Republican discourse throughout the debate on the 1862 bills suggested that professional soldiers represented the antithesis of the free labor values the party sought to promote. Republicans associated the regular army with both conservatism and privilege. Even worse, they cast the institution as treasonous, because of the officers who had defected to join the Confederacy. John Sherman informed his brother William T. Sherman that because of the "desertion of so many officers," he considered the old army "a manifest discredit" to the Union.[22] Michigan Republican Zachariah Chandler told his fellow senators that "the West Point Academy has produced more traitors … than all the institutions of learning and education that have existed since Judas Iscariot's time," while Maine's William Pitt Fessenden asserted that professional soldiers were "educated in a narrow, exclusive, miserable spirit," which made them hostile to volunteers.[23] Secretary of War Simon Cameron expressed a similar opinion in his first annual report. Cameron devoted considerable space to the "extraordinary treachery" displayed by the graduates of West Point and queried whether this was not a result of "a radical defect in the system of education itself."[24] Whether the association was justified, the Republican assumption that professional soldiers opposed the party's embrace of the common man won the regulars little support among the congressional majority.[25]

Republicans beat their anti-professional drum for more than a year after the war began. In the House of Representatives, Unionist Horace Maynard of Tennessee included the misuse of the regular army in a retrospective account of the Slave Power's historical misdeeds. Speaking as congressional debates over western expansion raged, Maynard condemned southern Democrats for their antebellum expansionist ambitions. Maynard stretched his case back to the era of the founding and Thomas Jefferson's Louisiana Purchase. "We gave it [the rebel power] three large States, carved out of the Territory of Louisiana," he began his recitation. "The purchase of Florida was in obedience to its demands, and so was the prosecution of the Seminole and Florida wars."[26] The Tennessee legislator ignored other wars of attempted Indigenous extermination that had occurred, most of which had no discernable connection to slave expansion. The Black Hawk War of 1832 or the multiple wars in the 1850s Pacific Northwest witnessed professional soldiers fighting to bring free states, not slave states, into the Union.[27]

Maynard laid territorial expansion and multiple wars of Indian land expropriation at the feet of southern Democrats and their allies in the army. Southern Democrats had stolen land from Natives in the South "so that the white man could enter with his peculiar institution, where otherwise it was forbidden."[28] In his zealousness to make a case against proslavery partisans, Maynard obscured the numerous instances of territorial theft that the army facilitated in free states and territories.[29] By tying the army to antebellum Indian wars and claiming that Indian wars waged by the army were done only on behalf of slavery, Maynard distanced his party from one of the great moral crimes of the nineteenth century. He also neatly linked professional soldiers to supporting both slavery and the ethnic cleansing of Indigenous peoples.

Maynard also connected the leadership of the antebellum army to the broader Republican case for the existence of a Slave Power conspiracy. Like Grimes, his Senate colleague, Maynard regretted the failure of northern politicians to resist the designs of the Slave Power instead of agreeing to their demands. "We have permitted both Houses of Congress, the Executive and Judicial Department of the Government, the Army and Navy, and our foreign diplomacy, to be controlled by this rebel interest," he recalled, "with the power all the while in our hands to do otherwise."[30] Including the leadership of the army in his list of untrustworthy federal institutions allowed Maynard to cast further suspicion on the loyalty of the regulars.

Republicans who considered the regular army problematic feared professional soldiers were antithetical to republican values. As such, they renewed colonial era accusations about standing armies as incompatible with democratic government. Soldiers, they said, were detached from the public and more loyal to their officers than to the government. This rhetorical strain had existed from the earliest days of the republic but was more often associated with Anti-Federalists like Thomas Jefferson, which formed the origins of what later became the Democratic Party. Republicans embraced this logic in their attacks on the army, however, and there was rarely a debate on military affairs in which they failed to invoke the specter of military despotism and the threat that standing armies posed to democracy. As British journalist Goldwin Smith explained to his foreign audience—in a nation that had experienced military rule after a brutal civil war, no less—when the war began, most Americans assumed that military despotism would result from the conflict "as a matter of course." "The first successful general," Smith explained, "would, without fail, overturn the constitution; and his army would, without hesitation, make itself the instrument of his treason."[31]

Unlike regular soldiers, citizen-soldier volunteers posed no threat to the republic. Wartime rhetoric often affirmed the degree to which the Civil War generation viewed volunteers as far less threatening to democratic institutions than regular troops. In July 1861, just days before the war's first significant battle occurred, the Republican-backed *Cincinnati Gazette* assured readers that they had no reason to fear a military despotism because "our [Union] troops are volunteers."[32] A small newspaper in the northern San Juan mountains of California concurred, assuring its readers that the war, if fought with a volunteer force, would never result in military rule. The editors noted that their readers might reasonably ask whether the armies then being assembled to wage war would "establish a military despotism, and destroy the very liberties they fought to rescue and maintain?" It would not be possible, the *Hydraulic Press* pronounced, because the volunteers had "visible occupations," "property," "wives and families," and "homes that are dear to them, and to which they long to return." The editorial also explained that all the men who would seek to make the army perpetual had already abandoned the Union cause and now found themselves "on the *other* side."[33]

Congressional Republicans assured the northern public that the nation's fortunes would not long depend on West Point officers. Practical experience in battle mattered more than book learning. "The atmosphere, the fume of the bivouac," declared *New York Tribune* editor Greeley, was much more likely to produce military genius than the textbooks of West Point.[34] A contemporary pamphleteer, in an attack on West Point graduates holding army commands, told his readers, "A country discovers its real heroes in the actual conflict of arms ... It is war, earnest and real war, and not parades or reviews, which alone can draw out a nation's spirit and its real men."[35]

Henry Wilson, a Republican senator from Massachusetts, speculated that the regular army under Jefferson Davis and John Floyd had been populated by men sympathetic to the Democratic Party (and who were, by implication, proslavery). Wilson echoed his colleague John Sherman's sentiments and claimed that professional soldiers were uninterested in the Union cause. "No doubt there are many officers in the army," he told the Senate on December 23, 1861, "whose hearts are not in this contest." He added, "I suppose that in former days the old Army was pretty nearly equally divided between the Whig and the Democratic parties, but when the new issues of the last few years came up, situated as they were, the largest proportion of the officers [in] the army sided with those who administered the government during the last ten years." When he looked at the list of regular army officers who had received appointments at the grade of brigadier general or higher in the new volunteer army, he claimed that of the 110 men appointed, "at least eighty are opposed to the present administration."[36]

Wilson's point of view mattered for the army's prospects. He was perhaps the most influential Republican leader in the arena of military affairs in the Civil War era. Before attaining that distinction, his career had seen the future vice president flourish as a political organizer. Wilson was consequential in forming the Free-Soil Party, a coalition of groups including Know-Nothings, Conscience Whigs, antislavery Democrats, and others who opposed slavery's western expansion. Though the Free-Soilers were short-lived, Wilson's experience as a coalition builder made him critical to the formation of the Republican Party. While not viewed as an outright Radical, Wilson subscribed to the belief that the chief aim of his party should be to dismantle and then destroy the influence and leadership of the Slave Power. One way to achieve that goal would be to acquire influence over the army and, when the time came, to help reorganize the institution from the ground up. Wilson began his work during the war and carried his passion for reforming the army into his authorship of the 1866 Army Reorganization Act—the most consequential piece of legislation relating to the army passed in the Civil War era.

The Republican habit of associating the regulars with conservative, pro-slavery values continued into the war's middle years. Indiana's George W. Julian, a radical antislavery voice in the House of Representatives, excoriated the influence of the antebellum Democratic Party over the military. "Democratic policy, in the year 1861," he began, "gave us as commanders [George B.] McClellan, [Henry W.] Halleck, and [Don Carlos] Buell, whose military administrations have so terribly cursed the country." Focusing his ire on officers who were known Democrats, Julian continued, "It impressed upon our volunteer forces in the field such officers as Fitz-John Porter, General [William] Nelson, General [Charles P.] Stone, and very many more whose sympathies with the rebels were well known throughout the country." What was more, Democrats had insinuated their politics into all aspect of Union military operations. "Those great hives of military patronage the Adjutant-general's Department, the Quartermaster's Department, the Commissary Department, the Ordnance Department, and the Pay Department are all under Democratic control," he asserted, "and have been during the war."[37]

Republicans, it seemed, would not be satisfied until they had rooted out Democratic influence within the army, whether on the front lines or in staff departments. As historian Jonathan W. White has argued, Republican efforts to purge the army of Democrats and Copperheads in the war's early years helped to influence soldiers to vote for Abraham Lincoln in the election of 1864.[38] Zachary A. Fry has likewise argued that congressional efforts to remove high-ranking Democrats from command allowed junior officers (elected by their peers from the ranks of the volunteers) to promote a Republican ideology among the citizen-soldiers of the Army of the Potomac.[39] Fewer Democrats among high-ranking officers, and Republican voters organically rising through the noncommissioned and junior officer ranks, helped to ensure that, at least among volunteer soldiers, Republican political views dominated Union war camps.

Rooting out Democratic ideology could take various forms. Radical Republicans argued for abandoning professional military education in preference of well-trained volunteers who could reinvigorate an ailing militia system that had fallen into disrepair.[40] Benjamin Wade, the most consistent opponent of the army in the Senate, joined his fellow Ohioan John Sherman in rejecting the need for West Point as a continued training ground for Union officers. Wade added a new element, suggesting that career soldiers represented an undesirable, and undemocratic, aristocracy in the United States. Wade claimed that the war proved that the United States Military Academy was not the sole national resource for turning out soldiers prepared to lead men. Because of the Civil War, Wade explained, "all over the country private military schools are springing up, and military tactics are being taught in our high schools." "I am in favor of that process which is going on," he continued, explaining, "I believe it is doing away with any necessity for this monopoly, this aristocratic branch of our government."[41]

Their constituents eagerly embraced their ideology. Special venom, among both legislators and their voters, was reserved for West Point. The graduates of the national military academy were widely thought to possess southern sympathies. One of Zachariah Chandler's correspondents spoke of the sorry state of the office corps in the Army of the Potomac and of the necessity of "purging the rottenness of this truly Democratic institution." Another complained that the Union could never hope for victory with officers only "half loyal to the cause." Yet another correspondent asserted that "regular army officers are so accustomed to bow down to slavery they don't know any better." An Indianapolis man wrote to George Julian that "McClellan, Halleck, [Benjamin F.] Butler, Sherman, Stone, Buell" all offered evidence that Union ranks were led by "democrats with secession sympathies."[42]

Economy and efficiency were frequent themes in Republican negotiations over military appropriations during the war. New Hampshire Republican John P. Hale forcefully reminded his fellow senators that the history of the regular army of the United States was one of inefficiency. He suggested that wartime military legislation could lay the groundwork for reforming the federal government's overpayment of the regulars. Hale claimed the regulars were notorious for collecting a paycheck while "sitting still . . . and doing nothing." Hale offered a resolution to reduce the pay of regular army officers during the war to the same scale as that of volunteer officers—and supposed that "if circumstances enable the country after the war to raise the pay of the regular army up to what it was," Congress might elect to do so.[43]

Multiple speeches that followed Hale's during the same day's deliberations raised economy in waging the war and ensuring that the conflict did not empower the regular army to increase its burden on the federal treasury. Only James A. McDougall, a Democrat representing California, questioned the Republican crusade for reduction. "It may be saving," McDougall said of the effort to reduce officer pay, "but it is not economy."[44] Devaluing the experience, education, and service records of regular army soldiers, he warned, might suggest a lack of faith in their efforts to help the Union win the war.

Senator Zachariah Chandler of Michigan also considered training regular soldiers to be economically inefficient. His line of argument pursued the favored Republican tactic of ensuring that the Civil War be fought as economically as possible for the federal government. Chandler reminded the chamber that "the average expense to the government of each West Point graduate for life is $75,000," the equivalent of $2.2 million today. Maintaining a large professional army required a large corps of trained officers. Chandler believed each of them was a burden "upon your treasury whether you want them or not." He then complained that despite not having to exert themselves or prove their abilities, "they are appointed brevet second lieutenants the moment they graduate, though you do not require them; and they are regularly promoted according to seniority." A professional military, Chandler claimed, created "an army of officers utterly worthless, scattered all over the land, leeches upon your treasury, whom you will never need."[45]

Chandler was not always a stickler for the facts. In a March 1862 speech arguing against increasing the ranks of the regulars during the war, Chandler again argued that volunteers had contributed far more than professional troops to the war effort. Once again, the Michigander sought to discredit West Point training. In the fighting at Fort Donelson, a victory for the Union army, Chandler claimed, "there was but one regular officer . . . [and] not a regular soldier there."[46] Like many Republicans, Chandler refused to give the regulars credit when he could laud the service of volunteer soldiers. Chandler knew as well as any of his colleagues that a brief glance at the Union order of battle for the fight at Fort Donelson could quickly discredit his claim. Ulysses S. Grant (class of 1843), James B. McPherson (1853), and Charles F. Smith (1825) were among the West Point graduates and regular army officers who led Union forces during the successful operation along the Tennessee River.

Chandler insisted that public education in colleges across the country could circumvent the pernicious influence of the professional army. "Michigan has already established a military department to her state university," he informed the Senate. "Let other states do the same thing," Chandler suggested. "Let the young men of the several states receive a military education at home, and very soon a spirit of emulation will spring up among the different states."[47] Such a transformation, Chandler believed, allowed white American males access to a military education if they desired, while also affording instruction in agriculture and industry (critical to the Republican vision for western expansion), and it would mean that every state possessed a substantial number of citizens prepared to respond to a military emergency. They would not be a drain on the federal treasury. Chandler's logic became central to legislation Republicans passed the following year, the Morrill Act.

The creator of the land-grant act, Vermont representative Justin S. Morrill, was similarly concerned that the nation's wartime military needs might lead to an enlargement of the professional force. Morrill intended his legislation to fund higher education in every state of the Union via the sale of public lands. The original version of the bill, introduced in the 1857 congressional session, did not include the provision for colleges to provide military instruction to their students.[48] Morrill added military training to courses in the agricultural and mechanical sciences when he reintroduced the bill in 1861. "Military instruction," Morrill commented, alluding to the North's lack of able officers at the start of the war, "has been incorporated [into the act] . . . upon the attention of the loyal states [to] the history of the past year."[49] Morrill, and his senatorial co-conspirator Benjamin Wade, preferred to give young men soldiering experience in civilian-run colleges. As the young congressman saw it, a continuing source of military skills among the citizenry would surely be needed as the country expanded.

Republicans sought to weaken West Point's hold on producing professional soldiers through their western legislation. Echoing their antebellum critiques of the regulars, Republicans continued, with no sense of irony, to embrace a Jeffersonian vision of diffused military power and a reliance on civilians to respond in the event of a military emergency. Republicans who resented the army's officer class as patrician preferred to democratize national military training. The Civil War's elevation of the citizen-soldier to almost mythic proportions also worked to bolster the Republican criticism of a large professional army.

The Republican offensive was not limited to West Point as an institution. It extended to the academy's individual graduates, with whom Republicans frequently demonstrated impatience. Increased scrutiny of professional officers prompted inquiries into the curriculum taught at the nation's flagship military academy. West Point in the Civil War era followed a curriculum most Republicans viewed as limited and moribund at best, and actively detrimental to the progress of American arms at worst. The bottom line for Republicans was that West Point graduates rarely campaigned as aggressively as politicians liked. Speaking as late as March 1864, for example, Jacob M. Howard, a Republican senator from Michigan, explained that the country derived "not the slightest benefit in the world" from educating men at West Point, and he opined that money spent by Congress on the academy was "thrown away."[50]

Republican attacks on West Point never wavered. The radical foes of the army devoted considerable time to tracing the war records of such prominent graduates as Buell, William P. Franklin, Halleck, McClellan, Porter, and Stone. The alleged failures of these officers were laid at the door of the national military academy, whose training had made them either incompetent or treasonous, and in numerous cases both. Benjamin Wade flatly accused the academy of causing the rebellion. He estimated that half of the regular officers were disloyal, aristocratic, and incompetent.[51] James H. Lane of Kansas believed that if the Union were to be defeated, the cause would be the southern sympathies of her generals. As an appropriate epitaph for the fallen nation, he suggested, would be "Died of West Point pro-slaveryism."[52]

As the war continued, Republicans were less likely to launch specific attacks against the regulars. This can be explained, in part, by the fact that as a percentage of the overall national military force raised during the war (2,778,000 enlistees), the regular army (62,000 troops) represented only 2.2 percent of Union soldiers.[53] Accounting for enlistment terms and casualties, 62,000 men served in a regular unit during the conflict. At any point during the war, there were never more than 25,000 men on the regular rolls—the authorized limit. Still, congressmen celebrated citizen-soldiers as the ideal representative of American military power, even before the end of the conflict. Throughout the war, when military legislation raised the possibility of increasing officer salaries or contemplated promotions in rank, Republican legislators demanded that volunteer soldiers be put on equal terms with professional officers, claiming that equality between the regulars and volunteers was "doing justice to the volunteer soldiery who have won our battles."[54]

It is worth briefly noting that the Democrats who remained in the national legislature during the war tended to quibble with military policy rather than with the army itself. This was especially true of the Copperhead faction of the Democratic Party, which virulently opposed the Radical Republican effort to turn a limited war to save the Union into an expansive fight for Black freedom and emancipation. Copperheads were convinced that the military pursuit of emancipation would wreak havoc on soldier morale. The editor of Copperhead sheet the *Philadelphia Age* exclaimed as much when he wrote, "The Negro mania has been as mischievous in the conduct of the war, as it has been in and is in politics." The pursuit of slavery's abolition led the editors to lament that "no man can tell where the demoralization of our army will end, or what calamity the future has in store for it."[55] For the Copperheads and Peace Democrats, a vote against the army really meant a vote against emancipation.

Democrats certainly did not exhibit the hostility Republicans manifested toward professional army officers—or at least they did not exhibit hostility toward General George Britten McClellan, whom many Republicans viewed as the ultimate example of a conservative, anti-emancipation, cautious West Point–trained officer. When he accepted the party's nomination for the presidency, McClellan gratified the Democrats' faith that he would reject the Radical Republican vision of the conflict. "The preservation of our Union was the sole avowed object for which the war was commenced," he wrote to the Democratic National Committee. "It should have been conducted for that object only."[56] Apparently the country did not feel as strongly as McClellan and his Democratic allies about the Republican quest for emancipation. Little Mac carried only three states in the president election of 1864 and received a paltry twenty-one electoral college votes, while the man he had once called "the original gorilla" retained the presidency with 212.[57]

BACKSEAT GENERALS:
CONGRESSIONAL REPUBLICANS MAKE MILITARY POLICY

When they were not debating the value of the professional army on the floor of the national legislature, Republican congressional leaders (most of the Radical disposition) frequently, and freely, voiced their frustration with the Lincoln administration's management of the war. Their critique—that Lincoln was too moderate on issues such as confiscation and emancipation—led several prominent Republicans to advocate for more legislative oversight of Union military policies. Men such as Zachariah Chandler, Charles Sumner, and Benjamin Wade in the Senate, joined by Thaddeus Stevens in the House, had campaigned in 1860 on outright opposition to slavery (rather than only forbidding its non-extension into the nation's western territories). As it became increasingly clear that the country would go to war over slavery, the Radical camp declared that the conflict should be waged not only to save the Union but also to end slavery—and culminate in equal rights for Black Americans.

In the early months of the Civil War, the Radicals realized they would need cooperation from Union armies to help consummate their antislavery goals.[58] They faced a thorny problem that arose from the separation of powers outlined in the Constitution by the army-fearing founding generation: they did not have sole control over the national armies that would wage the Civil War.[59] While their branch of the federal government had the power to declare war and to appropriate the money that would fund the Union war effort, their moderate colleague in the White House, Abraham Lincoln, held the title of commander in chief. Divided authority produced divergent ideas about how the war should be conducted.[60]

In their effort to assert their authority over national military affairs, Radicals in Congress agitated early and often for emancipation as a war aim. To their consternation, however, most of the army's leading officers did not share their goals. With Buell, John Adams Dix, Halleck, McClellan, Stone, and other Democrats controlling the army though the summer of 1862, Radical leaders saw little chance of achieving emancipation. As a group, professional soldiers, most of them educated at West Point, were not active in pushing for abolition in the field. Representative Martin F. Conway of

Kansas charged in the House that there was not "more than one sincere abolitionist or emancipationist among the military authorities."[61] Joseph Medill, the pro-Republican editor of the *Chicago Tribune,* warned Secretary of War Edwin Stanton that the latter would "discover scores of luke warm, half secession officers in command who can not bear to strike a vigorous blow lest it hurt their rebel friends or jeopardize the precious protectors of slavery."[62]

Republican legislators were particularly concerned with President Lincoln's exercise of presidential war powers. Many worried that the moderate president would follow the lead of the army and not take decisive action to use military resources to support emancipation. The Radicals abhorred the fact that when officers sympathetic to emancipation emerged from the army's ranks, the president contravened their military orders advancing abolition. When Major General John C. Frémont promulgated an order establishing martial law and emancipating the enslaved in Missouri on August 30, 1861, for example, Lincoln quickly ordered the general to rescind the proclamation, insisting that the officer (and onetime Republican presidential nominee) had exceeded his authority as a military commander.[63]

In the aftermath of the Frémont fracas, Radical legislators grew concerned with President Lincoln's exercise of presidential war powers. In a letter to Chandler, Wade wrote that Lincoln "has done more injury to the cause of the Union, by receding from the ground taken by Frémont, than McDowell did by retreating from Bull Run."[64] Lincoln defended his position, insisting that his job as president was to ensure that Union armies operated within the limits of domestic and international law.[65] "If the General needs [slaves] he can seize them, and use them; but when the need is past, it is not for him to fix their permanent future condition," Lincoln explained. "That must be settled according to laws made by lawmakers, and not by military proclamations."[66] The justification failed to satisfy the Radical camp.

Tempers boiled over by the war's first winter. Radical policymakers arriving in Washington for the December 1861 meeting of Congress intended to call the Lincoln administration to account for its conduct of the war. McClellan's inactivity, the decision to overrule Frémont, the Ball's Bluff disaster, and Lincoln's reluctance to adopt an emancipation policy stoked Radical fury.[67] The mounting rage of the faction and their determination to have a voice in the establishment of war policies evidenced itself in a wave of legislation. In the Senate, Lyman Trumbull proposed what would become the first Confiscation Act, writing to an acquaintance, "Action, action is what we want and must have."[68] Trumbull was joined in the House by Ohioan Samuel Shellabarger, who offered a resolution directed at censuring generals who returned fugitive slaves to their enslavers rather than granting them refuge behind Union lines. All the while, Radical senators urged their colleagues in the House to reject the readoption of the Crittenden resolutions, which sought to limit the war's stated aim to the preservation of the Union.[69]

Certain that Lincoln would not act unless pressed, Republican leaders turned to legislation to give Union officers inclined toward emancipation some latitude in which to operate. The first Confiscation Act, passed in August 1861, after Lincoln's repudiation of Frémont, authorized military leaders to seize the property (including property in slaves) of any individual participating in the rebellion, but it did not define the subsequent legal status of that property. The second Confiscation Act, passed in July 1862, after McClellan's failed campaign against Richmond, stated that any slaves owned by individuals who supported or took part in the rebellion, and all slaves in rebel territory captured by Union armies, would be "forever free of their servitude, and not again held as slaves."[70] The act exempted Unionist slaveholders from its threat of confiscation. The acts, though bold and legally creative, depended on military commanders who would enforce them to their fullest extent—and such officers were still a rare commodity 1862.

The Radicals also pursued a more direct channel for voicing their opinions on national military operations, establishing a committee to provide congressional oversight on the conduct of the war. Following a disastrous Union defeat at Ball's Bluff, legislators convened the Joint Committee on the Conduct of the War. Most concerning was the fact that the officer who had overseen the debacle, Major General Stone, was a known Democrat. Radical leaders hoped to dislodge the conservative elements of the army's high command and to use the committee "to bend the war to the goal of abolition."[71] Republicans George W. Julian (Indiana), John Covode (Pennsylvania), and Daniel Gooch (Massachusetts) represented the House. They were joined by Senate Democrats Andrew Johnson of Tennessee and Joseph Wright of Indiana, and by Representative Moses Odell of New York, from the House.[72]

Republican loathing for professional soldiers had reached a point of no return. Tired of inactivity and failure, one Republican constituent wrote to Zachariah Chandler that the Union "ought to have officers to command our army whose heart is in the work." One Ohio man complained to Benjamin Wade of Lincoln's inaction and claimed that McClellan was the "laughing stock of the people." One of Lyman Trumbull's correspondents recommended that Congress be firm and force Lincoln to make war "in earnest." "War costs money," he reminded Trumbull. "It is for you to grant it and impose conditions." Those who opposed a policy of emancipation, one Massachusetts man told Charles Sumner, were dragging out the war. Meanwhile, a Michigander advised Zachariah Chandler that "the people will sustain their representatives in the most radical steps they may take."[73]

Still, the Joint Committee was not universally accepted as the best option for investigating instances of military disaster. Abraham Lincoln's attorney general, Edward Bates, feared "the establishment of a precedent for congressional interference with the command of the army," which he thought might produce conflict between the military and the government akin to Revolutionary-era France.[74] Radicals such as Wade and Chandler could easily dismiss Bates's opinion—the Missourian was a slaveholder. Potentially more damning for Bates was the fact that his son Charles attended West Point, where he spent the early years of the Civil War training to become one of the professional soldiers so loathed by the Republicans—though luckily for his father's cause, he failed to graduate. When Senator Lafayette Foster of Connecticut argued that potential conflicts could be avoided if military mishaps were investigated by military authorities, the Radicals challenged his logic. Congress, argued Maine's William Pitt Fessenden, declared war and raised the money necessary to carry on war. When problems arose, was Congress to sit back and do nothing? "We must satisfy the people of this country that things go on well," he reasoned.[75]

The *New York Herald* disagreed with Fessenden's justification. The sheet, which often vacillated between the nation's two major political parties, summarized the committee's previous activities on April 10, 1863. There was no question, the editorialist asserted, that the committee was "a disgrace to the nation." Its members were "like a set of schoolboys playing soldiers when the schoolmaster is out." And the conclusions reached in the committee's reports were "about as valuable as the prattle of schoolchildren." The *Her-*

ald felt that the committee's continued investigations would have results opposite to their favored aim. Rather than make Union officers more aggressive, the threat of a committee investigation would encourage less risk taking on the field of battle, for fear of reprisals in the halls of Congress.[76]

Despite Democratic protests, Republicans across the country seemed to approve of the new investigative body. Finally, they said, there would be some accountability for military officers who erred in the course of their duty. One New York Republican gladly noted that investigating soldiers would finally call professional soldiers to account for their perceived miscues on the battlefield. "It seems," he told Chandler, "that regular army officers & doughfaces can make any amount of blunders & all will be right."[77] The letter reinforced several themes that ran through Republican discourse regarding the regulars. Above all else, professional troops were not to be to be trusted to conduct the war effort with any aggression or to push for emancipation. But perhaps more importantly, they were viewed as conservative by men and women far beyond Washington. The Republican message regarding the army had permeated the minds of the public.

As far as voters were concerned, it mattered little that none of the committee members had military experience. Even so, this lack of knowledge did impede their understanding of the war's more complex military aspects. According to foremost historian of the Joint Committee, Bruce Tap, their misguided ideas about waging war caused the members to "chronically [misrepresent] the reasons for battlefield victory and defeat." While Wade and Chandler held forth on the Senate floor about the conservatism of the army's officers, they used committee investigations "to discredit and replace many West Point educated Union officers."[78] One such officer, George McClellan, was a frequent target of the committee's ire. The "Young Napoleon" provided the committee with prominent example of the conservative West Point officer so loathed by the Radicals. In letters to his wife, Ellen, McClellan complained of having to appear before the "confounded committee" and complained that the inquisitors were constantly seeking to trip him up with their questions. Justifying his military decisions to a panel of civilians, McClellan explained, left his brain *"rather* tired out."[79]

Historians have often treated the committee harshly, though they tend to censure its members for their partisanship rather than their clear antimilitarism. The committee sought to meddle in the politics of the Union army—the same behavior they excoriated their Democratic colleagues for engaging in prior to the war. "This committee supposedly established to aid the war effort," wrote historian Harry W. Pfanz, "seems to have sought mainly to control the political thinking of the army's commanders." Bruce Catton (following the language preferred by the Radical-resenting T. Harry Williams) described the committee as "a fearsome Jacobin creation." According to Samuel Eliot Morison and Henry Steele Commager, the committee "hampered the executive, undermined army discipline, and discouraged the more competent generals."[80] Bruce Tap's work on the Joint Committee on the Conduct of the War offers the most impartial view but still argues that the committee's members deeply desired to push Union officers to be aggressive and acted zealously in that pursuit.[81]

Compared to the soldiers they interrogated; the legislators had little grasp of the detailed work required to win on the battlefield. And battlefield results mattered, for sustaining civilian morale, getting Republicans reelected, and forestalling foreign intervention in favor of the Confederacy. As historian Mark E. Neely explained, Republicans grew increasingly agitated with the failure of Union armies to achieve decisive victories, and party members revolted against "strategy" or the "military science" advocated by professional soldiers like McClellan.[82] Republicans blamed West Point–taught "strategy" for the lack of offensive campaigning undertaken by Union armies.[83] The committee did not hesitate to charge Union officers with coddling Confederates or opposing emancipation.[84] According to historian Marcus Cunliffe, the members of the committee "convinced themselves that the army was beset with apathy and defeatism, and that any officer known to be a Democrat was guilty of these sins until proved innocent."[85] The committee sought known Republican officers—as few as they were—to offer testimony on the failures of their Democratic colleagues.

Some, such as John Pope (of the West Texas artesian well expedition), did so eagerly. Pope received a hearty reception when he arrived in Washington to assume command of the newly created Army of Virginia in the early summer of 1862. His accession especially gratified the leading lights of the Radical faction. Secretary of the Treasury Salmon P. Chase demonstrated himself an ardent supporter of Pope, contrasting the newly arrived general with the conservative McClellan. Writing in his diary about Pope's wining and dining campaign in the capital, Chase recounted a dinner he shared with the Army of Virginia's new commander, during which Pope condemned McClellan's campaign on the Peninsula. "Genl. Pope expressed himself freely and decidedly in favor of the most rigorous measures in the prosecution of the war," Chase explained, and said that Pope "believed that, in consequence of the rebellion, Slavery must perish." In language that would have lifted Radical Republican spirits, Pope (given voice by Chase) declared that McClellan "was in favor of using every instrument which could be brought to bear against the enemy; and while he did not speak in favor of a general arming of the enslaved as soldiers, he advocated their use as laborers, in the defence of fortifications, and in any way in which their services could be made useful."[86] Behind the scenes of the campaign, as Radical pressure from Congress increased and Pope toured the capital, Lincoln and his cabinet were engaged in discussions about issuing an emancipation proclamation, with senior Union officials divided over the best course of action.

On June 25, just as the forces of McClellan and Confederate commander Joseph Johnston clashed at Oak Grove in the first of the Seven Days Battles, Pope spoke to that point before the House of Representatives. The general celebrated his own achievements in the war's Western Theater, slipped in a criticism of McClellan's ongoing failure to capture Richmond, and concluded by declaring that emancipation had to become the focus of the Union war effort. The Republican-dominated legislative body was, according to the pro-Republican *New York Daily Tribune,* "struck with Pope's frankness and ability."[87]

Pope offered similarly aggressive comments in his testimony before the Joint Committee on the Conduct of the War on July 8. The general spent the entire day giving answers to a series of questions about his plans for defending Washington and supporting McClellan. In addition, he offered his opinions of how the war ought to be conducted and provided his personal assessments of the generalship of his more conservative colleagues. Each answer perfectly reflected the Radical Republican desire to hear Union officers speak in favor of aggression against the rebels and action against slavery. Pope's pronouncements rang through the Capitol Building and seemed to suggest the possibility of a major shift in Union war policy.

Pope suggested that successful military operations required cooperation among army commanders. The subtext of his comments was that officers needed to share not only military goals but also political ones. When asked how his troops would operate in concert with the Army of the Potomac, Pope demurred, saying that two armies working together "should be commanded by generals of the same character and manner of operations." Pope then linked Union successes in the war's Western Theater to great cooperation among army commanders. "I think a portion of our successes in the west," he explained, "has been due to the fact that we have had nothing but entire harmony in our forces." Western troops, Pope asserted "pursued an aggressive policy from the beginning."[88] Throughout the interview, Pope consciously depicted himself as a foil for McClellan—and made certain his audience knew he was not one of the conservative Democratic officers the Republicans disdained.

Pope's statements stoked Radical resentment toward conservative Union officers. Horace Greeley's *New York Tribune* applauded Pope's declarations before the committee. Pope's arrival, the *Tribune* explained, rightly inspired "public confidence" in the Union war effort. "It is very much to be questioned," the editors wrote on July 23, "whether pro-Slavery generals can wage this war of ideas of successfully." Greeley's newspaper reminded sympathetic readers that in a conflict such as the Civil War, "heart is quite as essential as head or hand."[89] Pope's statements were met with celebration and the approbation of the Joint Committee. The Democrats brought up before the legislative investigators did not fair nearly so well.

Brigadier General Charles P. Stone served as the committee's most infamous target. Stone, an 1845 graduate of West Point, eagerly volunteered his services to the Union war effort at the outbreak of the Civil War. On October 20, 1861, George McClellan ordered Stone to conduct a reconnaissance of a Confederate position near Leesburg, Virginia. When one of his junior officers mistook some trees for a small Confederate camp, Stone gave his men permission to launch an attack across the Potomac River the following morning. The attack ended in disaster when Colonel Charles Devens arrived on the opposite bank to find a company of Mississippi infantry.

Panic seized the inexperienced Union commanders. Without orders, Colonel Edward Baker (also the senator for Oregon) used four boats to reinforce Devens—a mistake that cost Baker his life, as well as one thousand

Union casualties. Incensed at the death of their friend Baker, and certain that Stone must be a traitor, the Joint Committee investigated the incident and suggested that Stone be arrested. McClellan approved the order and Stone was held in a military prison without trial or formal charges for nearly six months. When word of the arrest reached Winfield Scott, he is reported to have said, "If he is a traitor, I am a traitor, and we are all traitors."[90] But the opinions of military officers, even those of Scott's stature, mattered little to the Republican partisans of the Joint Committee.

If their hounding of Stone was any example, the Joint Committee would not avoid controversy for the sake of harmony in the Union war effort. After the war, Emory Upton, a West Point graduate and veteran of some the conflict's most grueling battles, wrote approvingly of the Joint Committee in his *Military Policy of the United States from 1775*. Upton argued that "the power of Congress to raise and support armies unquestionably gave it the right to inquire how the military resources it had provided were being applied."[91] Senator Henry Wilson likewise encouraged the use of the committee as a check on both presidential and military power. The committee, Wilson wrote, "should teach men in civil and in military authority that the people expect that they will not make mistakes, and that we shall not be easy with their errors."[92] Wilson's belief that the committee could speak to both civil and military administrators signaled his confidence in its constitutionality.

Henry Wilson emerged from the Civil War with a zeal for reforming the professional army. Confident that Congress could do more than ever before to direct national military affairs, and bolstered by the energy of the Joint Committee's investigations as well as by the speeches of his Radical colleagues, he undertook the most comprehensive program of military reform in the country's history. Though not openly hostile to the regulars, Wilson's reform bill sought to combine Republican ambitions for the reconstruction of the South, reducing federal spending, and preventing the president from having too much control over the regulars. It was a supreme example of Wilson's legislative talents. It was also a clear signal to the nation's professional army that the period of growth and political support that soldiers and officers had enjoyed prior to the Civil War was over. The victors of Civil War would spend the rest of the century frustrated, underfunded, and lacking resources. The army's fortunes were on the decline.

Table 6. Membership of the Military Affairs Committee, 1861–1867

HOUSE	SENATE
Thirty-Seventh Congress (1861–1863)	
Francis P. Blair, Jr. (R-MO), Chair	Henry Wilson (R-MA), Chair
Samuel R. Curtis (R-IA)	Preston King (R-NY)
William A. Richardson (D-IL)	Edward D. Baker (R-OR)
James Buffinton (R-MA)	Henry S. Lane (R-IN)
Abram B. Olin (R-NY)	James H. Lane (R-KS)*
Gilman Marston (R-NH)	Henry M. Rice (R-MN)
Hendrick R. Wright (D-PA)	Milton S. Latham (D-CA)
James S. Jackson (U-KY)	Jacob M. Howard (R-MI)†
Thirty-Eighth Congress (1863–1865)	
Robert C. Schenck (R-OH), Chair	Henry Wilson (R-MA), Chair
John F. Farnsworth (R-IL)	Henry S. Lane (R-IN)
George H. Yeaman (U-KY)	Jacob M. Howard (R-MI)
James A. Garfield (R-OH)	James W. Nesmith (D-OR)
Benjamin Loan (UU-MO)*	Edwin D. Morgan (R-NY)
Henry C. Deming (R-CT)	William Sprague (R-RI)
F. W. Kellogg (R-MI)	B. Gratz Brown (UU-MO)
Moses F. Odell (D-NY)	
Archibald McAllister (D-PA)	
Samuel Knox (UU-MO)†	
Thirty-Ninth Congress (1865–1867)	
Robert C. Schenck (R-OH), Chair	Henry Wilson (R-MA), Chair
Henry C. Deming (R-CT)	Henry S. Lane (R-IN)
Gilman Marston (R-NH)	Jacob M. Howard (R-MI)
Lovell H. Rousseau (UU-KY)	James W. Nesmith (D-OR)
John A. Bingham (R-OH)	William Sprague (R-RI)
John H. Ketcham (R-NY)	B. Gratz Brown (R-MO)
James G. Blaine (R-ME)	James R. Doolittle (R-WI)
Sydenham E. Ancona (D-PA)	
Charles Sitgreaves (D-NJ)	

D = Democrat; R = Republican; U = Union; UU = Unconditional Unionist

* Member replaced

† Replacement member

THE PARADE

Painted in the aftermath of Robert E. Lee's surrender to Ulysses S. Grant at Appomattox Courthouse in April 1865, Winslow Homer's *Veteran in a New Field* offered an artist's view of the ideal culmination of Civil War military service. It was not medals, balls, and military honors, but a lone farmer with his scythe, tending to a field of wheat. Apart from an army jacket and canteen carelessly cast to the ground, the image hardly suggested the man had served in any army at all.[1] Homer's painting celebrated the end of war and the coming of peace. It also represented a challenge to any foreign nation or naysaying critic who doubted that the Civil War's great volunteer armies would disband peaceably.

When a woodcut of Homer's painting appeared in the pages of *Frank Leslie's Illustrated Newspaper* in 1867, the editors supplied their millions of readers with an explanation of the image's meaning. They first congratulated the United States for subverting international expectations and the example of history.[2] Many foreign nations expected the great Union armies to march on Washington and seize power, toppling the government of the democratic republic they had fought to preserve. In the British, French, or Spanish mind, Ulysses S. Grant, William T. Sherman, or Philip H. Sheridan each could easily become the next Caesar, Cromwell, or Napoleon. Second, *Leslie's* writers emphasized the superiority of the citizen-soldier over the army regular. "One of the most conclusive evidences of the strength of a republican form of government is the way in which the army has disbanded," *Leslie's* editors intoned, "each man seeking again the sphere of usefulness which he left temporarily, to aid the Government in its need."[3]

Veteran in a New Field, by Winslow Homer, 1865

Homer's painting captured the emotions of the Civil War's end, especially for those who found themselves on the winning side. The Confederacy and the doctrine of secession been crushed and a free labor republic had defeated a nation founded on the cornerstone of slavery. And the winning side had done so predominantly with temporary troops. And, to the nation's gratification, the men who served in those volunteer armies wanted nothing more than to go home. The *New York Times* exalted the disbandment of the Union armies, writing, "The nations of Europe are astonished by the news that though our gigantic war is but a few days over, we have already begun the disbandment of the great Army of the Union." The newspaper predicted that the transition to peace would be welcomed by many. The editors said the volunteers "will go to improve the coming season in tilling the land they have saved, and to set an example of our loyal and useful citizenship, such as only our army of citizen-soldiers can furnish."[4]

Nowhere was the rhetoric of the triumph of the citizen-solder more prevalent than at the Grand Review of Union Armies, held on May 23 and 24, 1865. For a nation that claimed to abhor standing armies, the two-day victory parade underscored the confidence of the American people that their soldiers posed no threat to the republic. Perhaps 150,000 troops, under arms, camped outside the gate of the national capital and paraded through its streets in front of thousands of onlookers, foreign dignitaries, politicians, and the victorious generals who had forged armies from a collection of farmers, factory workers, and laborers. Their rifle stocks and bayonets glinted in the late spring sunlight as they marched up Pennsylvania Avenue toward the Capitol. When the Ancient Romans had feted their victorious warriors along the Via Sacra, no weapons could pass through the triumphal gates into the city—and despite such precautions that once great republic had fallen to military dictatorship.

It mattered deeply to the citizenry that the nation that emerged from the Civil War should not become another Rome. And they said so, repeatedly. The Grand Review was, Wilfred M. McClay has written, designed to be "an object lesson in the new civics of nationalism."[5] The *Boston Post* previewed the parade for its readers, noting, "The war developed no Caesar, no Cromwell, no Napoleon." The editors celebrated the fact that the Union had survived without the usurpation of a dictator. "We may thankfully rejoice that it has developed none of the vices of a Caesar, a Cromwell, or a Napoleon."[6] Capturing the mood of a grateful nation, the volunteer soldiers likewise wished to conclude their service without controversy, embodying the ideal of the citizen-soldier. As Albert Harrison of the Fourteenth New Jersey Infantry explained, "I dont [*sic*] think it will be many days before our old Corps will be broken up & we shall go home rejoicing . . . We are to pass in Review through Washington & then return to camp. It will occupy nearly a day, but we can afford it as it will be the last time I trust."[7]

For numerous onlookers, the victory parade demonstrated that the events of the previous four years had strengthened the Union. New Haven's *Daily Palladium* informed its readers, "As no country has ever sent such valor to the field, so none ever welcomed such grand divisions back." The paper stated that Sherman's "conquering hosts" and "the legions of the Potomac army" would present "a splendid and imposing military spectacle." *Frank Leslie's Illustrated Newspaper* affirmed that "Alexander and Cyrus never gazed upon nobler armies or more heroic legions than those which passed through Washington during Tuesday and Wednesday, the 23d and 24th of May."[8] Nineteenth-century readers would have immediately understood the allusion. Cyrus and Alexander had forged two of the largest empires of the ancient world through their military prowess. Their soldiers were considered some of the greatest conquerors in history, yet *Leslie's* editors believed they could not match the power and prestige of the greatest Union armies.[9] The invocation called to mind spectacular military achievements, which were then supplanted in the minds of readers by the achievements of Grant's and Sherman's men.

Reflecting on the Grand Review two days after the parade, the *New York Times* stressed the centrality of the citizen-soldier to Union victory. The men who had taken up arms for the Union were cast in the mold of Cincinnatus. Like the storied Roman general, they had answered the call of their country and then laid down their arms when their duty was complete, their nation saved. They did not seek control of the government; they did not threaten the democracy. No dictators or oligarchs threatened to rise from the ranks of the great citizen army. "We may declare almost positively," asserted the paper, "that this American Republic will never again see such another array of armed men." The editors then enquired: "Who gives a thought to the bare fact that two hundred thousand soldiers have been reviewed in the National Capital?"[10]

The emphasis on the importance of the citizen-soldier appeared in newspapers throughout the country. The *North American and United States Gazette* in Philadelphia said of the review, "Never since Cain discovered war has there been so great cause for welcome of soldiers who have done their duty nobly and faithfully as now." The article also noted, "Never before, at any period, were great armies convened in the capital itself, undefended against its defenders and wholly at their mercy." The author of the article considered it a great testament that the returning Union armies posed no threat to the American government. "Law and order has been trampled down by armies sent out in their defense," the paper reminded readers. "In Greece, in Rome, in Germany, in France, in England—history is full of military usurpations."[11] No such usurpation threatened the Union.

Lois Bryan Adams, correspondent for the *Detroit Advertiser and Tribune,* noted the same citizen-soldier theme in her coverage of the review. "For two days past Washington has done nothing but watch our national heroes marching home," Adams wrote. "These are all citizens who know the value of their country and their government; they saw the danger menacing both, they made heroes of themselves, they have averted the danger, have given a progressive interpretation to the old Constitution, and are now quietly disbanding to go home and be citizens again." Adams believed "the heroes made by Kings and Emperors are not to be compared with these."[12] Adams looked on the achievement of the citizen-soldiers as having given new purpose to the Constitution and thus claimed that no heroes of history could surpass the Union veterans.

Soldiers who marched in the parade imagined a future away from the battlefield. They expressed gratitude for the warm welcome they received from their countrymen as they prepared to return to their farms and factories. First Lieutenant Frank M. Guernsey of the Thirty-Second Wisconsin Infantry often found himself at a loss for words during the review. "I cant [sic] begin to describe how we soldiers felt when we saw how the Nation threw open her arms and how warmly she welcomed us home, our work ended and the Union preserved," he wrote. "Every mans [sic] heart was big with emotion we knew that our long years of suffering and hardships had now a glorious end, and that we should soon go home to our loved ones and enjoy the fruits of our hard years of labor and danger."[13] For Guernsey, the prospect of never again having to endure such hardships added meaning to the Grand Review.

Other observers used the review to draw distinctions between professional soldiers and the volunteer Union troops. Articles in numerous newspapers concluded that despite the American veteran being a citizen rather than a professional soldier, he ranked among the greatest trained military soldiers in history. The *Caledonian* in Saint Johnsbury, Vermont, described the ovation received by the marching troops in similar terms, affirming the nation's gratitude for the citizens who saved the Union. "Neither did the legions of imperial Rome, returning in triumph along the Appian Way, or the conquering hosts of Napoleon the great when welcomed back from their Italian campaign by the Parisians, or the British guards when they returned from the Crimea," the paper exalted, "receive a more heartfelt ovation than is today being awarded to the Army of the Potomac."[14]

More than anything, soldiers viewed the review as their final military act, rejecting any notion that they wished to remain soldiers after their triumphal procession. St. Clair A. Mulholland recalled the Grand Review as signifying the point at which "the Regiment passed out of existence." "The members returned to their homes, to be welcomed by their friends and fellow citizens," he wrote, "to lay aside the uniform they had honored, and to once again become a part of the people—a good citizen because a good soldier."[15] Robert Burns Beath, in his history of the Grand Army of the Republic, echoed Mulholland's citizen-soldier theme, suggesting that the soldiers marching in the parade "were now present only that those necessary details might be completed which would enable them to take their places in the ranks of peaceful citizens."[16]

By October 26, 1865, General-in-Chief Ulysses S. Grant could proudly assert that only 210,000 men remained of the more than 1.1 million who were under arms just six months prior. Even better, Grant noted, "further reductions are still being made." The 1843 West Point graduate wrote that "800,000 men pass[ed] from the Army to civil life so quietly that it was scarcely known save by the welcomes to their homes received by them." The great Union leader acknowledged that many Americans may have had apprehensions of "disturbance and disorder at so vast a force being suddenly thrown upon the country to resume the occupations of civil life after having been so long absent from them." But their fears, he said, "proved entirely unfounded, the soldiers showing by their conduct that devotion to their country."[17]

Within four years, Grant would be installed as president, representing the Republican Party. To the great surprise of many, including his close friend William T. Sherman, he did little to support the regular army during his two terms in office. Sherman felt Grant's rebuke of the professional army so keenly that he admitted to a newspaper editor, "My faith in his friendship is shaken . . . and when again he wants it, it may be less than he supposes."[18] With the president posing no obstacle to their plans after 1868, the Republican majority in Congress seized their best opportunity yet to steer the ship of state to their desired harbor. They sought various ends—chief among them economization (a reduction of the vast bureaucracy created by the war), demobilization (achieved almost entirely within a year following the end of hostilities), and national reunification according to their terms. The final goal required the use of the army, as former Confederate states proved hostile to having Black freedom and civil rights foisted upon them. Free elections and fair conditions in which the former Confederate states would produce new constitutions depended on the presence of federal troops.

The Republican Party had little choice but to rely on the army to achieve its goals. George Boutwell, a Republican representing Massachusetts in the House, explained the situation plainly. Military occupation represented the only "practicable way of furnishing protection to life, liberty, and property" in the former Confederacy.[19] As far as Republicans were concerned, the army represented the backbone of their Reconstruction program. Soldiers gave their policies force and protected Americans who would otherwise have lived under constant threat. It follows, then, that the Republican Party's postbellum treatment of the army offers one way to understand the party's broader commitment to Reconstruction. Supporting soldiers meant supporting the programs that would bring aid to newly liberated freedpeople and prevent former slaveholders from regaining the political and economic power they possessed before the war.

Recovering Republicans' attitudes toward the army in the wake of the Civil War, in other words, allows historians to track the party's ideological commitment to Reconstruction. Historians have typically accepted the Hayes–Tilden compromise following the election of 1876 as Reconstruction's traditional end date. Close attention to military affairs, however, reveals that Republicans decreased their investment in Reconstruction beginning in 1870, and army data suggest that the largest reduction of troops in the South came not after the mandated reduction in 1876 but between 1869 and 1871. If Reconstruction's success depended on policing former Confederates and maintaining martial law in ex-Confederate states, the sharp decline in resources for the South after 1870–71 suggests that either the federal government considered the process largely completed or that goals of economic reduction took precedence over ensuring racial equality throughout the South.

Looking closely at Republican political policies vis-à-vis the professional army forces a reconsideration of the timeline for Reconstruction. It also offers a tentative answer to a question that historians have debated for nearly a century: What accounts for the failure of Reconstruction? One significant factor is that the Republican Party could not sustain its support for the army. When forced to choose between economization and maintaining a strong military presence across the former Confederacy, Republicans debated until they were blue in the face and then almost always chose to save money.

Republican leaders—many of them experienced enough to have served in Congress before the war, in the age of the Slave Power—continued to nurture their suspicions of the professional army. Lack of trust in the nation's soldiers combined with a craze for cutting federal spending so that the Republican war against the army also meant the untimely demise of the party's program for Reconstruction.

4

THE REPUBLICAN ARMY, 1865–1872

The wonder excited by the raising of the vast army which saved the Union from destruction was even surpassed by the wonder excited by its prompt and peaceful dissolution.

—James Gillespie Blaine, 1865

Late in life, Major General John A. Logan wrote a history of the volunteer soldier in America. Logan, who served in the Army of Tennessee in the Civil War's Western Theater, championed the volunteer veterans of the Civil War until his death in 1886. From 1867 to 1871, he served in the House of Representatives as a Republican from Illinois. In the Forty-First Congress, Logan chaired the House Committee on Military Affairs. In this capacity, he lobbied for a substantial reduction of the regular army of the United States. Logan's monograph about the achievements of volunteer soldiers, posthumously published as *The Volunteer Soldier of America,* encapsulated the Republican Party's attitudes about the regular army's conservatism and diminished value to the nation. A veteran who criticized some of the very men he had fought with against the rebels, Logan starkly revealed the uphill climb facing army professionals in acquiring congressional backing for their endeavors after the Civil War.[1]

Logan detailed how the broader Republican Party rationalized cutting back the regular army after the military clash of 1861–65. In Logan's judgment, professional soldiers were "a highly privileged class," and "beyond the reach of the sovereign people." He considered the regular army "foreign to the constitution and the best interests of the republic."[2] Logan and his colleagues in Congress developed new arguments for controlling the regulars. They asserted a congressional prerogative for managing military affairs that also challenged executive power. Legislators concentrated on how they could use soldiers to implement their Reconstruction policies, so much so that one historian has suggested that Congress exercised complete control over the army in the South.[3]

The tendency to favor Reconstruction meant that lawmakers like Logan gave less attention to the challenges facing the regulars in the West. Instead, they focused on the goal of curtailing the political power of former rebels and instituting Black suffrage in the defeated South. In 1870, for example, Kansas Republican Samuel C. Pomeroy admitted that the Republican Party intended to reduce the regular army even if it hindered the work of the regulars. Speaking about legislation to decrease the army, introduced by Massachusetts senator Henry Wilson, Pomeroy declared, "If the senator [Wilson] will show that this bill would reduce the expenses [of the army], though the whole western frontier were thereby exposed, I might submit to the reduction."[4] Pomeroy made clear the Republican preference for economization.[5]

Between 1865 and 1870, three Republican-controlled congresses systematically slashed the size of the standing force from 50,000 in 1866 to 30,000 in 1870, with the goal of 25,000 in the years that followed.[6] Republicans justified this action by continuing to make the case that a large standing army was unnecessary in times of peace. The party's leaders had to acknowledge, however, that the army served as a political instrument necessary for implementing Radical designs for Reconstruction, which included protecting African Americans, punishing those who remained disloyal to the Union, and attempting to ensure equal protection under the law in the former Confederacy.

Republicans contradicted themselves by supporting the army's use for Reconstruction while simultaneously attacking professional soldiers as a threat to the republic. Lawmakers gave soldiers and officers authority to oversee elections, arrest citizens who threatened free Blacks, and administer martial law in the South. Still, Republican senators such as James Grimes of Iowa proclaimed, "I know of no necessity for increasing the army," while adding more work for the army's officers and soldiers.[7] The party's willingness to use soldiers to enforce congressional Reconstruction under-scored that for all their proclamations of standing armies as antithetical to republican values, they understood they needed professional troops to advance their policies.

Table 7. Army Expenditures as a Percentage of the Federal Budget, 1860–1877

Year	Federal budget ($)	Expenditures ($)	Portion of federal budget (%)	Expenditures in 2023 dollars ($)
1860	63,131,000	16,410,000	26.0	591,491,530
1861	66,547,000	22,981,000	34.5	781,275,655
1862	474,762,000	394,368,000	83.1	11,681,492,530
1863	714,741,000	599,299,000	83.8	14,229,546,176
1864	865,323,000	690,792,000	79.8	13,163,327,556
1865	1,297,555,000	1,031,323,000	79.5	18,928,889,687
1866	520,809,000	284,450,000	54.6	5,352,132,484
1867	357,543,000	95,224,000	26.6	1,924,875,951
1868	377,340,000	123,247,000	32.7	2,596,605,985
1869	322,865,000	78,502,000	24.3	1,726,870,833
1870	309,654,000	57,656,000	18.6	1,316,713,398
1871	292,177,000	35,800,000	12.3	877,892,295
1872	277,518,000	35,372,000	12.7	867,396,822
1873	290,345,000	46,323,000	16.0	1,154,870,992
1874	302,634,000	42,314,000	14.0	1,110,445,559
1875	274,623,000	41,121,000	15.0	1,118,379,051
1876	265,101,000	38,071,000	14.4	1,064,458,043
1877	241,334,000	37,083,000	15.4	1,056,582,962

Source: Data compiled from Cambridge University Press, *Historical Statistics of the United States,* Millennial Edition online, https://hsus.cambridge.org. Accessed May 2023.

Table 8. Army Distribution by Year, 1866–1877

Year	Total troops	Reconstruction	West	Coasts
1866	57,072	29,978	24,592	3,770
1867	57,194	21,560	24,592	4,700
1868	51,066	19,661	21,735	4,257
1869	36,953	10,756	17,781	6,140
1870	37,240	8,761	18,718	5,129
1871	29,115	8,601	16,078	3,971
1872	28,322	4,806	20,112	2,960
1873	28,812	3,233	21,152	2,470
1874	28,640	3,236	20,426	2,116
1875	25,513	1,870	18,542	2,641
1876	28,565	0	19,802	2,976
1877	24,140	0	17,917	3,436

Source: Data compiled from Cambridge University Press, *Historical Statistics of the United States,* Millennial Edition online, https://hsus.cambridge.org. Accessed May 2023.

Table 9. Membership of the Military Affairs Committee, 1867–1885

HOUSE	SENATE
Fortieth Congress (1867–1869)	
James A. Garfield (R-OH)*	Henry Wilson (R-MA), Chair
William A. Pile (R-MO)*	Jacob M. Howard (R-MI)
John H. Ketcham (R-NY)*	William Sprague (R-RI)
Henry D. Washburn (R-IN)*	Simon Cameron (R-PA)
Grenville M. Dodge (R-IA)*	Oliver Morton (R-IN)
Green B. Raum (R-IL)*	John M. Thayer (R-NE)
Isaac R. Hawkins (R-TN)*	James R. Doolittle (R-WI)
Charles Sitgreaves (D-NJ)	
Benjamin M. Boyer (D-PA)	

Table 9. (*continued*)

HOUSE	SENATE
Forty-First Congress (1869–1871)	
John A. Logan (R-IL)*	Henry Wilson (R-MA), Chair
Amasa Cobb (R-WI)*	Jacob M. Howard (R-MI)
James S. Negley (R-PA)*	Simon Cameron (R-PA)
Jasper Packard (R-IN)*	Oliver Morton (R-IN)
Joel F. Asper (R-MO)*	Jahn M. Thayer (R-NE)
William L. Stoughton (R-MI)*	Jospeh C. Abbott (R-NC)
John S. Witcher (R-WV)*	Carl Schurz (R-MO)*
Frank Morey (R-LA)*	
Solomon L. Hoge (R-SC)*	
George W. Morgan (D-OH)*	
Henry W. Slocum (D-NY)*	
Forty-Second Congress (1871–1873)	
John Coburn (R-IN)*	Henry Wilson (R-MA), Chair
William L. Stoughton (R-MI)*	Simon Cameron (R-PA)
William G. Donnan (R-IA)*	Oliver Morton (R-IN)
Frank Morey (R-LA)*	Adelbert Ames (R-MS)*
George E. Harris (R-MS)†	John A. Logan (R-IL)*
John B. Hay (R-IL)	J. Rodman West (R-LA)*
Henry W. Slocum (D-NY)*	Francis P. Blair, Jr. (D-MO)*
Lewis D. Campbell (D-OH)*	
William Terry (D-VA)†	
Forty-Third Congress (1873–1875)	
John Coburn (R-IN)*	John A. Logan (R-IL), Chair*
William G. Donnan (R-IA)*	Simon Cameron (R-PA)
John B. Hawley (R-IL)*	George E. Spencer (R-AL)*
Jospeh R. Hawley (R-CT)*	Powell Clayton (R-AK)*
Lewis B. Gunckel (R-OH)	Bainbridge Wadleigh (R-NH)
Charles Albright (R-PA)*	James K. Kelly (D-OR)
Clinton D. MacDougall (R-NY)*	Matt W. Ransom (D-NC)†
Jacob M. Thornburgh (R-TN)*	
James W. Nesmith (D-OR)	
Pierce M. B. Young (D-GA)†	
Eppa Hunton (D-VA)†	

Table 9. (*continued*)

HOUSE	SENATE
Forty-Fourth Congress (1875–1877)	
Henry B. Banning (D-OH)*	John A. Logan, Chair (R-IL)*
Alpheus S. Williams (D-MI)*	Simon Cameron (R-PA)
William Terry (D-VA)†	George E. Spencer (R-AL)*
Philip Cook (D-GA)†	Powell Clayton (R-AK)*
John M. Glover (D-MO)	Bainbridge Wadleigh (R-NH)
John Reilly (D-PA)	Ambrose E. Burnside (R-RI)*
Augustus A. Hardenbergh (D-NJ)	Matt W. Ransom (D-NC)†‡
Clinton D. MacDougall (R-NY)*	Theodore Randolph (D-NJ)
Jacob M. Thornburgh (R-TN)*	Francis M. Cockrell (D-MO)†
Stephen A. Hurlbut (R-IL)*	John B. Gordon (D-GA)**†
Horace B. Strait (R-MN)	
Forty-Fifth Congress (1877–1879)	
Henry B. Banning (D-OH)*	George E. Spencer, Chair (R-AL)*
Edward S. Bragg (D-WI)*	Bainbridge Wadleigh (R-NH)
Levi Maish (D-PA)*	Simon Cameron (R-PA)
Alvah A. Clark (D-NJ)	Ambrose E. Burnside (R-RI)*
James Williams (D-DE)	Henry M. Teller (R-CO)
George G. Dibrell (D-TN)†	Preston B. Plumb (R-KS)*
John H. Evins (D-SC)†	Theodore Randolph (D-NJ)
Horace B. Strait (R-MN)	Francis M. Cockrell (D-MO)†
Harry White (R-PA)*	Samuel B. Maxey (D-TX)†
Anson G. McCook (R-NY)*	
Benjamin F. Marsh (R-IL)*	
Forty-Sixth Congress (1879–1881)	
William A. J. Sparks (D-IL)	Theodore Randolph (D-NJ), Chair
Benjamin Le Fevre (D-OH)*	Francis M. Cockrell (D-MO)†
Edward S. Bragg (D-WI)*	Samuel B. Maxey (D-TX)†
George G. Dibrell (D-TN)†	La Fayette Grover (D-OR)
Joseph E. Johnston (D-VA)†	John B. Gordon (D-GA)†‡
William E. Smith (D-GA)†	Ambrose E. Burnside (R-RI)*
Christopher C. Upson (D-TX)†	Preston B. Plumb (R-KS)*
Harry White (R-PA)*	J. Donald Cameron (R-PA)

Table 9. *(continued)*

HOUSE	SENATE
Forty-Sixth Congress (1879–1881) (continued)	
Anson G. McCook (R-NY)*	John A. Logan (R-IL)*
Benjamin F. Marsh (R-IL)*	Wade Hampton (D-SC)**†
Thomas M. Browne (R-IN)*	
Forty-Seventh Congress (1881–1883)	
Thomas J. Henderson (R-IL)*	John A. Logan (R-IL), Chair*
Anson G. McCook (R-NY)*	Ambrose E. Burnside (R-RI)*
Thomas M. Bayne (R-PA)*	J. Donald Cameron (R-PA)
George W. Steele (R-IN)*	Benjamin Harrison (R-IN)*
Oliver L. Spaulding (R-MI)*	William J. Sewell (R-NJ)*††
Henry J. Spooner (R-RI)	Francis M. Cockrell (D-MO)†
George R. Davis (R-IL)	Samuel B. Maxey (D-TX)†
William A. J. Sparks (D-IL)	La Fayette Grover (D-OR)
Christopher C. Upson (D-TX)†	Wade Hampton (D-SC)†
Jospeh Wheeler (D-AL)†	
Edward S. Bragg (D-WI)*	
Forty-Eighth Congress (1883–1885)	
William S. Rosecrans (D-CA)*	John A. Logan (R-IL), Chair*
Henry W. Slocum (D-NY)*	J. Donald Cameron (R-PA)
Charles H. Morgan (D-MO)*	Benjamin Harrison (R-IN)*
Frank L. Wolford (D-KY)*	Joseph R. Hawley (R-CT)*
Robert M. Murray (D-OH)*	Francis M. Cockrell (D-MO)†
George G. Dibrell (D-TN)†	Samuel B. Maxey (D-TX)†
John C. Nicholls (D-GA)†	Wade Hampton (D-SC)†
William A. Duncan (D-PA)	Johnson M. Camden (D-WV)
Daniel W. Connolly (D-PA)	
George W. Steele (R-IN)*	
Thomas M. Bayne (R-PA)*	
Theodore Lyman (R-MA)*	
James Laird (R-NE)*	
Byron M. Cutcheon (R-MI)*	

* Union army	‡ Member replaced	†† Medal of Honor recipient
† Confederate army	** Replacement member	

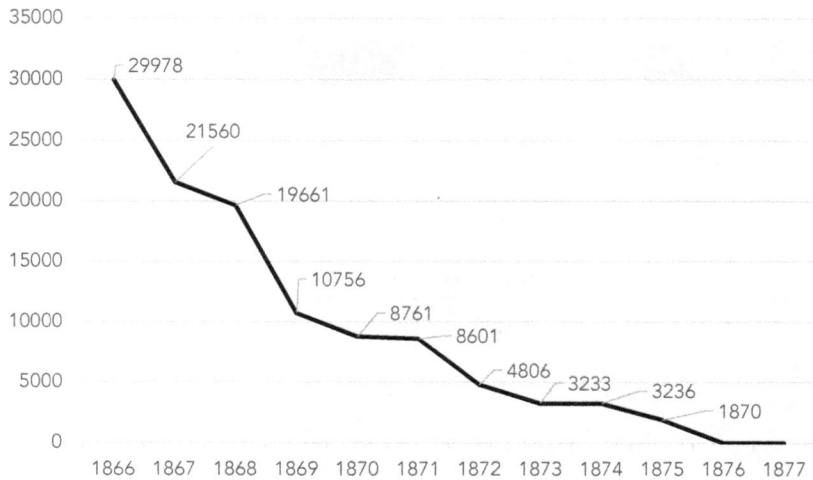

Graph 4. Troops posted on Reconstruction service, 1865–1877

Reconstruction-era Republicans were not monolithic in their views. Differences existed between moderate and Radical wings of the party. The Radicals advocated the most strenuously for African American citizenship and suffrage. Radicals believed the South had been defeated in a long and costly war and that Congress could dictate the circumstances under which the rebel states rejoined the Union. Senator George Julian, for example, proposed that "one rule be adopted for white and black," and that the nation should rid itself of "the vile spirit of caste which has brought upon the country all its woes."[8] Thaddeus Stevens, the Radical Pennsylvania representative, believed "the rebellion was an act of fiendish cruelty against the best Government on earth."[9] True to Radical policy, Stevens insisted that Congress had the sole authority to readmit the rebellious states, following "a reorganization in southern institution, habits, and manners."[10]

Moderate Republicans sympathized with the views of their more extreme colleagues but they hoped for more gradual change in social and political upheaval, and that it would come with the consent of southern whites. They sought federal guarantees of African American freedom and wanted southern law enforcement to safeguard the rights of freedpeople. They voted for the creation and maintenance of relief agencies such as the

Freedmen's Bureau. In contrast with the Radicals, "moderate Republicans viewed Reconstruction as a practical problem, not an opportunity to impose an open-ended social revolution upon the South." There had no intention of abandoning emancipation, but they were not "enthusiastic about the prospect of Black suffrage."[11]

Even though they constituted less than a majority in both houses, Radicals enjoyed enormous influence in shaping policy. According to historian Eric Foner, Radicals constituted "nearly half of the Republican members of the House and a lesser but still significant portion of the Senate."[12] Regardless of their overall proportions, Radicals were the driving force behind legislation governing Reconstruction. Radical influence grew as moderates came to share their belief that Congress had the right to dictate the terms of Reconstruction. The policies of Andrew Johnson, including leniency toward former Confederates and the exercise of the veto power over congressional legislation, pushed moderates into an alliance with Radicals. Both wings of the Republican Party wanted to seize oversight of the Reconstruction process from the president. Moderate William Pitt Fessenden of Maine, for example, called the Joint Committee on Reconstruction, which investigated southern behavior and recommended an aggressive legislative posture that led to the Fourteenth Amendment, "an imperative duty resting upon the representatives of the people in the two branches of Congress."[13]

Both Radicals and moderates strove to address the national debt amassed during the Civil War, which exerted a measurable impact on the regular army's financial support.[14] Military expenditures and the size of the regular army represented a significant cost to the government.[15] In the final two years of the Civil War, army spending accounted for nearly 80 percent of all federal expenditures. Throughout the Reconstruction era, Republican legislation reduced that percentage to an average of 15 percent by 1870, compared to the average of 20 percent of overall expenditures before the war.

The largest drop in the military budget as a percentage came after 1870, the year that Georgia became the last state readmitted to the Union. By 1871, all the former Confederate states had representatives once again seated in Congress. In 1870, the army's share of the federal budget plummeted (see table 7), while spending on veterans and on paying down interest on the national debt increased, taking up "more than half of all funds the government disbursed in the postwar decade."[16] Republicans believed that veterans deserved more federal dollars than professionals currently enlisted in the military. Logan served as a champion of veteran interests, serving as the first commander in chief of the Grand Army of the Republic, which lobbied for veteran affairs.

Democrats, meanwhile, created an unusual alliance with Radical Republicans by opposing funding for regulars in the South. Between 1865 and 1870, Radical Republicans and Democrats opposed manpower and budget increases, although for different political reasons. Republican representative Benjamin Butler led a loose coalition of Democrats and Radicals who, in 1868, wished to reduce the size of the army. Butler, a former volunteer general who "nursed a bitter grudge against the army from his own wartime experience," helped to engineer more reductions in 1869.[17] Democrats sided with Republicans on army reductions because weakening the army overall undermined the institution's effectiveness in occupying the South, allowing white Democrats in the region to have fewer constraints on punitive actions against freedpeople and white Republicans.[18] As historian Robert Wooster explained, "Democratic attacks against Republican-dominated Reconstruction and against a powerful federal government carried over to the army."[19]

Republicans empowered the regular army to transform the South via the Military Reconstruction Act. Enacted over the veto of President Johnson in March 1867, the measure established martial law in the South and placed the army in the role of enforcing a political reorganization that included Black suffrage. The law divided the former Confederate states (excluding Tennessee) into five military districts, assigned an army officer to each area, and required the commanding general "to protect all persons in their rights of person and property, to suppress insurrection, disorder, and violence, and punish, or cause to be punished, all disturbers of the public peace and criminals."[20] Soldiers also adjudicated who could vote and conducted registration drives that included Black males. In doing so they also disenfranchised white people they considered disloyal. Finally, the various state legislatures had to ratify the Fourteenth Amendment, which recognized the citizenship of Black Americans and established federal protection against discriminatory laws and practices.

The Republicans' embrace of regular troops for Reconstruction service grew out of both convenience and necessity. At the end of the Civil War, thousands of volunteer troops remained spread across the former Confederacy. Republicans and high-ranking army officers prioritized mustering the remaining volunteers out of service and returning the army to its professional-only status. For the better part of 1865 to 1866, however, volunteer troops still garrisoned numerous installations across the former Confederacy as they awaited their opportunity to go home. By the time Congress passed the Military Reconstruction law in 1867, no volunteers remained in the service. The legislation relied solely on regular troops for its implementation.[21] It remained for Congress to decide how to deploy a declining force to cover expanding needs.

The Thirty-Ninth Congress tackled this problem in an army appropriations bill that fixed the size and organization of the postwar military. Legislation appeared under the sponsorship of Radical Republican Henry Wilson in the Senate and Republican Robert C. Schenck of Ohio in the House.[22] Both chambers debated the bills from February until July 1866.[23] The final bill fixed the regular army at 50,000 troops—an increase over the 1865 force, which had been set at 25,000. Though larger than the nation's previous peacetime army, the troops faced a more extensive set of tasks to accomplish, with the addition of Reconstruction service. A larger army was necessary in 1866, according to one historian, because it served as the government's "armed bureaucracy," since the country lacked "reliable alternatives."[24]

The act mirrored broader Republican goals in several ways, especially by providing for the organization of Black regiments. African American regiments during the war comprised volunteers; this represented the first time that the nation had recruited Black men for regular duty. On the surface, the measure appeared egalitarian, but throughout the conversations regarding the Black regiments, legislators revealed their racial biases, as when they stipulated that the Black troops could only be deployed in the West, to avoid racial conflict in the South.[25] The legislation also provided for Indian scouts to serve short terms as required.[26] Finally, a provision underscored the desire of lawmakers to undercut West Point as the principal institution for military training. Echoing the Morrill Act of 1862, the legislation provided for military education in colleges, which advanced the attack on the national military academy that had begun during the war.

The total number of troops suggested by Wilson fell below the numbers recommended by some of the army's leading officers. Ulysses S. Grant sought 80,000 men for the regular force, hoping to include twenty regiments of African American soldiers.[27] Sherman speculated in a letter to his brother, Ohio senator John Sherman, that the Radical Republican plan for Reconstruction required an army of 100,000 men across the South.[28] The bill disappointed Major General Phillip Sheridan by neglecting to increase the cavalry available for western service, which he had suggested as necessary to meet the challenge of the larger geographic demands on the regulars.[29]

Yet something was better than nothing. Whatever their disagreements about the size of the army in the legislation, military officers detested sitting in limbo and expressed concerns that delays in settling the numbers hampered their ability to undertake their various missions. William T. Sherman exhorted his brother John to hurry the army bill along: "We need the Army Bills to get to work."[30] Grant wrote a similar plea to Secretary of War Edwin Stanton, stressing that army officers were losing time while Congress debated their status. Without a clear sense of troop levels, Grant could not compose a plan of operations for the postbellum army or manage the distribution of troops to various military posts.[31]

Prior to the Civil War, more than 90 percent of regular troops had clustered either in the Southwest or on the Pacific Coast. These states and territories comprised some 961,000 square miles. After the Civil War, military planners altered the army's western mission in response to gold rushes in Colorado (1859) and Montana (1862). In addition to California, Oregon, Texas, and the territories of Arizona, New Mexico, and Washington, the army had to maintain a presence in the present-day states of Colorado, Montana, North and South Dakota, Utah, and Wyoming. This gave the regulars more than 1.5 million square miles of western territory to cover. The addition of 10,000 men over the army's antebellum size also compensated for the military occupation of the former Confederacy, a task that added more than 770,000 additional square miles of land to oversee.[32] To this the army also added the defense of the nation's seacoast fortifications, on both the Atlantic and the Pacific. Typically, 10 percent of troops (two or three regiments) were reserved for this duty. William Tecumseh Sherman later recalled that the postbellum army looked less like an army and more like "little squads of men strung along a frontier of fifteen hundred or sixteen hundred miles."[33]

During the Senate debate, an array of amendments reflected the political interest in African American enlistments within the Republican-dominated chamber. Fessenden added an amendment placing white and Black officers on the same footing for promotion, noting that African American troops had rendered valuable service during the war and deserved compensation equal to that of white soldiers. New recruits were offered thirteen dollars per month. In the initial wave of enlistments, however, Black regiments would be officered by white men with a least two years of military experience.[34] Wade, one of the army's staunchest adversaries, wanted to add four African American cavalry regiments for western service. By sending Black troops to the frontier, Republicans hoped to avoid racial conflict arising from posting African American men to the former Confederacy to enforce Reconstruction among a recalcitrant white population. Prominent army officers such as George H. Thomas, George G. Meade, and Grant supported this view. They considered Black troops capable for Reconstruction service but saw them as what Grant termed a "demoralizing" influence in the South.[35]

Republicans in the House, meanwhile, questioned the propriety of funding the regular army when the nation owed a greater debt to the volunteer veterans. Kentucky's Lovell H. Rousseau, a political maverick who had risen to major general of volunteers during the war, claimed that the House had to choose between spending money on pensions for volunteers or on regular soldiers. In the name of economy, the chamber had to decide how to spend a smaller sum of money from the federal treasury. Rousseau wanted money cut from the regular army and added to the pension for veterans. His vitriol toward the regulars was notable. "The volunteer army of this nation put down the late rebellion," he exclaimed, "and they could have done it as well if there had been not a single West Pointer in the whole Army."[36]

Rousseau did not limit his disdain for the professional army to his congressional speeches. Just over a week after denouncing the regulars before Congress, Rousseau assaulted another congressman, Josiah Bushnell Grinnell, over remarks the latter had made about Rousseau's military record during the Civil War. The two had recently been feuding about another military issue—the maintenance of the Freedmen's Bureau in the former Confederacy. Grinnell wanted more power given to the bureau's agents, a select group of professional soldiers who were tasked with aiding the transition to freedom for Blacks across the South, while Rousseau suspected that the professional troops were abusing their authority. Rather than continue a reasoned debate, Rousseau beat Grinnell with his cane on the east portico of the Capitol, causing significant injuries to his colleague on the Committee on Military Affairs. A congressional panel reprimanded Rousseau for his trouble and the Kentuckian resigned his seat. In the special election to replace him, the Bluegrass State's electors returned Rousseau to fill the vacancy he had caused. In a final twist of irony, when Rousseau failed to secure reelection in 1867, he sought an appointment as an officer in the regular army. He was posted to Alaska.[37]

Democrats in the House joined with Republicans to oppose an increase to the army. Francis C. Le Blond, an Ohio Democrat, admitted he knew little about military matters, yet he maintained that only course of action that would satisfy him would be to reduce the peacetime standing army.[38] Le Blond's politics differed drastically from his Republican colleagues'. His wariness about the army stemmed from its use in the former Confederacy to effect a Radical agenda. As they looked to redeem the South from Radical Republican rule, Democrats realigned with southern whites to challenge Republican dominance and restrict Black voting. Because soldiers protected African American voters, Democrats abandoned their antebellum support for the army, leaving the regulars without the congressional support they had once enjoyed.

Republican objections to the House bill revealed the party's focus on the South at the expense of the West. Vermont's Frederick E. Woodbridge offered a clear summary of his party's position on the necessity of a peacetime army. He reminded colleagues that "a large standing army is inconsistent with republican institutions." Woodbridge described himself as "anxious . . . to reduce the expenditures of the government." The second-term representative noted that he would support military spending in one area: "the former rebellious States."[39] In terms of the West, Woodbridge also made a telling statement, saying that troops would be needed in what he called the Great Northwest—the present-day states of Idaho, Montana, Oregon, Utah, and Washington. The territories Woodbridge identified were potentially lucrative, containing untold quantities of lumber and mineral wealth. Their potential seemed worth protecting with regular troops. The Southwest, once the army's largest arena of operations, did not strike him as important.[40] He had this in common with at least one prominent army officer, William T. Sherman, who bluntly stated in his annual report for 1867 that New Mexico and the Southwest would never provide a return on the investment the federal government had made in acquiring the territory and facilitating white settlement therein.[41] The soldier and the politician alike rejected the importance of a region with significant racial diversity in favor of one that promised to be much more homogenous in its racial composition.

Newspapers reported avidly on the House debates, with major Republican and Democratic newspapers both arguing for a reduction in the army's size. Greeley's *New York Tribune* pleaded with the "economists in Congress" to "save us from the passage of this most needlessly oppressive measure." Greeley told his readers that "war is going out of fashion" and that every soldier added to the army cost the government five hundred dollars before the man joined a regiment. Greeley saw no reason for the added burden on the treasury. To him, the national economy already groaned under unprecedented taxation.[42]

The editors at the politically idiosyncratic *New York Herald* did not significantly differ from their inner-city rival. The *Herald*'s editors claimed that the country needed "the most efficient army with the smallest amount of materials and at the least expense." The *Herald* believed that the primary goal of the Republican should be reductions, in both size and cost. Congressional conversations about increasing army spending to maintain a reserve corps of veterans for service, meanwhile, produced complaints. The editors pointed to "a great deal of twaddle and affection of sentiment" about "the maimed veterans of the war."[43] Though it was meant as a rebuke of Republican sentimentality, the *Herald*'s final observation underscored the habit of disdaining the professional soldier and championing the veteran volunteer.

The Republican press walked a fine line between acknowledging the need for troops in the South and advocating for decreasing federal spending through military reductions. Maintaining a large standing army constituted a poor economic choice, the *Vermont Chronicle* explained, "especially when the country is weighed down by the burden of an enormous debt." The editors added one important caveat, however, in stating that a force should be retained to maintain order in the South.[44]

Others argued that the country did not need an army of the size proposed by either Wilson or Schenck because the nation was at peace. Philadelphia's pro-Republican *North American* noted that Wilson had sought guidance from the army's leading officers in crafting his bill. The editors asserted that the opinions of "the leading generals . . . should not be too closely adhered to in time of peace." The *North American* claimed that army officers only wanted to "make places and fat salaries and perquisites for about ten times as many officers as there should be on the payroll." The editorial then engaged in a familiar recitation of the faults of the regular army, saying, "The officers [will] yield to the influence of southern society, and soon become the mere partisans of the aristocracy." The most important point the writer strove to make, however, was that the Civil War had proven that volunteers were preferable to professional soldiers and that the American people had "no desire for an armed peace" overseen by "an army of drones."[45]

The Senate bill left newspaper editors across the country dissatisfied. Commentary in Republican and Democrat papers asserted that even in the scaled-down version legislators had provided for too large an increase in the regular force. The Republican editors of the *North American* informed their readers that the bill "will saddle upon us an army from 50 to 75,000 men." The newspaper argued that "the material does not exist in this country where of a large standing army can be maintained." More than anything, however, the newspaper repeated sentiments about the regular army that had filled the halls of Congress throughout the war years: "As for efficiency, the war proved conclusively that the regulars were no better than the volunteers."[46] As both chambers looked to organize an effective postbellum force, their wartime assessments of the regular army's performance had become conventional wisdom in the press, distributed to readers via newspaper columns.

The Republican *New York Times* ran editorials advising against an increase to the army.[47] One editorialist pointed out that money spent on the army might be better invested in the infrastructure of western expansion. Calling himself "Young America," the writer encouraged sweeping changes to the regular army. "At a time like this when the government has such need of monies to subsidize railroads," he explained, "all these meritorious savings ought to be looked after." The author had little sympathy for the professional soldiers who lost their jobs, claiming that officers were paid beyond their value. "If it be objected that some of the discarded veterans, if thus turned adrift, would be left rather poor," the writer claimed, "I can only say that is their business, not ours."[48] The letter underscored the disconnect between professional soldiers and civilian editors, who did not consider the work of the regulars as worthy of government spending as investment in infrastructure.

The Army Reorganization Act became law on July 28, 1866, and it represented the high point for the postbellum army in both funding and manpower. Congressional discussion of professional soldiers, however, did not end with the bill's adoption. As Reconstruction progressed and the Thirty-Ninth Congress shifted into its second session, legislators thought strategically about using the army to institute their policies. They also shifted their focus to using professional troops to undermine the authority of President Andrew Johnson.

In the winter and spring of 1867, the second session of the Thirty-Ninth Congress featured intense debate over the professional army in two areas: military Reconstruction and appropriations. Throughout the discussion of the bills, Republicans raised their traditional critique of the regular army but also admitted to the necessity of employing the regulars in the South. Looming over every conversation about the direction of Reconstruction was the growing chasm between the executive and legislative branches.[49] Andrew Johnson's leniency toward former Confederates and his increasing use of the veto power pushed congressional Republicans to assert even greater control over the regular army.[50]

Nowhere was the tension between the Republican ideology about the army and the importance of the regulars to reconstructing the South more evident than in the arguments over military Reconstruction. Senate Republicans used the debate, which absorbed their attention in early February 1867, to assert a congressional prerogative for managing Reconstruction. The discussion put many Republican legislators in a difficult position. While arguing that the army was necessary because there was "no civil authority" in the South, the same congressmen continued to view the regulars as untrustworthy. Maine's Lot M. Morrill explained that President Johnson had governed the South since the end of the Civil War "by his absolute military authority." If Congress did not take control of the army, Morrill warned, conditions in the South would lead to "murder, cruelties, and oppressions."[51] Republicans believed the civil rights acts were not being enforced and that the army was needed to insure equal application of the law.

Nevada Republican William M. Stewart grudgingly supported the Military Reconstruction Act, but only because it represented the best way to reorganize the southern states. Yet he cautioned about the use of unchecked military power, reminding colleagues that army officers were human beings susceptible to corruption. According to Stewart, southerners had fine wines, places of entertainment, and fashionable society that rivaled anywhere in the country. He believed that wealthy, white southerners could sway soldiers through various "allurements." He feared that officers could become reluctant to relinquish the power they held over civilians; that they would send false reports back to superiors of southern problems so they could remain in control.[52] Ultimately, he supplied no evidence for these assertions, portraying them as commonly held assumptions. In doing so, Stewart raised two of the most common themes in the Republican critique of professional officers: their supposed attraction to conservative politics and their unwillingness to yield power once it was given.

Stewart provided insight into how a select few Republicans saw the difference between the use of the military to police southerners and to confront Native peoples. As a representative for a western state, Stewart thought about the army not only as a tool for Reconstruction but also as an integral element of expanding federal authority in the West. Stewart argued strongly for transferring all matters concerning Indigenous Americans from the Interior Department to the War Department.[53] He considered the western arrangement cumbersome and unnecessarily expensive, because two bureaus overlapped in administering the region. Stewart posited a theory that it was more efficient to have the army in sole control.

Many of his concerns were founded on racist ideas about the people who lived in each region of the country. Despite his earlier statements about the possibility of white southerners seducing officers, he expressed no similar fears about the potential for soldiers in the West to be seduced by Indigenous ideas, politics, or ways of life. Stewart assumed that nothing about Native peoples could appeal to the interests of white soldiers.[54] He mentioned no "allurements" as he had in discussing the southern gentry, and regarding the West, not once did he raise the least uneasiness about the abuse of military power.

Nevada's senator was the only member of Congress who advocated for the army as a western administrative force as well as a southern one. When other Republicans considered Stewart's proposition to transfer the administration of the Bureau of Indian Affairs to the War Department, they could not move past their perception of the army as a conservative organization.

Taking a different slant from Stewart, Michigan's Radical senator Jacob Howard said that army officers would practice fraud as often as civilian administrators, and that the Senate should not "mistrust the management of Indian affairs to military hands."[55]

In the House, Radical Republicans continued to hedge their support for the army despite the desire to bring order to the South. Massachusetts representative Nathaniel P. Banks revealed a degree of personal resentment toward the regulars that informed his objections to the bill. Banks, whose war record as a major general of volunteers exemplified the uneven performance of most political generals, felt aggrieved toward the professional soldiers he had encountered during the war.[56] Banks listed numerous doubts about army officers overseeing Reconstruction. "My conviction," he told the House, "founded upon personal experience, compels me to say that I do not think the administration of the officers of the regular army will tend to the reestablishment of a loyal and Republican government."

Banks then turned to the familiar critique of the supposed political conservatism of the army's officer corps. "History does not justify us in expecting the restoration of overthrown Republican or Democratic governments through the intervention of purely military governments or of standing armies," he began. Then, echoing the concern of Senator Stewart of Nevada, he referred to the southern "aristocracy," which he considered "influential, educated, wealthy, powerful, and absolute in its control of public action beyond any aristocracy elsewhere existing." Drawing on his years of experience with regular soldiers, Banks asserted that "the regular army will fraternize with this aristocracy against this democracy; and so far as this occurs we should be deprived of the only basis we can have for the restoration of a loyal or democratic government in this country.[57] Banks believed that professional soldiers once again would fall back under the influence of the southern aristocrats who had dominated military affairs prior to the Civil War.

Republicans were searching for a way to control the army so that they could prevent the corruption that they feared would overtake the regulars. One major step toward this goal came in the annual appropriations bill for 1867. Tucked within the eventual law, a provision required that "all orders and instructions relating to military operations [be] issued through the General of the Army." It also stipulated that army officers could only be removed from command by the Senate, not by the commander in chief. Finally, a provision stripped the president of the power to issue orders to the army without the approval of the legislative branch.

This language sought to limit President Johnson's interference with army operations in the former Confederacy. Throughout 1866 and the early months of 1867, Johnson feuded with Major General Philip H. Sheridan, in command of Texas and Louisiana, over the general's vigorous implementation of Republican Reconstruction policies. Sheridan eventually removed public officials who contradicted Republican dictates, including dismissing the governor of Texas.[58] Sheridan's actions concerned Johnson enough that the president, in turn, removed Sheridan from command and replaced him with a Democrat, Winfield Scott Hancock.

Sheridan's removal offered a metaphor for the delicate position army officers occupied in the South. It also prompted a moment of reflection of the part of Ulysses S. Grant, who appealed to President Johnson to leave Sheridan in command. The "unreconstructed element" in the South, Grant explained, needed to see that the regular army could maintain control. By removing one of that army's best officers, Grant said, the president undermined the whole project of Reconstruction. Sheridan's removal—the removal of military authority—Grant explained to Johnson, "will embolden [former Confederates] to renewed opposition to the will of the loyal masses." While Sheridan considered his removal a relief from an "unsought burden," he insisted in his memoirs that he understood why he had been asked to perform Reconstruction service and hoped that history would recall his effort "to guard the rights of everybody in accordance with the law."[59] He could only do so if the national government sustained him in that service.

Johnson's unwanted intervention in military appointments gave congressional Republicans further evidence that the president opposed their program of Reconstruction. Republicans convinced themselves that Johnson wanted to limit military power in the South to garner political backing from white southerners. Johnson's earlier vetoes of the military Reconstruction and Freedman's Bureau bills revealed he opposed military intervention in the South because the country was, he claimed, not in a state of war and thus an occupation could not be legally justified.[60] Enacted on March 2, 1867, the new law required all military orders from the president to funnel through Grant. The general-in-chief was one of the professional officers who enjoyed the trust of lawmakers. They hoped to use him to curtail the implementation of policies repugnant to Republicans.[61]

The financial provisions of the law underscored that Republicans paid relatively little attention to the West. Congress appropriated $699,817 for rebuilding or altering fortifications on the Eastern Seaboard or in the Midwest. Only two military installations west of the Mississippi River received any money. Fort Union, New Mexico, received $10,000, while Congress appropriated $15,000 for repairs at Fort Leavenworth, Kansas. This pattern aligned with broader government spending trends that historian Richard Franklin Bensel detailed in his work on the postbellum economy. Bensel observed that Republicans favored internal improvements in the Northeast over those in the South or the western territories.[62]

The final bill also included language to disband white militias across the southern states. This provision, advocated by Wilson, aimed to aid army officers in their Reconstruction work. After the Civil War, white southerners attempted to reconstitute their antebellum militia organizations in more violent guises, including the Ku Klux Klan, White Leagues, and Red Shirts.[63] Organized by Confederate-friendly provisional governors, southern militias wreaked havoc on the already fragile civil governments during the first two years after surrender. Armed and often uniformed in Confederate gray, these militias formed shadow governments that undermined the legitimacy of Republican efforts at political reform by arresting, disarming, and assaulting freedmen and their white allies.[64] Considering the resurgence of this tradition of paramilitary politics, Republicans expressed their concerns over the racial composition of southern militias and proposed to rewrite the nation's militia law. In 1867, Wilson included a rider to the Army Appropriations Act that disbanded the white militias in all the former Confederate states except Tennessee.[65]

Multiple factors played a role in Wilson's desire to ban militia organizations in the South. For one, these paramilitary groups, organized by states, had targeted freedpeople for violence and stripped them of weapons under the excuse of reclaiming arms issued to soldiers during the war. Others, like James Lane of Kansas, saw militias as adding to problems for the army in keeping the peace and thus jeopardizing the mission of the soldiers. "I can see no possible propriety in sending a regular force there to keep the peace," he explained, "and at the same time arm them [former rebels] and authorize them to organize a local militia in the states until their status and condition is established by Congress."[66] Lane believed white southerners needed to demonstrate their loyalty unequivocally before reconstituting militias. Expecting regular soldiers to support the legal work of Reconstruction while having to suppress militia activity, Lane suggested, was not an effective use of the army.

Other Republicans questioned the wide-ranging powers claimed by the Radicals. According to James R. Doolittle of Wisconsin, one of the more conservative members of his party, limiting the president's executive powers established "from the Potomac to the Rio Grande a military despotism more absolute than any other civilized country within the last two hundred years."[67] Doolittle alleged that Radicals had exceeded constitutional boundaries. His language invoked the charges that Radical Republicans had often leveled at the Democratic Party throughout the war, portraying professional soldiers as aristocrats who served the interests of southern Democrats.[68]

With Reconstruction well under way and Republicans confident in their administration of the South, military legislation targeted larger army reductions. In 1868, the House and the Senate once again presented legislation to reduce the size of the regular army. With the presidential election looming, both chambers strove to indicate to voters that they took seriously the need to economize. The House bill proposed a reduction to a standing army of 25,000 soldiers and officers. In the Senate, Henry Wilson pursued a reduction to 30,000.[69] Wilson reported that the army had comprised more than 1 million men at the close of rebellion; by 1866 it had been reduced to approximately 55,000. The bill gave the executive flexibility to cut that number in the next fourteen months to 25,000, which Wilson claimed would save $6.5 million.

Though Wilson's bill passed, congressmen clamored for even greater reductions. Claiming that the Committee on Military Affairs had not proposed a large enough decrease in the number of troops, Democrats and Republicans alike strove for this goal. Democrats focused explicitly on removing troops from the South. In response, Wilson reminded colleagues that they had voted to use the army in the South, making a major reduction incompatible with their Reconstruction program. Maine Republican Lot Morrill wanted a "reduction to the minimum," or 40,000 men fewer than the 55,000 in the ranks in 1866. Morrill's proposal would have taken the army back to its antebellum size. He posited that cutting the number of troops saved the government on transportation and commissary spending. Fewer men to move and mouths to feed, Morrill reasoned, increased savings to the government.[70]

Wilson defended the bill as encouraging reductions compatible with his colleague's concerns, albeit accomplished more gradually. He emphasized that his committee proposed to reduce the army to 30,000 men, or by more than twenty-five regiments, as soon as the need for troops in the South abated. He predicted that such a reduction could be made within ninety days. In the summer of 1868, Wilson's assessment proved correct. As seven former Confederate states rejoined the Union, the government removed nearly 10,000 soldiers from the former Confederacy. The total number of troops in the army decreased accordingly. As more states in the former Confederacy reestablished political relations with the Union, Wilson explained, more troops could be withdrawn. Wilson added that Congress should not act too hastily, since they had a duty to sustain the reorganized governments by protecting loyal people from violence.[71]

Soldiers and civilians alike worried at the chaos that might follow declining troop levels. One Freedman's Bureau officer, John William De Forest, recalled explaining to one African American man in South Carolina that "the Yankees are here to see that you have justice." Once federal troops left, De Forest told the man, he could not expect the same degree of protection.[72] John W. Alvord, a minister and promotor of schools for freed Blacks across the South, explained that the lack of soldiers in Alabama had opened the door for white southerners to burn down several schools. "Only military force for some time to come," Alvord wrote, "could prevent the frequent outbreak of every form of violence."[73] "No white radical or colored will be allowed to vote at the next election for president," one Georgia resident worried in 1868, "if the government don't give us protections."[74] Republican government in the South, in other words, depended on the presence of professional soldiers, so Republicans faced a significant choice: let troop levels decline and risk backsliding on the gains of Reconstruction or set aside their crusade for economization at the expense of the army and continue to use professional troops to maintain order in the South.

Troop distribution figures underscored the relationship between Republicans and support for the army in Reconstruction. From 1868 through 1872, congressional actions demonstrated how the Republican Party intended to use the army. These years witnessed former Confederate states returning to the Union and a corresponding reallocation of resources toward the West (see table 8). After 1868, when seven states returned, officials cut in half the number of troops posted to the South (see graph 4, page 114). Rather than reinforcing western posts with newly available soldiers in 1868, however, congressmen pursued an overall reduction of the army. In 1870, when the three remaining Confederate states rejoined the Union, troop levels in the South again declined by half. On that occasion, however, authorities shifted troops to the West—four thousand withdrawn from the South in 1871 boosted western totals from 16,000 to 20,000 in 1872.

Though western numbers were higher than they had been in the antebellum army, the regulars were spread more thinly across a larger geography. During the decade before the Civil War, the federal government funneled most of its military resources into the Southwest and the Pacific Coast. The Great Plains experienced some attention from the government, but its strategic importance to the regular army emerged only late in the 1850s, during the Colorado gold rush.[75]

The increase in troops, though seemingly significant on paper, did not provide enough soldiers to meet the new geographic challenge. After the Civil War, the regulars acquired an addition 800,000 square miles of territory to patrol on the Great Plains. In 1866, for example, Sherman told the territorial governor of Montana that he had only one regiment of cavalry to cover Kansas and the territories of Colorado, Dakota, Montana, Nebraska, and New Mexico.[76] Prior to the Civil War, there had been one soldier for every sixty-four square miles of western territory occupied by the army; in 1868 there was one soldier for every seventy-one square miles.

Army officers expressed frustration at the divided duties of the professional force because of Reconstruction service. Western commanders, especially, wrote that Reconstruction denied them the troops needed to do their western work. In 1868, Sherman underscored the difficult position of the army within the larger apparatus of the federal government. He noted that the army performed multiple, often unrelated duties: aiding in surveys of public land, accompanying the progress of western railroads, establishing mail routes, ensuring the security of horse relays, and maintaining a consistent presence in the trans-Mississippi West "as though that region of the

country were in profound peace." "Over all these matters the military authorities have no control," Sherman mused, "yet their public nature implies
public protection."[77] Sherman consistently believed that unless Congress
increased the resources available to the army, his troops could not meet the
demands placed upon the regulars.

Democratic legislators returning to Congress in 1868 also complicated
the political picture for the regular army. Though still occupying only 20
percent of congressional seats in the Thirty-Ninth Congress (forty-five seats
in the House and nine seats in the Senate), Democratic legislators could
not be counted on as pro-army voters. Across the former Confederacy, continued military presence thwarted Democrats maintaining power in state
legislatures. Kentuckian Garrett Davis invoked the threat of military despotism. If the government was going to spend money on the military, he believed it would be better spent on ships and sails than on boots and saddles.
"I am especially favorable to the Navy because it in no degree imperils or
endangers our institutions and our constitutional and popular liberties," he
explained, "and those very considerations induce me always to be distrust-
ful of, and inimical to, a standing army." Davis also challenged the Senate's
assertion of control over the army, and said that Andrew Johnson, not Congress, ought to oversee troop reductions. The issue was pressing, Davis said,
because "there is no need for the occupation of the ten southern States by
any military force."[78]

The growing Democratic chorus for reduction increased the opposition
to the army in Congress. Senators from Indiana and Pennsylvania joined
Davis's call for immediate reduction, while Wilson and Maine's Lot Morrill insisted that reduction would follow the readmission of the southern
states.[79] As historian Gregory P. Downs has noted, Democratic resistance
to increasing the army grew throughout the postbellum period—and placed
Democrats in a political alliance with Radical Republicans. When Democrats finally regained control of Congress in 1878, they exacted retribution
for Reconstruction by attaching further army-weakening riders to appropriations bills.[80]

The reduction of the regular army in 1870 may have been the most consequential peacetime congressional action taken in military affairs since the
army increase of 1854. For the first time since the end of the war, congressmen could contemplate a significant reduction of the army, due to the prog-

ress of Reconstruction. The final bill, passed on July 15, 1870, provided for a 30,000-man standing army, inducement to obtain voluntary resignations of officers by paying them one year's pay and allowances, a voluntary retirement option for officers with thirty years' service, and the discontinuance of the offices of general and lieutenant general. Logan advocated heavily for striking from army rolls officers deemed "unfit," and the final bill provided for a five-man board to conduct hearings on officers identified by the secretary of war as unfit for service due to causes other than disabilities. If the board deemed them unfit, the president would discharge them from military service. The provision reflected Logan's disdain for professional officers but was presented as a cost-saving measure.[81]

Newspapers across the country approved of the plan to reduce the regular force. Philadelphia's *Evening Telegraph* applauded Congress's sense of economy. The editors did not see the need for a large army when "there is at present in civil life a hundred-fold larger body of trained officers." The army should be reduced to a skeleton, the paper explained, because experienced soldiers could fill the ranks at a moment's notice. Like congressmen who believed the regulars had done nothing to aid the Union in the Civil War, the *Telegraph*'s editors ranked the knowledge and experience of the war's veteran citizen-soldiers higher than that of professionals.[82] With so many experienced veterans ready to respond in the event of a military crisis, the country needed no large professional army.

The 1870 army debate also revealed the impact of veterans on the changing party composition of Congress (see table 9 for committee breakdowns). As Union veterans returned to the civilian life, they made their way into almost every profession, and many found themselves in positions of political power. In the Forty-First Congress, all the members of the House Committee on Military Affairs were Union veterans, led by John A. Logan of Illinois. Logan opposed the concept of a professional army. In his massive *Volunteer Soldier of America* he extolled the virtues of the militia while condemning the career army officer as a parasite dedicated to the preservation of the military class and indifferent to the well-being of the nation. Logan's efforts to ensure passage of the Army Enlistment Bill of 1870 highlighted his theories, which were shared by many of the volunteer veterans overseeing military affairs.[83]

Logan called for reductions in the size of the officer corps by 480 men. He proposed that the secretary of war appoint a five-man board to study the performance of every commander below the rank of brigadier general. A careful evaluation of the officers required to operate an army of 30,000 would force unqualified officers to resign their commissions. In addition, he urged that the number of major generals and brigadier generals be cut by 50 percent, with the superfluous soldiers dismissed from service. The bill also provided for the expiration of the ranks of general and lieutenant general after Sherman and Sheridan retired. A reduction in pay for general officers immediately followed the cutbacks.

Finally, Logan said that Congress should repeal section 2 of the Army Appropriation Bill of 1867—the provision that had limited the president's authority to issue orders directly to the army and required congressional approval of all decisions about the army's operations and commanders. This last provision indicated that Republicans believed the country had completed the work of Reconstruction. With Johnson out of office, the seceded states restored to the Union, and Grant in the White House, no reason existed to continue to exclude the president from managing the army.

Logan asserted that the American army had a staff large enough for a force of a million men. He stated that the United States Army had more officers than any similar organization in the world. He assured the representatives that his proposals covered but a portion of the potential areas of reduction. He forecast that the bill would save $3 million of the $37 million spent annually on the army. He sarcastically attacked the staff commanders by rhetorically asking why a man had to graduate from West Point to be appointed quartermaster general. "If you put a man in charge of the commissary department you have to make him a brigadier general. Brigadier general of what? Of beef and molasses and pork and beans."[84]

Not all Republicans agreed with Logan on the need for reductions in the officer corps. Pennsylvania Republican William D. Kelley pointed out that Logan's legislation lacked appreciation for the Civil War service of many army officers. "We ought to be saved the shame," he said, "of having it recorded in history as an act of ingratitude on the part of this Government that we struck [the army] out the moment we felt we could do without them." The proposed bill, Kelley said, would prove the aphorism that "republics are ungrateful." Republican John P. C. Shanks of Indiana (a brevet major general of volunteers) shot back, saying Kelley slandered the service of the war's volunteers. Why did Kelley not object, Shanks asked, when the volunteer colonels and captains and lieutenants "who periled their lives" in the Civil War were mustered out of service? Logan accused Kelley of caring nothing for the "crippled and wounded officers" or the "poor and wretched" veterans, all because Kelley had attempted to suggest that regular army officers also had rendered service worth some acknowledgment by the federal government.[85]

Logan also targeted the office of commanding general, the post filled by Sherman. He concluded that under existing law the president faced a difficult time in removing the general. With Sherman listening intently from the gallery of the House, Logan questioned why Congress saw fit to assign the rank of general of the armies to Sherman when George Washington had never attained that status. Discussing the proposed reduction in Sherman's pay, Logan stated, "I am willing he should have all the credit to which he is entitled. But because I am willing to give him credit as a great general, that is no reason why I should tax the wooden-legged and one-armed men, and the widows and orphans." Logan urged the House to pass his bill to indicate to the American people that "Congress intends to maintain control over the Army."[86]

Reducing the size of the officer corps appealed to Republicans who desired to shift professional soldiers into the civilian economy, where their West Point engineering training would serve the broader Republican program of national development. Pennsylvania Republican Joseph B. Donnelly suggested that a West Point education also suited graduates to work in industry or railroads—especially when the regular army had "no service to perform."[87] Donnelly's statement echoed the opinion of President Ulysses S. Grant, who told Henry Wilson in 1866, "I do not look with regret on officers of the Army leaving the Army in time of peace to take responsible and important places in Civil life." Grant, then general-in-chief of the army, explained, "A West Point education eminently fits them for such positions."[88] As if to prove Grant's point, dozens of West Pointers went into the railroad industry after the war.[89]

Some Republicans, meanwhile, continued to consider West Point training suspect. James S. Negley chimed in with a typical Republican condemnation of the "deeply imbued feeling of superiority" of the "aristocratic element of immaculate West Point," affirming that Logan's bill would bring change to a system that had created an officer corps that stood in opposition to the country's development. Negley pointed to men such as Jefferson Davis, Robert E. Lee, and David S. Twiggs as examples of the traitors West Point had produced. More than five years after the war's conclusion, after years of trusting the army to oversee Reconstruction, Republicans remained steadfast in their depictions of the regular army as a home to "anti-republican" values.[90]

Republican newspapers endorsed Logan's bill. The *Chicago Tribune* explicitly linked the end of Reconstruction with the congressional effort to reduce the army. The "immediate demands of the country" had been met, allowing the occupation of the South to end. In April, the *Advocate of Peace,* a magazine from the American Peace Society, celebrated the "large reduction" of the army and the elimination of "the host of superfluous officers on large pay, military sinecures, the great vampires upon the national treasury."[91]

Between 1865 and 1870, only congressman Henry W. Slocum defended the army against the charges that Republicans leveled at professional soldiers and West Point graduates. Though he wanted to say a word on behalf of the army, Slocum still voted to reduce the regulars. A Democrat from New York, Slocum had graduated from West Point in 1848 and finished the Civil War as a major general in command of the Army of Georgia. Rebutting charges that the academy had produced disloyal soldiers, Slocum proposed to name "ten graduates of the academy who were not only loyal but fought for the Union." Finally, Slocum said that if West Point graduates were aristocrats, "they are the funniest set of aristocrats that were ever collected in any country." Most of the academy's students, Slocum explained, arrived at school with not enough money to pay for their dinner. When Slocum's classmate Sheridan turned up at the academy, for instance, "he had not a dollar in his pocket."[92] Slocum concluded his speech by saying he intended to support Logan's bill because he was a Democrat and wanted the army out of the South.

As their work in the southern states decreased in volume, troopers returned to western posts and faced lives of monotony and isolation. Writing in 1897, a captain in the regulars reflected on the 1870 reduction of the army, revealing how soldiers perceived their treatment. "The opposition of late years to any increase of the regular army, even to give it bare efficiency, is well known," Arthur P. Williams wrote, "in spite of the recommendations and urging of all our generals." Williams then revealed that soldiers knew the argument against the army was based on saving money. "The principal ostensible objections to the increase of the army," he noted, "is on the ground of its uselessness, or the dread of increase of national expenditures." A society at peace, Williams continued, would rarely love its army and would "look upon all soldiers as idle, useless and even vicious members of the community, who are always seeking to plunge the country into a war."[93]

Williams understood that politicians loathed the army because it did not align with the nation's political culture. The mania for reduction, however, masked the reality that if Americans were to acquire uncontested control of the continent and expropriate the land of thousands of Native people, they needed an army. But as the United States entered the 1870s, it was an army that keenly felt the consequences of political neglect. Though Republicans did not intend to slight the West in military affairs, their political goals regarding the South often blinded them to western needs. As the Republicans reached their postwar ascendancy, the regular army approached its nadir.

INTERLUDE
THE GENERAL

General William T. Sherman had had enough. Enough of micromanagement, enough of scorn for his authority, enough of Washington, DC, and more than enough of politicians. On September 3, 1874, he received permission from President Ulysses S. Grant to move the headquarters of the United States Army to Saint Louis, Missouri. Though ranked and titled General of the Armies, Sherman believed he had little authority over the men and officers of the ailing regular force he commanded. Rather than while away his hours in a stuffy office in the War Department (practically in the backyard of the White House), where meddlesome politicians could seek him out at their leisure, he decamped to the Mississippi River and oriented his attention west.[1]

While in Saint Louis, unencumbered by the daily demands of Washington business and relieved of his ongoing feud with Secretary of War William Belknap, Sherman focused on finishing the first volume of his memoirs. Published to great fanfare by D. Appleton and Company in 1875, the work sold 10,000 copies in its first month.[2] And that was despite the volume ending before Sherman had told the story of how he invaded Atlanta and burned its manufacturing districts to the ground, and with most of his storied march to the sea still to come. Readers eager to know how Sherman's tale finished would have to wait more than a decade for volume 2, published in 1886—two years after Sherman turned sixty-four and retired from active service. By then the Ohio-born officer and 1840 West Point graduate had spent nearly four decades of his life, off and on, in the uniform of the United States Army.

Until he assumed command the Army of the United States in 1869, Sherman enjoyed the life of a serviceman. But with rank came responsibility.

William Tecumseh Sherman as general-in-chief of the army, ca. 1870.
Courtesy of the Jerald B. Everts Collection.

Sherman tolerated army bureaucracy, but he balked at politics. And as the head of the nation's professional fighting force, politics suddenly mattered more to Sherman's day-to-day existence than managing his shrinking army and its expanding responsibilities. Even more troublesome was the reluctance of his old friend President Grant to intercede with the legislators of the Republican Party in favor of the army. Just when it seemed the regulars might have a friend in the White House, one of their own, they learned they did not. It turned out Grant had little will to lead politicians with the force and resolve he had used to bring about Union victories on the battlefields of the South.[3]

More annoying to Sherman than Grant's disinterest in the army, however, was Secretary of War William Belknap's tumultuous management of the War Department. Sherman had hardly been on good terms with Edwin Stanton, the embattled secretary of war in the Lincoln and Johnson administrations, who had publicly chided the general for his handling of the surrender of Joseph E. Johnston's Army of Tennessee at Durham Station, North Carolina, in May 1865.[4] Despite their tiff, Stanton respected Sherman's ability to lead and manage an army; he had merely wanted to caution the general about playing politics at the end of the war. Unlike Stanton, Belknap cared little for Sherman's reputation or abilities and treated the army's leader as if he did not exist, issuing orders without Sherman's approval and making military contracts that Sherman knew nothing about.

When he recalled in his memoirs his reasons for moving the army's headquarters to Saint Louis, Sherman focused almost entirely on Belknap's role in pushing the general out of the day-to-day management of the army. Belknap, Sherman claimed, had seen fit to "usurp all the powers of the commanding general" when he took over his cabinet post. It served the interests of the country and the army better for him to spend the final years of the Grant administration in Saint Louis, Sherman concluded, and to escape "the mortification of being slighted by men in Washington who were using their temporary power for selfish ends." Sherman proved especially unhappy when Belknap slashed his salary in the name of postwar reduction, although Sherman still received higher wages than the chief justice of the Supreme Court or the president's cabinet officers. Sherman's relief from the secretary's tyranny came in 1876, when the House of Representatives impeached Belknap for his part in the Indian Ring trading scandal.[5]

As part of his effort to sideline Sherman, Belknap spent his early days in the War Department lobbying Congress for the sole power to appoint and license army sutlers. Sutlers were integral to the army economy and to life in the American West. They sold almost any goods imaginable from their post traderships, providing soldiers and civilians alike with access to clothing, tobacco, candy, and even weapons that were not otherwise available in the sparsely developed West. Sutlers received lucrative contracts, often worth thousands of dollars each year, to establish trading posts at U.S. military installations. Controlling the sutlers meant controlling men with significant sums of money.

As a member of Grant's cabinet, Belknap drew an annual salary of $8,000 (the equivalent of about $184,000 per year in 2023). As of 2021, the annual salary for members of the presidential cabinet was $221,000, meaning Belknap made only slightly less in 1870 than the equivalent cabinet member makes today. Still, the salary was not enough to meet the needs of Belknap's wife, Carita, who soon devised a plan to use her husband's authority over post sutlers to supplement the purportedly meager paycheck offered by the federal government. This plan became better known as the Indian Ring, or trading post scandal, which exposed Belknap's malfeasance to the nation.

In 1870, Carita lobbied her husband to appoint a New York contractor, Caleb P. Marsh, to the Fort Sill tradership in what was then Indian Territory. Annoyingly for Mrs. Belknap, her husband had already appointed an experienced sutler to Fort Sill, one John S. Evans, who did not want to quit his post. As a compromise, Marsh drew up an illicit partnership contract that allowed Evans to keep the tradership at Fort Sill. Evans would pay Marsh $12,000 per year in quarterly installments. Marsh was then required to give half of his $12,000 to Carita. The payments nearly doubled the couple's annual funds, but Congress quickly caught on.

In February 1876, word reached the House of Representatives that Belknap had been accepting kickbacks from traderships on western posts. Pennsylvania Democrat Hiester Clymer launched an investigation into the War Department. Clymer's sense of justice was fueled, in part, by a chance to get revenge against the Radical Republicans, who he believed had misused the army in upholding martial law in the South during Reconstruction. When he was hauled before the national legislature to explain himself, Marsh testified to the Clymer committee that Belknap had taken payments as part of Marsh's partnership agreement with Evans.[6]

President Grant received a warning that the House intended to bring impeachment charges against Belknap on March 2, as he settled down for breakfast. By 10:20 that morning, Belknap had tendered, and Grant had accepted, his resignation. When the Clymer committee received word of this action, Clymer and his colleagues were outraged, claiming that Belknap had only resigned to escape impeachment. The fact that Belknap was no longer employed by the government, the committee stated, did not mean he should not be held responsible for his corrupt activities. The members unanimously passed a resolution to impeach Belknap, though at the time of the events there existed no constitutional precedent for impeaching a former government official who had reentered civilian life.[7]

Regardless of whether Belknap would be put on trial (he was, but was acquitted), he no longer presented an obstacle to Sherman. The army's general-in-chief celebrated Belknap's removal by transferring his headquarters back to Washington. By that time, with Reconstruction no longer a pressing military concern and fewer areas of active need for troops to fight Natives in the West, the army faded into quasi obscurity, at least as far as national politics was concerned. Sherman felt confident enough in the army's safety from further political attacks that he wrote to John Pope that when it came to army issues, "indifference . . . marks the great mass" of congressmen.[8] But it had been a difficult road to that point, and Sherman knew it well, having overseen much of the army's tumultuous return to the West after the Civil War.

In the postbellum West, the professional army was a skeleton of its former self, particularly when compared to the army built just two decades earlier by Jefferson Davis. Whether in Texas, Montana, or Colorado, professional troops experienced frustration and setbacks in the gap between the duties they were asked to perform and the resources they were supplied to carry them out. By 1871, the Republican Party had determined that the best way to handle the professional army was with a slow death by political neglect. Professional troops despaired of their treatment but had no sympathetic ears to receive their pleas for aid. The Republican war against the army had finally reached its conclusion.

5

WESTERN MILITARY CHALLENGES, 1865–1872

A general Indian war could not be carried on with the present military force ... or anything like it. Regiments would be needed where now are only companies, and long lines of posts would have to be established for the protection of regions which ... are now wholly uncovered.

    —Francis Amasa Walker, Commissioner of Indian Affairs, 1872

In November 1865, frustration boiled over in the pages of an Omaha, Nebraska, newspaper. In the months that followed the surrenders of Confederate armies across the South, westerners awaited the return of the regular army to the West. Regular soldiers could finally resume their traditional duties of protecting settlers and dislocating Native people who contested white claims to western lands. As the winter approached, reality set in for numerous observers on the Plains: nobody in Washington seemed in any hurry to send troops back to the West. In the *Omaha Weekly Herald,* the editor leveled a broadside against Secretary of War Edwin Stanton, "the pestiferous, bull-headed potentate of the War Office." Stanton was concerned with advancing the politics of the Radical Republican Party, the paper claimed, "while the great interests of the West are neglected, spurned, and spit upon."[1]

The army's leading officers were aware of the perceived imbalance between the South and the West in the allocation of military resources in the immediate wake of the Civil War. When William T. Sherman undertook an expedition across the interior West in 1866, he fretted over expansive geography and minimal manpower. In command of the Division of the Missouri, which encompassed the area between the Mississippi River and the Rocky Mountains, spanning from the Rio Grande to the Canadian border, Sherman puzzled over the large military problems facing such a small army. When he arrived in the small town of Pueblo, Colorado, for instance, a cadre of citizens presented him with a petition begging for military protection. About halfway between Denver and Santa Fe, Pueblo lay along the Arkansas River in a relatively exposed location. Citizens worried (Sherman thought erroneously) that Ute, Cheyenne, and Arapahoe soldiers might take advantage of their isolation and attack the settlement. Whatever his sympathies for Pueblo's denizens, Sherman explained that more residents had signed the petition requesting protection than the number of troops he had available at any of his western garrisons. There were simply not enough regular soldiers to afford, as Sherman put it, "perfect protection."[2]

In histories of the Civil War and Reconstruction, the army has been regarded as an engine of social and political change in the American South. Soldiers offered an avenue to freedom for the enslaved during the war and implemented Reconstruction policies enacted by Republicans afterward, as they helped foster, according to historians, "emerging visions of freedom and citizenship."[3] In the West, soldiers not only aided the development of national railroads and overland immigration routes but also served as the instrument for advancing settler colonialism through constricting Indigenous freedom. Few historians have asked whether an army that faced these missions simultaneously in two different regions had the resources to accomplish the tasks set by the federal government. For the period from 1865 to 1871, the answer would have been mixed.

The army's western experience immediately after the war reveals an additional dimension to the connections between the South and the West in the Civil War era.[4] The myriad tasks set for the army in the Reconstruction South directly influenced the resources of the institution as it returned to the West. The country's top military thinkers negotiated the challenge of the multiple and sometimes incompatible demands that faced the regulars. Leading officers felt themselves unable to protect "life and property on the plains" and were "infinitely embarrassed" by their shortcomings.[5] One historian has recently suggested that "competing demands for troops for Western territories sharply limited the army's reach in the South."[6] It also could be argued that the demand for troops in the South—at least until 1872—limited the army's reach in the West.

In some areas of the West, just as in some areas of the former Confederacy, the army could project federal power. But the reach of officers and soldiers was limited by both geography and resources. These pockets of power have since been understood by historians as a model for governance termed the "stockade state."[7] According to stockade state theorists, although military power was strong and visible in some areas of the West, in other areas, when settlers called for military protection, none could be supplied. In 1868, for example, Sherman complained that the army was "very short of cavalry all the time."[8] Since the founding of the country, the federal government's ability to control peripheral western regions often had been predicated on the advance of the professional army into zones of contested sovereignty.[9]

Where federal power did visibly exist, it did no go uncontested. In the immediate aftermath of the Civil War, Indigenous resistance to white settler colonialism not only challenged military authority but also won back territory that the army had claimed in the name of the federal government. As Lakota warrior White Bull recalled in his memoirs, for example, the summer of 1866 featured "the most sustained warfare the whites had ever encountered." Native knowledge that western forts "were removed from supply sources . . . and food supplies" as the army reorganized gave resisting Natives "a strategic and tactical advantage of which they were well aware."[10] The army's readjustment to service as the nation's "frontier constabulary" was neither swift nor certain.[11] As Republicans debated how best to use the army, regular troops made a disorganized return to the West.

Military turmoil worsened as the War Department attempted to muster out the federal volunteers who remained in uniform in the summer of 1865. Many volunteer units had not yet served the three years they had promised the federal government when enlisting for Civil War service.[12] Given that these volunteers were trained and equipped for campaigning, some units were sent West in the hope they could help General-in-Chief Ulysses S. Grant respond to reports of Indian "hostilities" and French threats on the border with Mexico. Unfortunately for the War Department and for the regulars, citizen-soldiers had no intention of fighting any enemy who was not wearing Confederate gray. As one Union volunteer explained in the summer of 1865, "cavalry will undoubtedly be sent up on the Indian frontier," and like most of his fellow volunteers, Algernon Badger had no desire to "chase Indians." "After the work of the past four and half years it would seem like boys play."[13]

Most volunteer troops retained after the formal Confederate surrenders shared Badger's sentiments, a fact that officers quickly realized.[14] In the Division of the Missouri (briefly the military division of the Mississippi), 1,487 commissioned officers and 25,487 enlisted men served in October 1865. One year later, the department's commander, Sherman, reported 578 commissioned officers and 13,953 enlisted men, or a drop of roughly 46 percent. This reduction left the commander with fewer troops than the army had used to occupy the Southwest and Pacific Coast in 1860; meanwhile, he had to disperse them over an additional 800,000 miles of territory.

Much of that region included current-day Wyoming and Montana, where white settler encroachment on Indigenous land prompted staunch Native resistance. After gold was discovered in Montana in 1862, eager fortune hunters blazed the Bozeman Trail through the heart of Lakota, Cheyenne, and Arapaho territory. The traffic threatened to displace thousands of Native people. In the aftermath of the 1864 Sand Creek Massacre, many Southern Cheyenne turned north and joined forces with the Northern Cheyenne, Lakota Sioux, and Arapaho, moving through present-day eastern Colorado and western Nebraska into the country surrounding the Powder and Tongue Rivers. There, they gathered in large numbers in the winter and spring of 1865. The Native coalition attacked a small contingent of volunteer troops on the North Platte River in July 1865, killing Lieutenant Caspar Collins and twenty-seven other soldiers.[15]

Two army officers stood in the path of the Indigenous efforts to reclaim the Powder River country: Brigadier General Patrick E. Connor and Major General Grenville M. Dodge. In response to Native resistance to white encroachers on the Bozeman Trail, Connor and Dodge planned that a force of 4,500 volunteer troops would conduct a three-pronged offensive against the tribes in the Powder River country. After months of delays, when the campaign finally got under way in August 1865, more than two thousand of the troops failed to materialize.[16] Between the time of the surrender of Confederate armies across the South and the late summer of 1865, the War Department had demobilized the volunteer force Dodge and Connor counted on for their expedition. This swift demobilization of the Civil War's federal volunteers placed pressure on the military situation in the West in ways that are underappreciated by historians.

Volunteer troops posted to the West in the summer of 1865 flatly resisted participating in non–Civil War military actions.[17] In late July, Connor complained to Dodge of mutinous troops, revealing that on July 21 "part of the First Nebraska Cavalry stationed at Kearny claim, as the war is over, that they are entitled to discharge, and have mutinied. I have ordered Colonel Heath to suppress it with grape and canister." Dodge responded on the same day with a similar report. Soldier discontent seemed to spread across the frontier. "All the troops are giving me great trouble," Dodge reported from his Saint Louis headquarters. "Infantry at Fort Leavenworth mutinied; cavalry (some of it) the same; but are now on the march under new reorganization of commands."[18] Both Dodge and Connor prepared to use coercive measures to keep troops in uniform.

Volunteer troops who might have helped aid the transition from temporary volunteers to regular units were not willing to extend their service to help the professional army. The War Department ordered soldiers transported from Washington to march along the Bozeman Trail to Fort Kearny and Fort Laramie, but when the soldiers came on the scene, the federal government reversed their orders and bent to pressure to send the volunteers home. Dodge complained that all the rigmarole had occurred "without any benefit whatever being received from them, and also after we had been at the expense of equipping them fully, and also transporting supplies to the plains for their use." Because the volunteers demanded to return home, Dodge ended up with fewer than six thousand troops, "many of them mutinous, dissatisfied, and inefficient." Dodge reminded superiors of the challenges facing him without more resources: "It must be borne in mind that I had about 2,600 miles of overland mail and telegraph line to protect in addition to carrying on the campaign."[19]

The War Department could not guarantee Dodge the support he requested. When General John Pope of the regular army assumed command of the Department of the Missouri, he ordered Dodge to send the remaining volunteer troops home. Dodge telegraphed Captain George Price on August 15 that "General Pope has sent me positive orders to reduce the troops on the plains, as soon as your expedition is over, to 4,000 men." Pope wanted the troops placed "at prominent posts on an overland route." Pope nixed

Dodge's campaign plans and ordered the units mustered out. "The 14th, 15th, and 32d Illinois Infantry started this morning for Springfield, Ill.," Pope told Dodge. "They are to ride the 'iron horse' to their State and soon to be citizens again."[20] Despite the acknowledged need for troops on the Plains, Pope could not force volunteer troops to remain in service. The men that Dodge needed so desperately had become citizens once again.

In 1865 and 1866—as Congress debated what the reorganized army would look like—high-ranking officers could offer only piecemeal protection in much of the West. In 1886, William T. Sherman divided his troops among four subdepartments: four regiments of infantry and two hundred Indian scouts in the Department of Dakota; one battery of artillery, one regiment of cavalry, three regiments of infantry, and two hundred Indian scouts in the Department of the Platte; one battery of artillery, two regiments of cavalry, eight companies of the Tenth Cavalry (United States Colored Troops), three Colored Troop infantry regiments, and 150 Indian scouts in the Department of the Missouri; and one battery of artillery, four companies of the Tenth Cavalry (United States Colored Troops), two regiments of infantry, and fifty Indian scouts in the Department of the Arkansas. In total, this was more troops than there had been in the whole of the antebellum army, but they were stretched thinly across significantly more territory.

In his public correspondence and official reports, Sherman repeatedly emphasized the size of territory to be overseen by his troops. In describing the Department of the Missouri, the largest military department in the West, the general attempted to communicate the scale of his operations to an audience with little familiarity with western geography. "This military division embraces the vast region from the Mississippi River to the Rocky Mountains, of an average breadth of one thousand three hundred and fifty miles," he explained, "and length of over one thousand miles, viz: from the southern border of New Mexico to the British line." Sherman singled out the mountain territories as important to national development, noting the vast stands of pine trees, array of minerals, and fertile mountain valleys "worthy [of] the liberal and fostering care of the general government."[21] Sherman insisted that the soldiers and officers of the regular army remained the government's best option for performing that work.

Sherman's claims that he had done all he could with the troops he had on hand did not meet the expectations of white settlers. Across the West, governors and citizens wrote letters and petitions complaining of lack of protection from the army. In 1866, the governor of the New Mexico Territory, Robert B. Mitchell, emphasized to General-in-Chief Ulysses S. Grant that "the number of troops stationed in this country since the commencement of the late rebellion has been totally inadequate for the protection of the lives and property of its inhabitants." Mitchell reminded Grant that Republican policy attached great importance to developing the West's natural resources for profit. "There is not today one half the wealth in this country that there was at the time of its annexation to the United States," Mitchell exclaimed, "and this is due entirely to the failure of the Government to give that protection that it then guaranteed."[22] Mitchell noted that throughout the 1850s, the federal government had invested in military protection in New Mexico. The postbellum West looked markedly different.

Army officers also noticed a shift in priorities from the antebellum years. No longer did military leaders consider the Southwest the most important region for committing troops. Sherman referenced the army's historical involvement in the Southwest in a letter regarding the military management of New Mexico. He referred to "vast outlays of men and money" that failed to "extract a feeling of gratitude from the People" of the territory. In a memorial to Congress, weighing in on the question of committing men and resources to protecting New Mexico's citizens, Sherman advised against that path. "Every officer & soldier of the U.S. Army sent to New Mexico goes to a worse than Siberian banishment," he explained, with characteristic understatement. "The vast territory is a desert waste," he emphasized, "and only inhabited by the remnants of old Spanish & Indian settlements left there centuries ago by a bolder & more hardy race in search of Gold & Silver that exists in the Desert mountains." The only reason Anglo-American settlers had moved to New Mexico after 1846, Sherman speculated, was to profit by supplying livestock and food for the professional troops "banished there."[23] It was a strong, if misinformed, assertion of New Mexico's worthlessness, to Sherman's mind.

Sherman's description of the region's inhabitants revealed the general's misguided and uninformed sense of the history of the Southwest borderlands. The language referencing "remnants" of a "bolder race" drew explicitly on the ideologies of the cultural superiority of Anglo colonizers and the assumption that until white people arrived in New Mexico and Arizona the region had remained only sparsely settled—because the cultures of the original occupants did not register with Sherman's conception of "civilization."[24] Sherman discounted the fact that many Hispanic residents considered themselves culturally white, and he ignored the extensive evidence of complex Indigenous civilizations.[25] Ultimately, the officer suggested that unless white people settled in the Southwest in greater numbers, and could sustain themselves without relying on federal military contracts to provide their income, the region could never become a part of the United States. Only white occupancy, Sherman argued, gave the Southwest economic, cultural, or political value.

The bottom line for Sherman was money. He based his reluctance to commit troops to the Southwest on the cost of the operation. The general understood that he had to operate within the goals of reduction favored by the Republican Party. To maximize limited resources, Sherman proposed that soldiers be concentrated only between the Arkansas and Platte Rivers to protect the transcontinental railroads and to provide escorts for western-bound migrants. Perhaps to emphasize his disdain for the Southwest, Sherman offered a preposterous and politically impossible solution that he hoped would save the government untold sums. If Congress would give Arizona back to Mexico, Sherman wrote, "I will agree to knock two regiments of cavalry from our estimates" of necessary manpower.[26] Sherman repeated some version of the request almost every year in his annual report, until he retired from active service.

Most army officers were realists about what the federal government could provide in terms of troops. In late 1866, Grant offered Secretary of War Edwin Stanton a thoughtful assessment of the nation's military situation. Grant's letter contained two important observations about the Republican Party's use of the army. First, Grant acknowledged that the West would not be a priority for the nation until "it becomes practicable to withdraw a portion of the troops from States lately in rebellion." Second, he admitted that it might not matter how many troops the federal government committed to western service, because it would never be enough to prevent violence between Natives and white settlers.

Mitigating violence was a far larger challenge than the professional army could address. Only developing roads and railroads across the West, Grant thought, would end military resistance on the part of Native peoples. Like many mid-nineteenth-century Americans, Grant subscribed to the racist ideology of the "vanishing Indian," the notion that Native people would "disappear" from the West as it filled with white migrants and railroads.[27] Still, Grant, like Sherman, acknowledged the need to work within the limits set by the Republican Party for the size and mission of the regular army.[28]

Taking a tack opposite to the country's highest-ranking soldier, other voices from within the army expressed alarm over congressional plans to reduce the size of the national force. The *Army and Navy Journal* declared its dread of a "penny-wise, pound-foolish economy, which looks to 'cutting down' the Army till what is left is wholly incapable of performing the duty assigned to it." Editors worried whether Congress would be "fully alive to the importance of a military establishment, not only in resisting actual invasion, in suppressing actual insurrection, and in discharging all attempts to disturb the peace of the Union." The same article complained that rather than send diplomatic envoys to represent the United States to foreign nations, the federal government should invest in the army as a representation of the image the country wanted to project to the world. American soldiers, the editors reasoned, were worth showing off to the world.[29] The writers for the *Army and Navy Journal* were disappointed that victory in the Civil War had not convinced the federal government of this, nor had the war made Republicans more amenable to giving greater aid to the regular army.

Ongoing congressional debates over army funding delayed troop deployments and forced frontier garrisons to operate with skeleton staffs through 1867, even though the demands of overland travel still pressed upon the soldiers at frontier posts. In 1866, Sherman pointed to the construction of a 550-mile wagon road from Fort Laramie, Wyoming, to Virginia City, Montana, as a project hampered by the turmoil of transitioning from a volunteer to regular force as the military still conducted police action in the South. "By reason of the discharge of all volunteers, and the late period at which we were provided a regular army," he explained, "we were too weak to attempt it this year, and must do so the next." Even then, he admitted to his brother, Senator John Sherman, "after the bill passes it will take months to enlist the men, and in meantime all volunteers are clamorous for discharge, and must be discharged as soon as winter lets them come in."[30]

Sherman's prediction proved correct: lagging supply trains and troop reductions compromised the army's ability to mount offensive expeditions throughout 1867. In that year's annual report from the Department of the Platte, a subdivision of Sherman's larger western department, Major General Christopher C. Augur recited a familiar list of obstacles that had prevented his troops from campaigning. Auger's complaint covered every conceivable deficiency in the army's management: "the great delay in getting supplies in readiness at Laramie . . . there being no depot of any kind in this department—and more emphatically the inadequacy of my force to make as contemplated and at the same give sufficient protection to insure confidence along the railroad and other routes."[31]

The same complaints were replicated in dozens of annual reports from western commanders. In his 1868 annual report, Grant issued a summary of all reports submitted from western commanders that emphasized one conclusion: a reduction in troops would be disastrous to the army. "The troops on the plains are all needed," Grant wrote, and added for emphasis, "troops are still needed in the southern States." Sherman likewise asserted that the army could not "reduce our military forces on the frontier." Sheridan, meanwhile, explained that after he had dispersed 2,600 soldiers to comply with Sherman's instructions to dedicate military protection to all overland travel routes and rail lines, he had fewer than eight hundred troops to conduct offensive operations or respond to requests for troops in the whole of the Department of the Missouri. "It was impossible," Sheridan said, "to accomplish a great deal in so extensive a country." Responding to every report of a Native attack on mail trains and cattle herds received from frontier settlements in the Department of the Dakota, meanwhile, occasioned "constant activity" for Alfred Terry's troops.[32] Though sometimes separated by thousands of miles, western officers consistently reported that they were lacking resources to meet the array of missions assigned to their forces.

The scarcity of troops left most posts undermanned. On December 31, 1866, the 14,000 soldiers under Sherman's command occupied fifty-nine separate military installations or were en route to locations within the Division of the Missouri. The force at any location ranged from one company of infantry and one of cavalry at Fort Union, New Mexico, to ten companies at Fort Wallace, Kansas, eight of them cavalry. Most typical were installations like Fort Garland, which played host to one or two rotating companies of infantry and cavalry in the Colorado Territory's isolated San Luis Valley. The troops in the division made up 168 companies of infantry and cavalry, plus four batteries of artillery. Had troops been divided evenly among the instal-lations, each could claim 2.8 companies of forty to sixty men and officers.[33]

This meant that numerous posts averaged fewer than one hundred occu-pants, without accounting for sickness and desertion. Company command-ers constantly reported that they did not have enough troops to perform basic tasks, including post repairs and upkeep, the maintenance of supplies and care of animals, or escorting mail trains. When A. L. Hough joined the Thirteenth Infantry in the early 1870s, he found the regiment not only over-burdened by its missions in Wyoming and Utah but also suffering from low morale, high desertion rates, and a severe manpower shortage. Upon taking command of Company C, Hough recorded that there were only eighteen men in a unit whose normal size ranged from sixty-five to seventy troops.[34]

Beyond troop shortages, the army's reoccupation of western military installations seldom equated with military preparedness. As one officer fresh from West Point explained of new recruits to the army in 1870, "Our knowledge of the 'old,' ante-bellum army was almost nothing, and while rec-ollections of our great conflict were most vivid, they were not allied with the regiment to which we then belonged, nor, indeed, for the most part with the regular service."[35] The soldiers who went West after the Civil War were likely more accustomed to the combat operations of the Civil War than to the various duties—including Native campaigning—required in the West.[36] Lack of experience also defined the officer corps. In 1867, only 21.5 percent of regular army officers had any antebellum experience, and of that percentage, fewer than 1 in 4 men had obtained field officer grades prior to the war.[37]

Troops across the West had plenty to occupy their time in every sector. In summarizing the reports made by army departmental commanders in 1871, Secretary of War William Belknap compiled a list of duties that the U.S. Army had performed during the preceding year across the whole of the trans-Mississippi West. The secretary reported to President Grant that civil authorities made one hundred applications for troops in the space of ten months. Regulars patrolled the US–Mexico border. Other troops arrested bandits who had entered the United States after robbing a Hudson's Bay Company store in Canada. Troopers assisted civil officials in Wyoming to control striking coal miners and responded to requests by officials regarding Mormon leaders in Utah. Soldiers evicted white squatters from Indian lands in Kansas and finished the year by arresting traders in New Mexico who were caught selling livestock stolen by Comanches in Texas. Commenting on Belknap's report, Sherman stated that the army performed "admirably" in protecting citizens on the "sparsely settled frontiers of the West."[38]

These conditions bred discontent among soldiers, especially as their wages and chances for promotion decreased. Pope speculated that falling wages and increasing labor demands on military posts drove soldiers to desert. The West offered such men opportunities in a labor-starved region. This situation contrasted with soldiers on Reconstruction duty. Pope explained that for soldiers in eastern posts, "there is no opening in any civil pursuit for a soldier who deserts the Army."[39] In the West, on the other hand, as one enlisted infantryman explained, "all this unpaid labor, carried out from day to day, month to month, by men enlisted for military service, created almost universal dissatisfaction and desertions became frequent."[40] From 1865 through 1877, according to one historian's estimates, desertions amounted to almost one-third of the army annually.[41] Congressional reductions failed to help matters. An 1870 army reorganization bill dropped wages of private soldiers from sixteen to thirteen dollars per month, and as a result, desertions "largely increased."[42] In practical terms, this meant that the army never included as many men as it counted on paper, leaving posts without a full complement of troops.

Army officers felt that Congress constantly escalated their institution's duties without providing commensurate increases in resources. Forever railing against the economic "mania" that seemed to grip Congress annually, the *Army and Navy Journal* criticized the government's shortsightedness. The editors mentioned several pieces of legislation under debate by the national legislative body. The list included a treaty to annex Saint Thomas, a treaty to annex Santo Domingo, a bill to grant belligerent rights to the people of Cuba in their war against Spain, and the "Utah Bill," which proposed to suppress polygamy in the territory. These measures, the *Journal* declared, all fell under the rubric of "army-increasing propositions."[43] At the same moment, legislators pondered another army reduction bill. Reading the weekly and monthly columns from the perspective of the army suggests that the federal government never successfully grasped the reality that confronted the military: too much work to do and too little to do it with.

Some troops occupied with activities such as post repair or protecting mail routes received almost no traditional tactical training. This became abundantly clear to Colonel D. B. Sackett, who traveled along the Missouri River to inspect army posts in 1867. In his reports, Sackett repeatedly noted that the new recruits to the regular army, serving at reoccupied frontier forts, did not receive regular drilling or marksmanship practice. At Fort Berthold, Dakota Territory, Sackett noted, "The company has neither drill or [sic] target practice for the last year."[44] Troops at Fort Union and Fort Sully, also in Dakota Territory, experienced similar conditions. Officers lacked the motivation to provide soldiers with guidelines for conduct during military engagements, and the War Department seldom pressured officers to prepare enlisted soldiers to fight, suggesting federal authorities' widespread disinterest in the military readiness of the frontier.

The inexperienced officers at Fort Phil Kearny learned of their ill-preparedness less than four months after Inspector General William B. Hazen's 1866 visit. Just before Christmas, Captain William J. Fetterman led a command of about eighty to their deaths in a fight with two thousand Lakota, Cheyenne, and Arapahoe soldiers. The Fetterman Fight, in which the entire outfit perished, represented one of the worst military disasters for the United States in its decades-long experience of Indian–army warfare. At the Fetterman Fight, Native soldiers concealed themselves in the ravines near Fort Kearny and effected a perfect ambush.[45] United States troops performed more capably in the main battle of the subsequent summer—the Wagon Box Fight—but again found themselves outnumbered and unable to take the offensive. And the troops along the Bozeman Trail could only defend their isolated posts, unable to take any aggressive action against the coalition of Indigenous soldiers led by Oglala Lakota leader Red Cloud.[46]

The series of fights that became known as Red Cloud's War ended in 1868 with the Treaty of Fort Laramie. The treaty had three significant results. First, the United States was forced to recognize Native title to the Powder River and Black Hills country as well as to commit to protect Native interests from white squatters or attempted settlement. Second, the army agreed to abandon three major installations that ran through the region, tearing down Forts C. F. Smith, Reno, and Phil Kearny. Third, the government agreed to close the Bozeman Trail. Augur, commander of the Department of the Platte, concluded that the war had convinced Red Cloud of "weakness on our part." Augur feared that the success of Red Cloud would spur other

Indigenous nations to seize upon the weakness of the army throughout the region—especially in the Smoky Hills region of Kansas.[47]

Though the integrity of the treaty lasted for less than a decade, the military success of Red Cloud against the United States Army forced the federal government, and the regular army, to admit to the "Lakotas' right to rule the northern plains as they saw fit."[48] The combination of Lakota strategic planning, the timing of their major resistance efforts, and the army's uncoordinated effort to defend government installations on the northern Plains contributed to one of the greatest Native victories in the history of the Indian wars.[49]

THE MILITIA PROBLEM

As the army struggled to reestablish itself in the West, territorial governors voiced their desire to employ temporary militias rather than regular troops to protect settlers. Professional officers, in turn, were suspicious of the political impact of such authorizations of force. Sherman wondered whether he could trust the governors and other local politicians who were invested in organizing temporary military forces.[50] The Civil War generation saw its share of examples of the limitations of political generals—men who used their partisan connections to acquire commissions to lead volunteer regiments, usually creating chaos due their lack of ability.[51] Historian Robert G. Athearn speculated that "had the regular army been confronted only with the problem of containing the Indian tribes, without the many complications produced by territorial officials who envisaged themselves as Indian fighters or those who merely sought publicity, the postwar difficulties of the military might have been greatly reduced."[52] Because the federal government had to pay states or territories for the use of their local militias, territorial governors sought to tender troops to the regular army in the hope of receiving an influx of federal dollars.

White settlers across the West bombarded army officers with requests for authorization to organize militias to embark on violent campaigns against Indigenous people. Citizens willing to volunteer for militia service did not disguise their hatred for Native peoples; in fact, they often pointed to the emotion as an added qualification in seeking commissions. In September

1866, John R. Pulliam, who had served with Colonel John Baylor's Second Texas Cavalry Regiment during the Civil War, requested the command of a Texas militia regiment. Pulliam referenced his Confederate service and then explained, "I am well informed upon the Frontier—have interest there, and a special emity [sic] to the hostile Indian." The enmity, Pulliam explained, stemmed from Natives allegedly murdering fourteen of his soldiers in 1861 while his Confederate forces had occupied Fort Davis, Texas.[53] To make the case for his worthiness for a militia commission, Baylor offered his hatred of Indians as an asset.

The nation's professional soldiers knew that newspaper editors, settlers, and territorial governors collectively imagined a much larger Indigenous threat than any that actually existed. "This is the safest Indian country I was ever in," Captain Gustavus C. Doane of the Second Cavalry Regiment wrote to his wife in 1871. Doane saw no evidence for concern among the white settlers in Arizona. "The danger and the stampede is all in the newspapers," Doane claimed, asserting that civilian contractors had a vested interest in keeping up a steady barrage of false reports to ensure a continuation of government protection. He drove home his point by assuring his wife that he considered southern Arizona safer than New York—"and infinitely more so than Chicago." Doane condemned Arizona's settlers with the same vehemence he directed toward western journalists, accusing them of amplifying the Indian threat to continue bilking the government on supply contracts. Showing his low opinion of the (non-Native) locals, Doane exclaimed, "This country is full of tramps, thieves, and ten cent gamblers, both whiskey and water are sold per drink at about the same price at roadside doggeries."[54]

No matter their opinions on militias, local settlers, or the press, army officers remained duty bound to respond to threats. Aware of this, western governors exploited the army's commitments and pleaded incessantly to raise territorial militias for Indian fighting, especially when the federal government failed to deploy the regular army in large numbers. On June 4, 1867, Alexander Cameron Hunt, the territorial governor of Colorado, informed the second-highest-ranking soldier in the nation that "an Indian war now exists over a country two thousand by one thousand miles in extent." Hunt explained to Sherman that he knew the general had "not troops to guard half so much territory." Despite his concern for Colorado's fledgling ranch settlements, Hunt also admitted, "I have no money or credit with which to equip the five hundred men standing ready to go on a campaign."[55] More important for Sherman's decision-making, Hunt had only a vague assertion of a threat to justify the use of temporary troops for his territory's protection. There certainly was no general Indian war on the scale he claimed.

Sherman did not immediately endorse the formation of a militia in the Colorado Territory. In a telegram to Hunt, he stressed that the federal government had no law in place to pay for such temporary troops. He added, "I don't believe you will have imminent trouble with the Indians there if your people will be ordinarily prudent." Sherman stressed to Hunt that most conflicts could be avoided if white settlers refrained from instigating them. The message failed to calm the governor, who forwarded a plan to "carry the war to the villages of the Indian," proposing a multicolumn march. He added, however, that Sherman should "have no fears of our making war on Indians now peaceable." In the weeks that preceded Hunt's campaign plan and request for militia funding, a military commission in Sherman's department had been investigating the events of the 1864 Sand Creek Massacre and the conduct of John Chivington in the Colorado Territory. Hunt's language and promise not to attack peaceable Indians proved an eerie echo of the same statements made by Chivington and John Evans, Colorado's wartime territorial governor.[56]

Despite his misgivings, Sherman authorized Hunt to raise three 50-man companies of volunteer militia, but he wrote privately to General G. P. Ihrie, the army paymaster in Denver, that he thought "the Indians are already off for the North or for the Arkansas [River]." He also informed Ihrie that "the volunteers in question cannot be paid at all till Congress appropriates specially," adding, "we don't intend to buy horses at all."[57] Sherman knew that the federal government had no interest in paying for a territorial militia in Colorado and that he could not, in his capacity as departmental commander, compensate the men or divert his department's resources on the basis of rumors he doubted had any veracity.

In directing Hunt to organize a small band of troops, Sherman allowed the governor to believe he had come to the territory's defense in the face of a supposed Indigenous threat. Sherman felt confident, as he indicated to his paymaster, that the militia would not engage in any kind of combat, since he considered Natives no longer a threat to Colorado's Front Range. The 150-man force allowed by Sherman (but not authorized by any federal authority) lasted for ten days. They never found the horses they needed. The *Army and Navy Journal* criticized the men who volunteered for the expedition, reporting "some settlers are anxious, it is said, to enroll themselves" but worrying that any citizen eager to enlist in a temporary militia regiment lacked restraint. The editors worried that Coloradans might try to emulate the actions of Chivington.[58] They could not have made their disdain for the militia any clearer.

Army leaders simply did not trust politicians—whether in Washington or the West's territorial capitals—to be fair about their military needs. Before granting Hunt's request, Sherman indicated he believed territorial governors had ulterior motives in asking to raise volunteer units. Writing to Grant in May 1867, Sherman explained, "I know that in New Mexico and in Colorado it would not be safe to trust the Governors, for they would gain popularity by getting their people employed in nominal service by the United States."[59] Grant and Sherman assessed the intentions of western governors correctly, knowing that territorial politicians used rumors of Native incursions to increase support for themselves among constituents.

It troubled the army's leading officers that it did not seem to matter whether reports of violence or requests for troops overstated the problem or had any truth to them at all. As an organization, the army's primary duty was to respond, if possible, to reports of military crises and either address the threat or manage the aftermath. If troops arrived and found no threat, as they often did, all that they achieved was spending time and government funds on a mission that distracted them from larger campaigns or post maintenance. Falsified threats wasted already overstretched military resources. The only way to prevent territorial officials from raising local militias was to send them professional troops; otherwise, they must suffer the consequences of allowing untrained civilians to create havoc with Indigenous people and the army itself.

Grant took Sherman's warning seriously and explained to the War Department the problems attendant to authorizing temporary territorial militias. A petition by white settlers in New Mexico requested two regiments of local militia to operate throughout the territory to "subjugate the Indians, place them on reservations, protect our citizens and open and develop this rich country." Grant urged Stanton to avoid giving locals any such military authority. "Local organizations are believed to be the most expensive and least efficient means of affording protection against Indians," Grant explained, telling Stanton that if New Mexico needed protection, the troops needed to come from the regular army.[60]

Working through his frustration, Sherman prepared a circular explaining the militia laws and regulations of the United States. Sherman's explanation boiled down to the assertion that militias were only to be relied upon as a last resort, if the regular army absolutely could not respond to a military crisis. Sherman shared the circular with Stanton and Grant, requesting their counsel. Both suggested that Sherman refrain from publishing the circular. If he distributed it, they believed that territorial governors might use the letter to justify raising larger militias. Governors, thought Grant and Stanton, could easily claim they had exhausted all other avenues for acquiring military protection. No matter how carefully he explained the situation, Sherman could not get territorial governors to understand that the government had no need for militia soldiers and would refuse to pay for them unless they were forced to call them out for service.

Even when politicians got their way in eliciting military action, it did not always go well. In 1867, former Union general Thomas Francis Meagher, acting in a nonmilitary capacity as territorial governor of Montana, called five hundred volunteers into service in the Gallatin River valley. Local newspapers printed copies of correspondence that purported to demonstrate Sherman's and Stanton's acquiescence in the call for volunteers.[61] Despite a belief among the citizenry that Meagher issued the call with the proper authority, the service of the volunteers ended in acrimony when the regular army finally sent a small force to build federal forts in central Montana while refusing to pay the militia for its service.[62]

A subsequent encounter between the regular army's officials and the militia in the Montana Territory revealed the distrust of the former toward local military organizations. Upon being ordered to disperse by Alfred Terry, the army commander in the territory, the militia rioted and raided the regular army's supply trains. In his annual message to the territorial legislature, Governor Green Clay Smith explained that "a large number who had been mustered into service, upon receiving orders to muster out, disobeyed the order, possessed themselves of quartermaster and commissary stores, some two hundred and fifty horses and mules, and deserted."[63] In his annual report, Sherman suggested that Smith had actually countermanded Terry's orders and "retained in service these volunteers, and has brought about a conflict with the Crows and other Indians outside of the settled limits of the territory, when he knew that the government desired very much to retain peaceful relations with them."[64]

The War Department investigated the pillaging of the army's supply trains by the temporary territorial militia. The report suggested that the July 1, 1867, death of Meagher had damaged the cohesion of the troops. En route to Fort Benton to receive a shipment of ammunition for the militia, Meagher fell overboard from the steamboat *G. A. Thompson* and drowned in the Missouri River. Unruliness among the militiamen, however, resulted from more than just his demise. Thomas B. Marquis, a member of the militia, later remembered, "The first Montana Militia was composed largely of ex-ruffians of the Missouri–Kansas border. As soldiers they were utterly unruly. One company drowned its first captain. Desertion was a matter to be determined merely by personal inclination."[65] In short, this militia conformed to every stereotype that had convinced officers such as Sherman to exclude them from auxiliary service with the regulars.

Sherman repeatedly asserted that the militias should not be trusted. While writing to Pope about shifting regular troops into the Montana Territory in 1867, Sherman requested that a regular officer be posted in the vicinity "to check the tendency of the Volunteers to bring about trouble for the sake of curing it." Sherman knew the militia used threats of an Indian invasion to manufacture work for themselves and receive a paycheck from the federal government. Sherman related the alarm in Montana to the outcry that had followed the US–Dakota War of 1862, which he believed had diverted crucial army resources during the Civil War. "Even as it is," Sherman explained to Pope, "I fear civilians of the style of T. Francis Meagher may involve the Frontier in a needless war—such as occurred in Minnesota some years ago."[66]

While Meagher encouraged the militiamen, the territorial governor had the law against him—no legislation existed for raising local militias in the territories. Over the course of the Montana affair, Sherman "emphatically refused" several of Meagher's requests for arms and equipment and declined to muster in the Irishman's five hundred volunteers. Sherman did not, however, neglect the reports of widespread depredations in the Gallatin valley. To determine the size of the threat, Sherman called for "a discreet officer" to go to Virginia City, Montana, and "judge the necessity of a call for volunteers." Major William H. Lewis reported that the region "had not been invaded by hostile Indians at all." Sherman concluded his recapitulation of the summer's events by stating, "The United States are not in any measure responsible for the call for volunteers in Montana." It took more than seven years of fighting with the federal government for the Montana militiamen to receive payment. In December 1874, Congress appropriated $513,343 to cover the cost of the illicit territorial militia.[67]

The Montana exercise underscored the difficulty for army officers in assessing threat levels and determining troop distributions. Sherman explained to Meagher in 1866 that he had only one regiment of cavalry to cover Kansas and the territories of Colorado, Dakota, Montana, Nebraska, and New Mexico. Sherman told Meagher, "It is idle to expect all my Cavalry in one remote Territory, leaving all the others without any and leaving the roads this side of you unguarded." Historian Robert G. Athearn observed that the Montana militia campaign fell apart because there were no Natives threatening any part of the territory. In fact, Athearn accused the militia of trying to "produce" an Indian war.[68] Historian James L. Thane Jr., described the debacle more bluntly: "During the summer of 1867, under Acting Governor Thomas Francis Meagher, the Territory of Montana spent $1,100,000 to repel an invasion by four Indians."[69] The entire exercise proved that the Native American "threat" existed more in the minds of white western settlers than in reality. Despite this, the army remained duty bound to provide federal assistance, and so the institution's resources were stretched even more thinly across the West.

Militia also posed a problem in Texas, where the army struggled to manage the simultaneous demands of Reconstruction and the western portion of the state. Most army officers in Texas focused on completing their Reconstruction duties and left western settlers feeling unprotected by the regulars. The problem in Texas was twofold. First, under the provisions of the 1867 army appropriations bill, white militia were outlawed in the former Confederate states. Even if they were necessary, they could not be organized without breaking federal law. Second, and more frustrating for the army, was the fact that the governor of Texas, James Throckmorton, manufactured the idea of an Indigenous threat on the state's western border to force Phillip H. Sheridan to transfer troops away from Reconstruction service and to the West.

Lack of men significantly slowed the army's ability to direct troops to reoccupy frontier posts. The regulars did not start the process in Texas until September 3, 1866, when Sheridan posted a cavalry force at Fredericksburg, west of Austin. Sheridan acted quickly because he had spotted notices in local newspapers calling for recruits to fill a new force of Rangers, to be paid by the state. Wary of seeing former Confederates mounted and armed, Sheridan informed Governor Throckmorton in no uncertain terms that no militia organizations were to be raised. Army officials frequently associated eager militiamen with the Confederate cause. Sheridan worried that enlisting them in the service of the federal government, even temporarily, empowered resistance to Reconstruction. He told Grant that "Gov Throckmorton's letters are rather 'Bunkum' I have not replied—silence is the best policy."[70]

The relationship between the army officer and the Texan politician deteriorated not long after Sheridan's missive. Beset by problems and juggling demands from multiple theaters with no troops to meet them, Sheridan lost his patience with the contentious Throckmorton. Sheridan removed Throckmorton from office by an order dated July 30, 1867, on the grounds that he was "an impediment to the reconstruction." The same order appointed Republican and Unionist E. M. Pease governor of Texas. Pease took office on August 8, 1867. Rather than win at the ballot box, where Throckmorton had unequivocally thrashed him (by a margin of 49,277 votes to 12,168) the previous year, Pease gained his governorship through political favors. Pease, like Throckmorton, failed to grasp the extent of the problem faced by the army in Texas. In his short tenure as governor (1867–1869), Pease also clashed with Sheridan and his principal lieutenant in Texas, Colonel Charles Griffin.[71]

Sheridan believed that public officials in Texas overstated the claims of Native transgressions to get the army out of the way of overseeing strife between whites and Blacks, but Sheridan and his subordinates remained committed to Reconstruction duty in the central and eastern portions of the state. Colonel Griffin, an ardent supporter of freedmen's rights who commanded the Texas subdepartment, patiently explained to newly invested Governor Pease his difficulty in distributing troops. Griffin told the governor that if loyal Texans could assist the army in performing the civil duties it had to undertake—fair elections and achieving justice for crimes against African Americans—he could move his soldiers to the frontier. But Griffin refused to commit troops to frontier protection while the unreconstructed element ruled the state. The colonel told the governor that his evidence indicated that for every white person killed on the frontier by Natives, twenty people died in the interior from Reconstruction violence. Until Texans submitted to Reconstruction, Griffin determined that the frontier (the portion of Texas west of present-day San Antonio) demanded little of his attention—or that of his troops.[72]

The problem of divided responsibilities between Reconstruction and the West endlessly frustrated Sheridan, and this frustration came through clearly in his 1867 annual report. "It is strange that over a white man killed by Indians on an extensive frontier the greatest excitement will take place," he mused, "but over the killing of many freedmen in the settlements nothing is done. I cannot help but see this, and I cannot help but tell it to my superiors, no matter how unpleasant it may be to the authorities of Texas."[73]

Just as Sherman did in Montana, Sheridan sent investigators to determine the truth behind claims of supposed Indian attacks on white settlements in West Texas. While awaiting word, he telegraphed Grant, sharing his suspicion that "the secret of all this fuss about Indian troubles is the desire to have all the troops removed from the interior and the desire of the loose lazy adventurers to be employed as volunteers against the Indians under the act of the State Legislature." In another letter to Grant, Sheridan confessed that he preferred to use troops in Texas "to protect Unionists and Negroes."[74] Sheridan's commitment to Reconstruction gratified congressional Republicans, but the situation underscored the difficulty the commander faced in simultaneously managing military Reconstruction and a western frontier, especially when a southern governor undermined his authority.

As the reality of the regular army's weakness dawned on Texans, a chorus arose urging the return of the Texas Rangers, or some other militia force, to protect the frontier.[75] Austin's *Daily Journal* apprehended "great misery, loss, and ravage when this savage war cloud breaks in blood and fire on our border." The newspaper appreciated the efforts of the regulars, admitting "the troops will do all they can, but the frontier is immense and force inefficient." "Hurry up the Rangers," the editorial concluded. Two weeks later, the same newspaper complained, "The War Department at Washington . . . telegraphed General Reynolds that no such force must be permitted to take the field and make war on the Indians." The *Journal* explained that unlike in the decade before the war, when the federal government paid for auxiliaries such as the Rangers, the federal government had no intention of paying for a similar postbellum organization.[76]

President Grant's orders to dispatch a regiment of cavalry to Texas failed to placate the press. The editor of the *Galveston News* asserted in bombastic fashion that a militia force would better serve the interests of the settlers than would the regular army. The writer doubted whether a new regiment "would prove any more efficient than the handful of government troops now nominally defending our frontier." The newspaper did not want to see any of the army's "pipe clay and regulation tactics," rejecting peace and preferring to carry out a war against the state's Indigenous people.[77] The editor's objection to the service of the regular army boiled down to the fact that the troops could not go on the offensive against Native peoples with any regularity; they had to stay close to garrisons and guard government property. And they had too little manpower to defend more than six hundred miles of West Texas borderland. The newspaper argued that the Rangers, or another militia force, could undertake the work of offensive warfare while the regulars maintained their defensive posture. Without a policy for accepting militia into federal service, however, the army could not contemplate the proposed scheme.

Because of the conflicting priorities of Reconstruction and frontier service, the regulars left the Texas frontier almost entirely unprotected during the summer of 1869. Cavalryman H. H. McConnell recalled, "The troops being pretty much all engaged in the work of reconstruction in the interior, the tier of counties adjacent counties to the Red River being exposed to the incursions of bands of depredating Indians." Like many army officers, McConnel cast all Indigenous people in Texas as hostile and engaged in what he judged to be illicit activity against white settlers. In that year, he explained, "only two small companies remained at Fort Richardson . . . building barracks, officers' quarters, and similar work, no time being left for the defense of the settlers, although it seemed to U.S. that was 'what we were here for.'" While he could explain the duty he had performed, McConnell could not offer a logical reason for the army's neglect of one of its traditional duties. "It seemed strange to me then," he recalled, "and I look back now and fail to understand, the utter indifference of the government to the condition of the Texas frontier at this time (1869–70)."[78]

As the needs of Reconstruction changed, so too did troop distribution. By 1870, 945 regulars were stationed at posts carrying out Reconstruction duty, 1,323 were posted along the Rio Grande border, and 2,146 were on the frontier (table 10). That was the critical year for a permanent shift in troop distribution, when the frontier claimed the greater number of available troops for the first time (graph 5).[79] That Reconstruction service had previously claimed the lion's share of troops in Texas illuminated congressional priorities. The War Department also transferred Texas to the Department of the Missouri from the Department of the South in 1870, a final sign that military officials believed the primary duty in the state had shifted from Reconstruction oversight to frontier occupation.

As the military occupation of the South dwindled after 1870 and 1871 and troops settled into more permanent dispositions across the West, the army looked set to transition into a new phase of its western work. Had an officer been able to survey the West in 1871, he might have had a reason for renewed confidence. Only 1 in 6 soldiers remained in the South. The army was weathering congressionally mandated reductions. In 1871, the War Department reported that expenditures had fallen more than $17 million from

Table 10. Distribution of Troops in Texas, 1867–1877

Year	Total	West	Reconstruction	Rio Grande
1867	4,722	1,256	2,706	760
1868	5,668	2,224	2,371	1,073
1869	4,589	1,514	2,069	1,006
1870	4,414	2,146	9,45	1,323
1871	3,821	2,690	3,68	763
1872	3,916	2,513	5,24	879
1873	4,178	2,920	63	1,195
1874	4,245	2,737	367	1,141
1875	3,012	1,929	321	762
1876	3,017	1,539	512	966
1877	3,067	1,703	600	764

Source: Gregory P. Downs and Scott Nesbit, *Mapping Occupation: Force, Freedom, and the Army in Reconstruction,* published March 2015, http://mappingoccupation.org. Accessed May 2023.

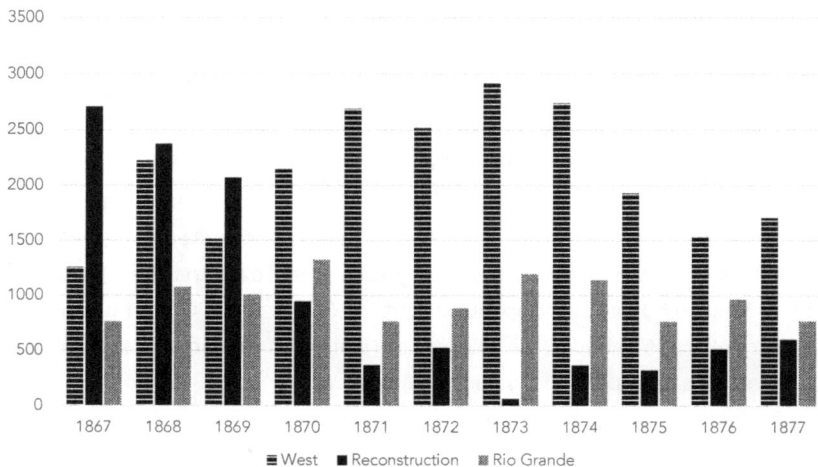

Graph 5. Distribution of troops in Texas, 1867–1877

the previous year. By the end of 1871, in accordance with the 1870 Army Reorganization Act, superfluous officers and "indifferent soldiers" were discharged, bringing the number of men in service down to 30,000. Over the course of 1871, the War Department received one hundred applications for troops from state and territorial governors from across the country, including in the South and the West. Where necessity required it, the secretary of war explained, the army responded "promptly."[80]

Still, challenges remained. Clothing and equipage, according to William W. Belknap, the secretary of war, remained "unfit for army use." Appropriations to facilitate the upkeep of army buildings also fell short. The secretary asked Congress to focus on the fact that they had not allowed enough money to "shelter the army in a manner essential to its comfort and health."[81] The cost of transporting troops across the country remained high, drawing about $1.5 million from federal coffers. More than $10 million worth of ordnance and small arms stores left over from the Civil War were sold in 1871 to help supplement the army's budget. To keep costs low, the army limited future weapons manufacturing to only the supplies required by the troops. The secretary noted the ongoing effort across the continent to shift soldiers to the use of breechloading small arms—a new tactical advantage that helped to overcome future disparities in troop strengths during engagements.

For soldiers and officers, life at western posts became increasingly routine. Infantry soldiers at Fort Davis, Texas, performed a variety of fatigue duties, such as reveille, assembly, drill, mess, tattoo, and taps. Enlisted soldiers constructed buildings, telegraph lines, and roads. They also hauled water, cared for horses and mules, chopped wood, and tended the post vegetable garden. Especially active days might see troops guarding stagecoaches and wagon trains, mapping the area, searching for water, or guarding railroad crews. At Fort Davis, soldiers most often left the fort to protect travelers, freight wagons, and U.S. Mail coaches traveling on the road from San Antonio to El Paso.[82] In his study of the soldiers of the Indian wars, Don Rickey, the acknowledged expert on the daily life of the frontier army, concluded, "Isolation, boredom, and monotony characterized the life at the western posts."[83]

Altogether, army officers reported that their work was becoming more manageable. Sheridan believed that across the interior West, only one sector, Arizona, demanded active campaigning. Sheridan expected active operations against Native peoples to transition from "administering punishment to giving protection" with increasing speed.[84] The army's second-in-command believed that once the army forced Indigenous people to reservations, soldiers would shift from campaigning to administration. Officers and soldiers alike looked to the rapid construction of various transcontinental railroads as a boon to their operations. The army's commissary general, A. B. Eaton, understood that advances in communications wrought by the railroads, and access to a growing abundance of local goods from increased white settlement, aided in bringing essential supplies to soldiers.[85] The spread of technology and the renewed federal commitment to settler colonialism put the army in a position to recover from the divided priorities of the immediate postbellum years. Though the national fighting force remained small and underpowered compared to that of the rest of the world, the army did its duty in providing whatever aid it could to bring about the white conquest of the West.

CUSTER'S LAST BEER

"One thing for sure," western chronicler Norman Maclean wrote, "it is an odd advertisement for beer."[1] He referred to the 1888 painting *Custer's Last Fight,* by Cassilly Adams. Purchased by the Anheuser-Busch corporation and turned into a lithograph by Otto Becker in 1896, the print was used to market Budweiser beer in thousands of bars and saloons across the United States. In the early decades of the twentieth century, Anheuser-Busch distributed more than a million copies of the print. The corporation's relentless marketing strategy all but ensured that generations of Americans were greeted by George Custer and his Seventh Cavalry troopers as they, in the fashion of Norm Peterson from *Cheers,* settled onto their favorite barstools for an evening of drinking and debate.

Just two decades after Custer's fight at the Little Bighorn, the army officer's name and image had become woven into the nation's consciousness. But Custer was more a figure of myth than a part of the nation's history. His demise, brought about by arrogance and failure to obey orders, was not eulogized so much as it was romanticized.[2] The Adams painting and Becker lithograph were just one example. William F. Cody, when he sought to sell to eager audiences across the globe the story of America's western expansion in the guise of Buffalo Bill, stitched "the Custer legend onto his own entertainment."[3] Even John Ford and John Wayne were drawn to tell their version of the Custer story, though Ford insisted his motion picture *Fort Apache* was a criticism of the arrogance he found rampant among postbellum frontier army officers like Custer. Speaking to Peter Bogdanovich in 1971, Ford admitted that "it's good for the country to have heroes to look up

Custer's Last Fight (1896), lithograph from a painting by Cassilly Adams, 1888

to," but as far as he was concerned, Custer ought not be among them. Ford wanted his audience to understand that Custer had done "a stupid job" on June 25, 1876.[4] Still, at the end of Ford's greatest cavalry film, the army are the winners.

Myth can explain why so many Americans would be forgiven for disbelieving the notion that anyone in the nineteenth-century United States opposed the regular army. While many Americans might remember seeing Emanuel Leutze's work in a dusty textbook, far more would readily call to mind *Custer's Last Fight* as a representation of the nation's westward growth. Or they would think of a film by Ford, a sketch by Frederick Remington, or a novel by Zane Grey or Louis L'Amour. Adolphus Busch, writers of dime novels, and motion picture directors knew soldiers made for good stories. And good stories get told, and read, and watched time and time again, until the myths within them are accepted as truth. So much so that a man who played George Custer on film could go on to be elected President of the United States—an office Custer had perhaps coveted for himself.

When he made his fatal blunder in 1876, Custer not only ensured his own legend but also sundered Republican plans to reduce the army to its smallest postbellum size. In a twist of irony, Custer's last stand provided the American regular army with its first moment of respite after more than a decade of diminution at the hands of the Republican Party. The only thing worse than having to increase the army, in Republican eyes, may have been the fact that the soldier who created the need was exactly the type of officer that Republicans had long insisted permeated the ranks of the professional force. Custer and his wife, Elizabeth "Libbie" Custer, were avowed Democrats, and the Civil War's "boy general" was an acolyte of the most feared conservative in the army's recent history, George McClellan.

The news of Custer's defeat at the hands of a coalition of Lakota, Dakota, Arapaho, and Northern Cheyenne soldiers did not make an instantaneous media splash. In fact, the news of Custer's demise hit eastern newspapers just as the nation erupted in celebration of its centennial birthday. The most popular periodical of the era, *Harper's Weekly*, did not report extensively on what the editors termed "the Montana Slaughter" until their July 22 issue—nearly a month after the battle itself.[5] Rumors of the death of Custer and his troopers reached Congress somewhat sooner than the editors at *Harper's* heard about it, though not until July 6, when in both the House and the Senate references were made to the possible death of Custer and his command. On July 8, the Senate passed a resolution requesting that President Grant confirm that some two hundred regular soldiers had died in Montana.

By the time the news reached Congress, the two chambers had already agreed to reduce the army to just 25,000 soldiers and officers in the following year. This represented a five thousand–man decrease from 1875, which would heavily tax infantry and artillery regiments. The measure delighted anti-army Republicans and Democrats alike. In contrast to the comparatively heady years before the Civil War, the army could no longer count on Democratic support. In the 1870s, when former Confederates and old southern Democrats began returning to Congress, chafing from their harsh treatment at the hands of the Radicals during Reconstruction, they fixed their political ire on the army—the on-the-ground manifestation of Radical Reconstruction. By using the army so forcefully during Reconstruction, in other words, the Radicals had all but guaranteed that the Democratic Party would learn to detest the regulars almost as much as the Radicals did.

Custer's debacle forced Congress to amend their reduction, however, and to agree to augment the army by 2,500 troops—all cavalry—who would be discharged as soon as the conflict with the Lakota and Dakota ceased. Pleased at the first supportive measure to cross his desk in more than a decade, William T. Sherman wrote to Philip Sheridan that they owed Custer their thanks. "Congress is now in session willing to give us all we want."[6] Sherman may have spoken too soon or been too zealous in his estimation of the beneficence of the national legislature. Just one year later, in the summer of 1877, a Democrat-dominated Congress failed to pass an appropriations bill and the officers and soldiers of the army went without pay from June to November. Only the congressional delegation from Texas argued for more troops, insisting that their state presented a multitude of military challenges requiring greater army investment. Their colleagues were uninterested in the pleas of the Texans, and the latter compensated with their famous Rangers.

Beyond the politics involved, the shock of the Custer news prompted public reflections on the role the regular army had played in postbellum expansion. In Congress, two key themes emerged in the speeches given in the wake of the battle. In one strain of argumentation, congressmen from the former Confederacy (many of them former Confederates themselves) eulogized Custer to sound the call of sectional reconciliation, saying that they could let bygones be bygones and celebrate the life of an army officer who had excelled on the field of battle and gone to his death doing his duty. In the second, members of Congress from the West pointed to the defeat of U.S. troops at the Little Bighorn as the natural consequence of the federal government's neglect of the region's needs, exemplified by the steady reduction of the army over the previous decade.

Representing Virginia as a Democrat, William Terry urged honor to Custer's memory by granting a pension for the relief of his wife, Libbie, and his father, Emanuel. Speaking to his Democratic colleagues, Terry urged them to vote in favor of the pensions because, he said, in addition to Custer's postbellum career, the officer's Civil War service had "displayed a gallantry scarcely any equaled and none surpassed." Unlike many of his colleagues, Terry had formed his opinion of Custer's abilities firsthand. When in command of the Stonewall Brigade in 1864, he received a wound while facing Custer and the First Brigade of the First Cavalry Division of Philip

Sheridan's Army of the Shenandoah at the Third Battle of Winchester. The Virginian's colleague, Samuel S. Cox of New York, made certain the House did not miss the importance of Terry's remarks, saying they were "in consonance to-day with the feeling of the American people." And since Terry had once fought against Custer, Cox considered it "a proud thing" that the Virginian made no objection to the pension bill.[7]

Mississippi's Lucius Quintus Cincinnatus Lamar II, a Democrat surely in the running for most impressive name in the Forty-Fourth Congress, likewise urged his House colleagues to "forbear to dwell on the darker memories of the war." Rather, Lamar—the chairman of the House Democratic Caucus—hoped they could all "cherish as a common heritage the glorious deeds performed by soldiers of both sides in that conflict."[8] This rhetoric conforms precisely to what historian Caroline E. Janney carefully parsed in her study of the limits of reconciliation after the Civil War. When it served a clear political end or helped to sell a narrative to a public audience, veterans could let bygones be bygones—as both Terry and Lamar indicated. It worked because the public wanted to embrace a narrative of shared American values such as "valor or devotion to one's cause."[9] Eulogizing Custer allowed former Confederates to emphasize those ideas and gain political and popular support.

As the House debated whether to allow for a temporary increase to the army, Democrat Martin Maginnis received a special opportunity to address the lower chamber. The *Congressional Record*'s depiction of Maginnis's speech indicates congressmen tripping over themselves to cede their time to the thirty-five-year-old Union army veteran, in a manner uncharacteristic of most nineteenth-century congressional debates. The reason so many wished to hear from Maginnis was that he was the nonvoting representative for the Montana Territory and had more knowledge than anyone else on Capitol Hill of the conditions Custer and his Seventh Cavalrymen had faced. Maginnis used his time to accuse the House of being "slow to move" in supporting western territories with the troops they constantly pleaded for. "The shadow of [the American] flag," Maginnis said, was "a mockery of the protection that it owed to its people." In short, westerners knew that the government had voted year in and year out to reduce the institution that could support them, and the Custer fight had resulted from that neglect.[10]

As is history's habit, the irony piled on long after the debates over Custer faded into political obscurity. Because Custer died so infamously and because he attracted so much attention in his lifetime, the generations of Americans who grew up in the late Gilded Age and Progressive Era did so idolizing the frontier troops that the Republican Party had spent three decades defaming. When their children produced works of culture in their own right, this glorification of the army continued. For the first five decades of Hollywood's history, regular soldiers roamed the silver screen as heroes, taming the West alongside cowboys, mountain men, and pioneers. It was not until 1970 that Americans encountered a thorough critique of the frontier army at their local cinema: director Ralph Nelson's *Soldier Blue,* a film about the 1864 Sand Creek Massacre, which was really about the war in Vietnam. Films such as *Dances with Wolves* (1990) and *Hostiles* (2017) have since offered further criticism of the army's part in American settler colonialism, though such stories are still a rarity.

In all fairness to Hollywood, pro-army films often followed the model of earlier works of culture, including paintings and literature. Frederic Remington, who was born just six months after the opening shots of the Civil War were fired at Fort Sumter, ceaselessly illustrated the United States Cavalry in its late frontier days. Like Remington, Theodore Roosevelt (born in October 1858) was captivated by the dash and derring-do of the western regular soldier. Roosevelt informed readers of his multivolume survey of western expansion, *The Winning of the West,* that understanding the process of Manifest Destiny required close study of the work of the regular army. Writing in 1894, Roosevelt declared, "The regular forces led the way ... The Federal forts were built first; it was only afterwards that the small towns sprang up in their shadow. The Federal troops formed the vanguard of the white advance. They were the mainstay of the force behind which, as behind a shield, the founders of the commonwealths did their work."[11]

Remington, Roosevelt, and Adolphus Busch alike realized that the regular army represented action and initiative to a nation that was turning away from its frontier past.[12] Their generation—the sons of fathers who had fought in the Civil War—lionized the regular army in the popular imagination. And their descendants have done the same in novels, films, and even works of history. Each author and artist had a reason—to commemorate the settling of the West, to urge American men to be as manly as their forebears, or simply to sell suds. Whatever the purpose, the narratives proved appealing. But as popular narratives often do, they traded details for a bigger picture: the regular army had conquered the West and paved the way for the pioneers and the railroad.

The army played an important part in the story of western settlement, to be sure, but it is necessary to look at those finer details. Doing so reveals that whatever the army accomplished in the Civil War era, it did so while its very existence was being fiercely contested. That contestation offers a new way to understand the politics and motivations of the Republican Party with regard to dismantling the Slave Power, winning the Civil War, and effecting the reconstruction of the nation. Antimilitarism played a much larger role in all these events than most historical works have considered. While it was not the most important plank in the platform of the Republican Party, anti-army politics changed how Republicans governed and could compromise their effectiveness, especially in their stewardship of the West—a place they coveted but never effectively managed.

The purpose of this book has not been to make an apology for the army, nor to suggest that the institution was so weak that it was not capable of the violent acts that soldiers and their officers carried out across the West. Rather, its goal has been to demonstrate that better integrating military history with studies of politics and culture in the Civil War era can indicate where the country could have pursued alternative paths. Republicans could have committed more troops to Reconstruction, and for a longer period. The party could have supplied soldiers to western outposts to police settlers who provoked Native nations and violated Indigenous treaty rights. Instead, the single-minded pursuit of dismantling the state that the Slave Power had constructed dictated all that Republicans did, and because the army had helped to build that proslavery state (or so Republicans believed), the regulars had to be dismantled as well.

It would shock veterans of the postbellum regular army to learn how the nation came to venerate them as heroes. In their lifetimes, they could not even get the federal government to pay them a pension on par with that given to Civil War, Spanish–American War, or First World War volunteers.[13] When he wrote about his colleagues from the postbellum regular army, George Baird had little hope Americans would remember his service. Regular army men, he said, "lie in unknown graves; their country never knew their names and has forgotten their services." He wanted his audience to know that all he and his colleagues had done had been in the name and the service of a government that often seemed to despise them. He explained that at Thermopylae, where Leonidas and his three hundred fell, "there was erected a memorial with the legend 'Stranger, tell the Lacedaemonians that we lie here in obedience to their laws.'" But Americans remembered their professional soldiers less well than the Ancient Greeks did their Spartans. In the West, Baird said, for the regular army men, "from the scattered, unmarked, forgotten graves of those unknown heroes comes the message, 'Tell it to Columbia that we lie where we fell in obedience to her commands.'"[14]

NOTES

Introduction: Westward the Course of Empire

1. In many respects, the United States had exceptional immunity from having to be on a constant military footing in the nineteenth century. As Sarah C. M. Paine has recently observed, "US leaders preferred checkbook conquest to the classic massed-armies approach." Paine, "Centuries of Security," 814. Because the United States had little to fear in terms of a land invasion, with both its northern and southern borders being far more stable than similar national borders in Europe, the country had little use for a large standing army and was primarily a maritime power, especially by the turn of the twentieth century.

2. "Settler colonialism" describes the marginalization or elimination of native peoples by nonnatives so that the foreigners can acquire, hold, and profit from the use of native land. It differs from extractive colonialism, in which a small cadre of temporary foreign administrators exploits native labor. As with extractive colonialism, the attitudes of settler-colonists continue to organize and influence a society long after the initial acts of dispossession. For the theoretical basis of settler colonialism, see Veracini, *Settler Colonialism;* and Hixson, *American Settler Colonialism,* esp. chap. 1. In the words of anthropologist Patrick Wolfe, "Invasion is a structure not an event." Wolfe, "Settler Colonialism and the Elimination of the Native," 388. Numerous recent studies examine settler colonialism in the American West. On Native child abduction and resocialization in state-sponsored boarding schools, see Jacobs, *White Mother to a Dark Race.* On the use of legal frameworks, particularly criminal law, to gain control over Native people, see Ford, *Settler Sovereignty.* On the use of police and law enforcement agencies to incorporate national borderlands and impose racial order, see Graybill, *Policing the Great Plains.* On the logic of violence as it relates to settler-colonial societies, see Blackhawk, *Violence over the Land.*

3. It also could be read, generously, as anti-imperialism. Nineteenth-century Americans associated militarism with imperial nations such as Germany and Prussia, which were pushing to expand their borders. See the delineation of these attitudes made by Trauschweizer, "On Militarism," esp. 513–515. American antimilitarism, then, was part and parcel of the broader cultural act of forgetting the violence of western territorial conquest—an assertion of Anglo innocence in the subjugation of Indigenous peoples recently summarized in Ostler and Jacoby, "After 1776," 321–336. Robert Teigrob raises a similar point of American anti-imperialism's

"often erratic relation to fact." Teigrob, "Empire and Cultures of Militarism in Canada and the United States," 32.

4. For the twenty-five years following the Civil War, Kevin Adams notes, more than 40 percent of regulars were foreign born. Adams, *Class and Race in the Frontier Army,* 4.

5. Or so said Ohio Republican representative Benjamin Stanton. *Congressional Globe,* 35th Cong., 1st Sess. (March 11, 1858), 1074.

6. Bacevich, *New American Militarism.*

7. See, for example, Cogley, *History of the Seventh Indiana Cavalry Volunteers.* Cogley suggested that his entire regiment loathed George Custer when they were assigned to serve under him, and he accused the general of forcing soldiers "to perform menial services for himself, which was an express violation of the law," adding that he believed his unit had been forced to march to Texas after the Civil War "simply to retain dandy officers like Custer a little longer in authority" (171–172).

8. The moniker "Slave Power" described a political cabal composed of southern slaveholders and their northern allies ("doughfaces"), who exerted disproportionate control over all three branches of the federal government. With less than one-third of the free population of the entire country, the slaveholding states nonetheless produced eleven out of sixteen presidents, seventeen out of twenty-eight Supreme Court justices, sixty-one out of seventy-seven presidents of the Senate, and twenty-one out of thirty-three Speakers of the House. See Richards, *Slave Power.*

9. Inbody, "Grand Army of the Republic."

10. Several factors distinguished the militia from professional soldiers. Regular troops enlisted directly in the army and served a substantial term (usually four to five years). The categories of militia and volunteer were more closely related, distinguished primarily by whether a state government or the federal government had authority over the enrollment, equipage, and oversight of the temporary troops. As Millett, Maslowski, and Feis, *For the Common Defense,* explains, militia soldiers responded to domestic insurrection and undertook other temporary duties, whereas regulars performed duties that required occupation of territory or extended campaigning, such as wars against Native peoples. This did not mean, however, that militias were not used during conflicts with Indigenous peoples, such as in the Black Hawk War or the First Seminole War, where as many as 30,000 served. See Hess, *Civil War Infantry Tactics.*

11. Like volunteer fire companies of today, but with mandatory participation by white men between ages eighteen and forty-five, the militia turned out to meet an emergency, after which the men returned to civilian life. They were by no means regular soldiers but instead were men who gathered periodically, if at all, supposedly to train. Militia musters also provided social gatherings for men—a time to drink and reinforce local hierarchies. More to the point, they existed in a nebulous relationship with U.S. military commanders because they often were controlled by local civilian authorities or state governors. As such, tensions always existed between regulars and militia auxiliaries. Regular soldiers typically considered militiamen suspect in their discipline under fire and in their military knowledge. Militias often ran when confronted with enemies composed of professional forces. Militias also cost more than any other form of troops, with one army officer estimating in 1846 that the temporary troops required an expense three times greater than that of regular soldiers. In 1846, army officer Henry Wager Halleck esti-

mated that a regular force of 20,000 men in a six-month campaign cost $150 per soldier. Halleck then explained, "The cost of a militia force, under the same circumstances, making allowance for the difference in the expenses from sickness, waste of camp-furniture, equipments, &c., will be two hundred and fifty dollars per man." In short or irregular wars, a category in which Halleck placed the Second Seminole War, the expenses of the militia, according to the data, "invariably exceed those of the regulars by *at least three hundred per cent.*" Halleck, *Elements of Military Art and Science,* 150, emphasis in original.

12. The federal government paid states directly for the use of these troops. Volunteer militia units came complete with officers and often attempted to operate independently of the control of the regulars. They also provided their own supplies and weapons. During and after the Mexican–American War, the federal government shifted to directly enrolling volunteers into federal service. Most men who fought in Union armies during the Civil War did so as federal volunteers. Because temporary troops composed of the citizen-soldier represented the ideal for a democratic republic, the regular army never gained the popular appeal of its volunteer comrades.

13. Following the lead of Amy Greenberg and others, "Manifest Destiny" will be capitalized throughout the work. See Greenberg, *Manifest Manhood.*

14. Leutze, in Justin G. Turner, "Emanual Leutze's Mural *Westward the Course of Empire Takes Its Way,*" pamphlet in DeGolyer Library, Southern Methodist University, Dallas, Texas, 10–12.

15. Historian Gary Clayton Anderson categorizes the actions of the federal government toward Native peoples as an ethnic cleansing. See Anderson, *Ethnic Cleansing and the Indian.* Jeffrey Ostler treats the history of the federal government's Indian policies as a genocide. Ostler, *Surviving Genocide.* Both logics were undergirded and justified through the rhetoric and ideology of Manifest Destiny and settler colonialism.

16. See, for example, the explication of how Americans memorialized postbellum Indian wars in Cothran, *Remembering the Modoc War,* or the landmark work of O'Brien, *Firsting and Lasting,* which vividly illustrates how early white settlers depicted the "extinction" of Native peoples in their early histories of American colonization; aggressively "replaced" Natives with Euro-American images, monuments, and property; and then promoted the idea that Native peoples no longer existed in the present, perpetrating the idea of the "disappearing Indian" and denying Native claims to "Indianness."

17. Turner's "Frontier Thesis" fed into the ideology of American exceptionalism, a point of view about the supremacy of the place of the United States in the world and in the history of nations widely embraced by Americans throughout the nineteenth century, and especially after the Civil War. For the most recent treatment of the embrace of this ideology, see Lang, *Contest of Civilizations.* The Frontier Thesis exerted immense power because it tapped into American fears that the nation would lose its identity once the West no longer needed to be settled. Traffic to the West, Turner said, had motivated most of the great political, economic, and social development in the nation's (still very short) history. Generations of American historians have levied criticism and critique at Turner, and the value of his work as history is doubtful. Its value as primary source evidence for the point of view expounded by the generation that pulled the United States from the 1800s into the American Century, however, is unmatched.

Turner and his intellectual descendants elevated the pioneer and the rugged individualist to supreme status in the process of western expansion and rarely considered the aid supplied by the state, which is why the regular army is largely absent from the earliest professional works of history on the West.

18. Utley, *Frontiersmen in Blue*, 5. Utley and the military historians of the middle and later decades of the twentieth century could write with greater freedom about the process of western settlement because their field had finally been freed of influence of economic determinism advocated by first wave of historians of American Empire, up to and including William Appleman Williams.

19. See Merk, *Manifest Destiny and Mission in American History*, which was among the first major works of history to question the inevitability of Manifest Destiny—and its success. Graebner, *Empire on the Pacific*, likewise forced historians to consider whether the process of Manifest Destiny was largely carried out in an ad hoc fashion or political planners clearly articulated a vision for settling the West.

20. See Kelly, "North American Crisis of the 1860s," 337–368; Richards *Breakaway Americas;* St. John, "Unpredictable America of William Gwin," 56–84. See also Isenberg and Richards, "Alternative Wests: Rethinking Manifest Destiny," in the recent special issue of the *Pacific Historical Review,* which argues for a robust scholarly reexamination of the idea of Manifest Destiny as a historical monolith.

21. Burge, *Failed Vision of Empire*.

22. The best example remains Ostler, *Plains Sioux and US Colonialism*.

23. This turn in the literature of the American West began in the 1980s, among the cohort of scholars including Patricia Nelson Limerick, Richard White, William Cronon, and Donald Wooster, who developed the "new western history." In particular, Limerick, *Legacy of Conquest,* asked probing questions about the nature and consequences of Manifest Destiny. On violence and its role in the history of the American West, see also Blackhawk, *Violence over the Land*; Kelman, *Misplaced Massacre;* Lindsay, *Murder State;* and Madley, *An American Genocide*.

24. This book will use "frontier" to describe the American West as it was both encountered and imagined by many of the monograph's principal actors. Nineteenth-century Americans viewed the frontier in Turnerian terms, as the zones of the West that had not yet come under the influence of American institutions or white settlement. One reason the frontier mattered so much when it came the regular army, moreover, and why the term is worth using in this text, is that soldiers who were on the "frontier" were far less of a threat to the republic. Keeping a "frontier army" away from the nation's centers of population and industry allowed the government to heed James Madison's warning that "a standing military force, with an overgrown Executive will not long be safe companions to liberty." "Madison Debates, June 29 [1787]."

25. In this way, Republicans functioned as an impediment to the creation of a more centralized federal government. For a sampling of the frameworks and debates on this issue, see Bensel, *Yankee Leviathan;* LaFeber, *New Empire*; Cummings, *Dominion from Sea to Sea;* Skocpol, *Protecting Soldiers and Mothers;* and Skowronek, *Building a New American State*. For a framework that considers federal power in the West, see Downs and Masur, *The World the*

Civil War Made. Downs and Masur offer the idea of the "stockade state," which suggests that federal power existed in the West but in limited spheres of influence.

26. Fully cognizant of the danger of engaging in "cameo" history, I have done my best to fully contextualize those places in the book where I have drawn on African American or Indigenous voices. Because most speakers presented here are white men, however, I am aware that even these efforts may seem disingenuous. I endeavored to follow the sources and I hope readers will understand how I arrived at the narrative presented herein. See Deloria, *We Talk, You Listen,* 39.

27. White, *The Republic for Which It Stands,* 104–105.

28. Adam Arenson, "John Gast's *American Progress*: Using Manifest Destiny to Forget the Civil War and Reconstruction," in Scharff, *Empire and Liberty,* 122–139 at 122.

Interlude: The Cadet

1. On July 1, 1828, Jefferson Davis was commissioned both brevet second lieutenant and second lieutenant in the infantry, the branch reflecting his middling rank in the list of that year's academy graduates. Heitman, *Historical Register and Dictionary of the United States Army,* 1:358.

2. Jefferson Davis to Mrs. Susannah Davis, August 2, 1824, in Roland, *Jefferson Davis Constitutionalist,* 1:2.

3. The number is almost certainly higher. For one brief exploration of total Confederate casualties, see Gary W. Gallagher, "Proximity and Numbers: Walter H. Taylor Shapes Confederate History and Memory," in Gallagher and Cushman, *Civil War Witnesses and Their Books,* 288n35.

4. A fourteen-volume project at Rice University, *The Jefferson Davis Papers,* which finished publication in 2015, offers a more complete set of Davis's writings and supersedes the Dunbar volumes as a scholarly edition of the papers.

5. Monroe et al., *Papers of Jefferson Davis,* 1:18; hereafter *PJD.*

6. All three of Taylor's daughters opted to marry soldiers. Ann Mackall Taylor wedded U.S. Army surgeon Robert C. Wood in 1829, Sarah married Davis in 1835, and Mary Elizabeth "Betty" Taylor married William Wallace Smith Bliss, eponym of Texas's Fort Bliss, in 1848. Taylor's son Richard also pursued military service, though as a volunteer in the Confederate army.

7. Included in *PJD,* 1:lx.

8. See, among other recent works, Karp, *This Vast Southern Empire,* esp. chap. 9; Waite, *West of Slavery;* Quigley, *Shifting Grounds;* May, *Manifest Destiny's Underworld;* Greenberg, *Manifest Manhood;* and Wolnisty, *A Different Manifest Destiny.*

9. See, for example Johnson, *River of Dark Dreams.* The West was also part and parcel of the capitalist project, but historians have most often focused on the region after the war. The influx of capital into the postbellum West, in aid of development, infrastructure, and internal improvements, reflected the apogee of this vision of controlling labor and the western landscape. See, for example, Black, *Global Interior.* For more on capitalism in the postbellum West, see also Robbins, *Colony and Empire;* and White, *Railroaded.* For an equivalent study of similar transformations in the New South, see Bryan, *Price of Permanence.*

10. Karp, *This Vast Southern Empire;* Waite, *West of Slavery.*

11. Brettle, *Colossal Ambitions;* Zvengrowski, *Jefferson Davis.*

12. Ammann, "Jefferson Davis: Secretary of War." See also Ramsdell, "Natural Limits of Slave Expansion," which concluded that the territory west of modern-day central Texas "would never have become suitable for plantation slavery" (97). Today we would understand Ramsdell's claim to state that plantation slavery could not have flourished on the western side of the 100th meridian, which runs just west of present-day Abilene, Texas. The 100th meridian marks the eastern edge of the Great Plains, and indicates the point at which annual rainfall drops off so significantly that large-scale agriculture becomes impossible without the aid of substantial irrigation.

13. Calhoun's most influential suggestion, organizing the army around an "expansible" model, was never officially adopted as policy. Calhoun invested heavily in repairing and increasing the nation's seacoast defenses, many of which would become a focal point in the Civil War. He also advocated for the creation of the Bureau of Indian Affairs, which was initially housed in the War Department, before it moved to the newly created Department of the Interior in 1849. The question of which cabinet office would control the bureau plagued Congress for several decades, with both War and Interior ministers arguing for their superiority when it came to serving the interests and needs of the nation's Indigenous people. The federal government ultimately opted to keep the bureau in the Interior Department, under civilian management. On Calhoun, see Elder, *Calhoun.* On the Bureau of Indian Affairs, see Genetin-Pilawa, *Crooked Paths to Allotment.*

1. The Proslavery Empire of Jefferson Davis, 1852–1856

1. Both Davis's predecessor in the office, Charles Magill Conrad of Louisiana, and his successor, John B. Floyd of Virginia, were slaveholders like the Mississippian. In his memoirs, Abner Doubleday charged Floyd with using his tenure in office to support slaveholders, writing, "The new President [Buchanan] was hardly inaugurated before his Secy of War, Mr. Floyd of Va., began to take action with a view to assist the secessionists when the moment came for them to act." Doubleday, *My Life in the Old Army,* 182.

2. In a study that examined select congressional votes from 1838 to 1855, William B. Skelton found that Whigs supported the army to the same extent as Democrats. Skelton also noted that during the era of the Second Party System (approximately 1828–1852), military policy was relatively insignificant "as an issue in party conflict." Skelton, *American Profession of Arms,* 296.

3. Davis sought to expand chattel slavery as it was practiced in the American South. It was a form of enslavement that typically involved white enslavers forcing enslaved Black men, women, and children to labor on agricultural plantations. Other forms of slavery existed in the United States, and in the American West, where legacies of both debt peonage and economies of captivity had operated before European arrival, through both French and Spanish control, and after the war with Mexico.

4. "Annual Report of the Secretary of War," 36th Cong., 2nd Sess. Military employment ranged from 77.6 percent of total federal employment in 1816 to 44.1 percent in 1851. See Ericson, "United States Military," 131.

5. From 1849 to 1860, for example, a total of 20,393 soldiers saw duty in Texas alone. Breeden, "Health of Early Texas," 363.

6. Hsieh, *West Pointers and the Civil War,* 91. Winders, *Mr. Polk's Army,* notes that the army "fared poorly" after the Mexican–American War (206). George T. Ness Jr.'s history of the antebellum army calls the regulars "a miniature army." Ness, *Regular Army on the Eve of the Civil War,* 1. One early book on the mobilization of Civil War armies speculated that there may have been enough regular troops in 1861 "for the policing of New York City," but not for the task of occupying the frontier. Shannon, *Organization and Administration of the Union Army,* 27. Historian James M. McPherson describes the antebellum army as "pitifully inadequate" and "tiny." McPherson, *Battle Cry of Freedom,* 250. Historian Mark R. Wilson similarly characterizes the antebellum national fighting force as "arthritic" and "moribund" in his analysis of state power in the decades before the Civil War. Wilson, *Business of Civil War,* 64.

7. *Daily National Intelligencer,* January 4, 1855.

8. *North American and United States Gazette,* January 20, 1855.

9. Woods, *Arguing until Doomsday,* 118–120.

10. Albert G. Brown to Jefferson Davis, January 1, 1853, *PJD,* 5:3–4.

11. Weigley, *History of the United States Army,* 189–190.

12. Jefferson Davis to Ethan Allen Hitchcock, June 3, 1853, *PJD,* 5:18–19.

13. Jefferson Davis to Montgomery C. Meigs, June 3, 1853, *PJD,* 5:19.

14. For the history and iconography of the liberty cap, especially as it related to the American Revolution, see Lurie, "Liberty Poles," 673–697.

15. Jefferson Davis to Montgomery Meigs, January 15, 1856, *PJD,* 6:7.

16. *PJD,* 6:8n4.

17. Pierce urged the increase in his first annual message to Congress, while Davis advised the same course in his annual report on the state of the War Department.

18. "Increase and Better Organization of the Army," 33rd Cong., 2nd Sess., H. Rep. No. 40, 2.

19. *Congressional Globe,* 33rd Cong., 2nd Sess., 514.

20. Ibid., 516.

21. This argument drew on rhetoric that had defined America's relationship to landholding and sovereignty since the era of the Early Republic. American officials spent the first decades of the nineteenth century proclaiming territorial sovereignty across vast swathes of the continent. Thomas Jefferson's acquisition of the Louisiana Territory, for example, proved to be the crown jewel in the third president's proposed "Empire of Liberty," which historian Peter Onuf argues purposely excluded Natives and those of African descent from citizenship or rights of sovereignty. Onuf contends that the views espoused by Jefferson would have been embraced by a majority of those in power and that Jefferson's imperialism was not incompatible with that of Andrew Jackson, though they represented divergent political parties. Onuf, *Jefferson's Empire.* Similar logic of empire via military coercion was widely accepted by the British and many American loyalists during the American Revolution. Gould, *Persistence of Empire.*

22. *Congressional Globe,* 33rd Cong., 2nd Sess., 517.

23. Ibid., 528.

24. Simpson, *Cry Comanche,* vii.

25. There is some statistical evidence to suggest that in terms of promotions and appointments, southern-born officers did benefit from pro-southern control over the War Department. In his deeply researched statistical study of the antebellum army, George T. Ness Jr. found that it took an officer, on average, twenty-two years to rise to the rank of colonel of cavalry, thirty-seven to become a colonel of infantry, and forty-four years to become a colonel of artillery. Only six regimental commanders in the antebellum force reached their new rank ahead of the average time, and "five were from southern states." Southern-born officers, moreover, controlled six of the seven geographic departments managed by the army in 1860. Only Major General John E. Wool of Troy, New York, in command of the Department of the East, represented the free states at the highest level of army command—and he commanded the fewest troops of any department, by some margin. Ness also noted that the administrative departments of Surgeon General, Quartermaster, Topographical Engineers, Subsistence, and Ordnance all were headed by southern-born officers in 1860. Ness, *Regular Army on the Eve of the Civil War,* 9-10.

26. Expropriation of Indigenous land also occurred outside of the American South, detailed most notably in Bowes, *Land Too Good for Indians.* The point about the relationship among capitalism, slave expansion, and Indian removal is especially pertinent in the wake of the Mexican–American War, which was waged, in part, to gain new territory for the expansion of slavery.

27. Adams, "An Annotated Edition of the Personal Letters of Robert E. Lee, April 1855–April 1861."

28. In his memoirs written after the Civil War, cavalryman William Woods Averell recalled that while he was posted to Carlisle Barracks, Pennsylvania, in 1856, "conversations in our mess and in quarters upon the questions of the day, and the possibilities and results of a conflict between the North and the South were prognosticated and discussed . . . [but] the views of all were crude and undeveloped. Whatever conflict may come would be within the Union. There was not any expression, and I believe there was no thought, of any possible disunion of the States." Averell's memory suggests that soldiers were acutely aware of the political questions at issue during the 1850s, but his admission of the uninformed opinions of many officers suggests varying degrees of investment in political issues on the part of his compatriots. Eckert and Amato, *Ten Years in the Saddle,* 71.

29. Lee to Joseph G. Totten, June 17, 1845, in Letterbook 1, DeButts-Ely Collection of Lee Family Papers, Manuscripts Division, Library of Congress.

30. Edmund Kirby Smith to Mother, July 31, 1856, quoted in Parks, *General Edmund Kirby Smith,* 89–90.

31. Lee, *Personal Letters,* 141.

32. Robinson, "Kiowa and Comanche Campaign of 1860," 398.

33. Sedgwick, *Correspondence of John Sedgwick,* 2:10. Despite being a capable officer, Sedgwick is perhaps known to Civil War historians for the elaphantine circumstances surrounding his mortal wounding at the Battle of Spotsylvania.

34. Averell, *Ten Years in the Saddle,* 59.

35. Unidentified newspaper quoted in Johnston, *Life of General Albert Sidney Johnston,* 192. Johnston's service as the secretary of war for the Republic of Texas from 1838 to 1840

doubtless bolstered his reputation among Texans. The state's residents were so attached to Johnston, in fact, that after his death at the Battle of Shiloh, in 1862, the legislature of Texas requested that his body be disinterred from a grave in New Orleans and moved to the Texas State Cemetery in Austin.

36. "Annual Report of the Secretary of War," 31st Cong., 1st Sess., 3. Language to a similar effect appeared on the first page of each of Conrad's subsequent reports.

37. *Appendix to the Congressional Globe,* 32nd Cong., 1st Sess. (April 29, 1852), 542.

38. Frazer, *Mansfield on the Condition of Western Forts,* 67. Mansfield, born in 1803, was one of the oldest officers killed in action during the Civil War, in the fighting in the East Woods at the 1862 Battle of Antietam.

39. To facilitate this transition in strategy, Jefferson Davis commissioned Captain William Hardee to produce a new infantry tactics manual for the rifled musket and improved munitions. Hardee based his *Rifle and Light Infantry Tactics* on the practices of the French *chasseurs à pied,* considered at the time to be the epitome of light infantry. These mobile units could operate independently of a larger body of troops and range farther from a supply base, two requirements of Indian scouting. The War Department convened a tactics review board at West Point in 1854 and made cadets demonstrate Hardee's drills. The department approved Hardee's text, giving the army something of value for work in the West. Hope, *A Scientific Way of War,* 195; see also Smith, "Fort Inge and Texas Frontier Military Operations, 1849-1869," 1-25.

40. "General Estimate of Funds Required for the Service of the Quartermasters Department at Fort Duncan Texas, in the Month of February 1861," Fort Duncan Records, 1857-1861, box 2H431, folder Misc. Papers 1860s, packet 2, Briscoe Center for American History, University of Texas, Austin.

41. "Monthly Report of Forage, November 1860," Fort Duncan Records, ibid.; the November delivery would have cost slightly more than ninety dollars.

42. "Reports of Persons and Articles Hired for November 1860," Fort Duncan Records, ibid.

43. Rister, *Robert E. Lee in Texas,* 89-90.

44. Hood, *Advance and Retreat,* 8.

45. Hood's Texans, from the First, Fourth, and Fifth Texas Infantry regiments, were, along with the Third Arkansas, the only Confederate regiments hailing from west of the Mississippi River to serve in the war's Eastern Theater.

46. Biggs quoted in Rister, *Robert E. Lee in Texas,* 90-91.

47. Data from Elder and Weber, *Trading in Santa Fe,* xx.

48. Wooster, "Fort Davis and the Antebellum Military Frontiers," 59.

49. Letter from E. C. Palmer to Governor H. R. Runnels, October 4, 1858, copied in Walter Prescott Webb Papers, 1857-1966, box 2M277, folder Research Notes: Indians, Briscoe Center for American History, University of Texas, Austin.

50. Adams, "Personal Letters of Robert E. Lee," 579.

51. The networks of slavery in the Southwest were incredibly complex. As detailed in Brooks, *Captives and Cousins,* slave raiding was common among both the Hispanic and Native communities. Women and children, as well as livestock, moved among societies by the thou-

sands. In the Southwest the concept of slavery embraced myriad forms and degrees of servitude or coercion, in addition to highly nuanced gradations of adoption into the slaveholding society. As a result, slavery penetrated the collective culture of the region. Because the forms of slavery practiced were not racialized in the same way as on a plantation or in chattel slaveholding, they were less culturally legible to the new American occupants of the Southwest borderlands. See also Reséndez, *The Other Slavery.*

52. Averell, *Ten Years,* 108, 110.

53. In Texas, historian Miguel Ángel González-Quiroga has written, local elites in the region adopted or tolerated Anglo settler attitudes toward slavery because "slavery was decisively bound up with the cotton economy and prosperity." After the Texas Revolution, however, Anglo racial attitudes toward Mexican and Hispanic people hardened. Slavery was abolished in Mexico in 1829. González-Quiroga, *War and Peace on the Rio Grande Frontier,* 37–38.

54. Kiser, *Borderlands of Slavery,* 25, 41, 52.

55. Averell, *Ten Years,* 133.

56. Lahti, *Cultural Construction of Empire,* 4.

57. Frazier, *Mansfield on the Condition of Western Forts,* 6–7.

58. Kiser, *Borderlands of Slavery,* 117–118.

59. Goetzmann, *Army Exploration in the American West,* 4–5. The growth of new historical fields of inquiry since the era of Goetzmann has introduced new questions about the environment, nature, and the relationship between science and colonization. Amy Kohout's monograph is one example of this newer wave of work, arguing that soldiers in the postbellum Indian wars and Philippine–American War placed their experience in and understandings of nature at the center of Progressive-era debates about American imperialism. Kohout, *Taking the Field.*

60. Pope (like Davis) was working under assumptions gathered from previous military surveys of the region, including one carried out in 1849 by Randolph B. Marcy. Marcy's map was an optimistic appraisal of both the land and the ease of passage across the southern Plains. Indeed, in his journals, Marcy noted that over the greater portion of the area he covered, the terrain was so perfectly level that "it would appear to have been designed by the great architect of the universe for a railroad," a prophetic statement that was soon tested by the surveys for the Pacific Railway. See "Route from Fort Smith to Santa Fe," 31st Cong.

61. Johnson, *Soldier's Reminiscences in Peace and War,* 129.

62. "Scraps preserved by N. M. for H. W. M.," Merrill Collection, 1833–1897, Henry E. Huntington Library, San Marino, California.

63. The expedition was such a failure that Walter Prescott Webb, in his extensive analysis of the quest to find water on the Great Plains, relegated Pope to a footnote in a fifty-page chapter on the history of water in the region. As Webb detailed, and Pope could not have known, the invention necessary to bring to the surface the water the young army officer found below the Llano Estacado was the windmill. Pope, being no Don Quixote, had to content himself with tilting at the high plains of the Permian Basin. See Webb, *Great Plains,* esp. chap. 8; on Pope, 535n42.

64. "Annual Report of Captain A. A. Humphreys," 22.

65. Cotterill, "Memphis Railroad Convention, 1849," 93.

66. *Texas State Gazette,* November 22, 1863.

67. For a full account of the exploits of the Camel Corps and the men who managed them, see Lesley, *Uncle Sam's Camels.*

68. Seward, *Slaveholding Class Dominant in the Republic,* 11.

Interlude: The Runaway

1. Frederick Douglass, "The Anti-Slavery Movement," speech included in Douglass, *My Bondage and My Freedom,* 363.

2. Civil War historian David Herbert Donald, in his biography of the senator, does note that the Burns case stoked Sumner's passion for abolition. See Donald, *Charles Sumner and the Rights of Man,* 260–267.

3. Sumner, "Crime against Kansas," 46–47.

4. Though it is often regarded as the least consequential of the measures included in the omnibus compromise, the issue of Texas was of great concern to many, including President Zachary Taylor. Taylor hoped the national legislature could reach an agreement that would keep Texans out of New Mexico. The president felt that "Southern men" in Congress were using the New Mexico issue "to bring on civil war." Taylor personally assured First Lieutenant Alfred Pleasonton, the twenty-six-year-old army officer then en route to join the Second United States Dragoons in the territory, that he had ordered reinforcements from the army to New Mexico to resist an invasion by Texas. If necessary, Taylor claimed, "I will be with you myself . . . before those people shall go into that country or have a foot of that territory. The whole business is infamous and must be put down." Taylor's assertion that he would, as president, ride at the head of the American army was the first instance since George Washington during the Whiskey Rebellion that the sitting executive seems to have seriously contemplated joining troops in the field. In suggesting such an action Taylor, like Washington, explored the idea that the title of Commander in Chief was not merely symbolic, spurred to this consideration by an extraordinary crisis, just as the first president had been. See Pleasonton's letter to Thurlow Weed, September 22, 1876, in Barnes, *Memoir of Thurlow Weed,* 2:180. On Washington during the Whiskey Rebellion, see Slaughter, *Whiskey Rebellion.*

5. Campbell, *Slave Catchers.*

6. Stevenson, *Journals of Charlotte Forten Grimké,* 65–66.

7. Higginson, "Massachusetts in Mourning," 5.

8. Thoreau, "Slavery in Massachusetts," in *Essays,* 172–189 at 175. Like his fellow transcendentalist Ralph Waldo Emerson, Thoreau viewed the military conquest of Mexico as the root of many of the nation's most divisive issues. Emerson had predicted in 1846 that "the US will conquer Mexico, but it will be as the man swallows the arsenic, which brings him down in turn. Mexico will poison us." See Porte, *Emerson in His Journals,* 275.

9. See Dana's remarks in *Boston Slave Riot,* 63.

10. Sumner, Crime against Kansas, 46–47.

11. Young, *God Greater than Man,* 15.

12. *Congressional Globe,* 35th Cong., 1st Sess. (May 13, 1858), 1073.

2. Republicans versus Regulars, 1854–1861

1. *Congressional Globe,* 34th Cong., 1st Sess., 399.

2. Varon, *Disunion,* 262.

3. Foner, *Free Soil.*

4. "To Pass H.R. 667, Bill Relating to Army Appropriations," House vote no. 473 in 1859 (35th Congress), February 21, 1859, GovTrack, https://www.govtrack.us/congress/votes/35-2/h473.

5. In Michael F. Holt's field-defining work on the Whig Party, for example, there are no index entries for "Army," "Military," or "United States Army," despite the monograph covering the period of the Mexican war as well as Bleeding Kansas. Jefferson Davis's term as secretary of war is mentioned in passing on page 776. Holt, *Rise and Fall of the American Whig Party.*

6. See Foner, *Free Soil;* Gienapp, *Origins of the Republican Party.*

7. The only men hailing from nonslaveholding states to chair the committee were, in the Senate, William Henry Harrison of Ohio (Nineteenth Congress and half of the Twentieth), James Shields of Illinois (Thirty-Third), and John B. Weller of California (Thirty-Fourth); and in the House, William Eustis of Massachusetts (Seventeenth Congress) and Benjamin Stanton of Ohio (Thirty-Sixth). Andrew Jackson chaired the Senate committee in the Eighteenth Congress; Martin Van Buren's vice president, Richard Mentor Johnson, chaired it in the twenty-second, twenty-third, and twenty-fourth House congressional sessions.

8. See, for example, Quigley, *Shifting Grounds.*

9. *Congressional Globe,* 31st Cong., 1st Sess. (March 25, 1850), 378.

10. Heitman, *Historical Register,* 1:242. Colonels John J. Abert, Edmund B. Alexander, Philip S. G. Cooke, John Garland, Thomas Lawson, Matthew M. Payne, Washington Sewall, and George H. Thomas all were Virginians from the old army who remained loyal to the Union. Overall, 35 percent of West Point graduates from Virginia remained loyal to the Union, 56 percent joined the Confederacy, 8 percent did not fight for either side in the war, and 2 percent resigned. See Wayne Wei-siang Hsieh, "'I Owe Virginia Little, My Country Much': Robert E. Lee, the United States Regular Army, and Unconditional Unionism," in Ayers, Gallagher, and Torget, *Crucible of the Civil War,* 37.

11. Charles Stearns to Charles Sumner, October 2, 1855, quoted in Mullis, *Peacekeeping on the Plains,* 44.

12. Edwin Sumner to Samuel Cooper, July 7, 1856, quoted in "Governor Geary's Administration," in *Transactions of the Kansas State Historical Society,* 373–374.

13. Holloway, *History of Kansas,* 375.

14. Reported in various newspapers. See, for example, *Burlington Free Press,* July 25, 1856.

15. Sumner, quoted in the *Daily American Organ,* July 10, 1856.

16. *Buffalo Daily Republic,* September 16, 1856.

17. *Chicago Democratic Press,* July 5, 1856; *Burlington Free Press,* July 25, 1856; *Hillsdale Standard,* July 29, 1856.

18. Wendell Phillips, quoted in *National Anti-Slavery Standard,* August 16, 1856.

19. *Carolina Spartan,* August 14, 1856; *North American,* July 18, 1854.

20. "Franklin Pierce to the Senate of the United States, August 4, 1856," 1.

21. Ibid.; Davis to Edwin Sumner and George Cooke, February 15, 1856, 2; Samuel Cooper to Sumner, March 26, 1856, 3; Davis to Sumner, May 23, 1856, 5.

22. Potter, *Impending Crisis,* 204–206.

23. See letter and notes in *PJD,* 6:41–42.

24. *PJD,* 6:111.

25. *Chicago Journal,* August 22, 1856; *New York Herald,* August 9, 1856.

26. *Congressional Globe,* 34th Cong., 1st Sess. (July 24, 1856), 1751–1752.

27. Ibid., 1752–1753. Whitfield's concluding line can be found in another speech delivered against the threat of military occupation. In Jefferson Davis's inaugural address as president of the Confederacy, in response to Abraham Lincoln's call for 300,000 volunteers to suppress the rebellion, Davis declared, "We seek no conquest, no aggrandizement . . . all we ask is to be let alone." Roland, *Jefferson Davis Constitutionalist,* 5:84.

28. *Appendix to the Congressional Globe,* 34th Cong., 1st Sess., 528.

29. *Congressional Globe,* 34th Cong., 1st Sess., 443. Keitt backed his threat with action and rose to be a colonel in the Confederate Army before he was mortally wounded at the Battle of Cold Harbor.

30. Krug, *Lyman Trumbull.*

31. Appendix to the *Congressional Globe,* 34th Cong., 1st Sess., 206.

32. Krug, *Lyman Trumbull,* 125–126.

33. William Henry Seward, *Speech of Hon. William H. Seward for the Immediate Admission of Kansas into the Union,* 14. On the abolition argument, see, for example, William Ellery Channing: "If one man may be rightfully reduced to slavery, then there is not a human being on whom the same chain may not be imposed." Channing, *Slavery,* 15.

34. *Congressional Globe,* 34th Cong., 1st Sess., 482.

35. Appendix to the *Congressional Globe,* 34th Cong., 1st Sess., 1095.

36. *New York Times,* September 2, 1856.

37. *Milwaukee Daily Sentinel,* July 10, 1856.

38. *National Era,* July 31, 1856.

39. Blassingame et al., *Frederick Douglass Papers,* 3:125.

40. *New York Herald,* August 24, 1856; *New York Tribune,* September 1, 1856.

41. *Western Democrat,* September 2, 1856. Nathaniel Banks, a Republican senator from Massachusetts, seems to have been the first person to use the phrase "Let the Union slide," at a rally in Portland, Maine, in 1855. When he was asked if he would be willing to maintain slavery in the United States, Banks replied that he would prefer to "let the Union slide."

42. In her history of the coming of the Civil War, historian Elizabeth R. Varon writes that disunion rhetoric "shaped and limited Americans' political and moral imagination, ultimately discouraging a politics of compromise and lending an aura of inexorability to the cataclysmic confrontation of North and South." Varon, *Disunion,* 2. Ultimately, the regular army represented an element of national Unionism—a federal institution that drew men from all sections and parties to serve the same interests. Threatening the survival of the army, on the part of the

Republicans, was an equally viable threat to the Union. For an explanation of why nineteenth-century Americans so valued the concept of Union, see Gallagher, *Union War;* Stampp, *Imperiled Union,* esp. chap. 1, "The Concept of a Perpetual Union," 3–36.

43. *Charleston Standard,* September 10, 1856.

44. "To Pass H.R. 667," House vote. For the Senate vote see "To Pass H.R. 667," Senate vote no. 640 in 1859 (35th Congress), February 26, 1859, GovTrack, https://www.govtrack.us/congress/votes/35-2/s640.

45. "Senex" to Jefferson Davis, November 18, 1856, *PJD,* 6:60. The identity of Senex is not known. The Latin word loosely refers to an "old man" and was a popular figure, in various guises, in Roman theater.

46. *PJD,* 6:60. The importance of Thermopylae's historical example lies in its demonstration of the power of an army defending its home soil—and the image of Leonidas and the three hundred final Spartan defenders of the pass valiantly fighting against the armies of Xerxes, which may have numbered in the hundreds of thousands. Herodotus claims the Greeks inflicted 20,000 causalities on the Persians over three days of fighting, losing perhaps two thousand to four thousand of their own troops. For a summary of the historical and tactical importance of Thermopylae, see Lendon, *Soldiers and Ghosts,* 59–61; the main source for the battle of 480 is Herodotus, *Histories,* 7:201–233.

47. Furniss, *Mormon Conflict,* 29.

48. *Mormoniad,* 5, 21.

49. Ibid., 22.

50. *Kanzas News,* May 22, 1858.

51. *Congressional Globe,* 35th Cong., 1st. Sess. (April 1, 1858), 1431.

52. *Congressional Globe,* 35th Cong., 1st Sess. (March 20, 1858), 1222.

53. *Congressional Globe,* 34th Cong., 1st Sess. (April 7, 1856), 456.

Interlude: The Senator

1. Jefferson Davis, "Speech in the US Senate (Farewell Address), January 21, 1861," in Cooper, *Jefferson Davis: Essential Writings,* 193–194.

2. Crane, *Red Badge of Courage,* 3.

3. "The loyal American citizenry," historian Gary W. Gallagher reminds us, "fought a war for Union that also killed slavery." Gallagher, *Union War,* 1.

4. Altogether, there were 1,098 officers in the U.S. Army in December 1860. For detailed statistics, see Bensel, *Yankee Leviathan,* 119.

5. Subtracting 4 million enslaved African Americans from the overall 1860 population of 31.5 million leaves 27.5 million—the total white population of the country. Of these, 5.5 million lived in eventual Confederate states. Thirty percent of the nation's white population lived in the slaveholding states, but Delaware, Kentucky, Maryland, and Missouri did not secede.

6. For statistics and quotation, see Hsieh, "'I Owe Virginia Little, My Country Much': Robert E. Lee, the United States Regular Army, and Unconditional Unionism," in *Crucible of the Civil War,* ed. Ayers, Gallagher, and Torget, 37.

7. Howard, Sherman, and Oliver, *Committee of Three.*

8. *Congressional Globe,* 37th Cong., 2nd Sess. (December 23, 1861), 164.

9. In 1862, Gideon Welles, Lincoln's naval secretary, indicated that this point of view extended to the cabinet: "Something more is wanted for a good general—talent, intuition, magnetic power, which West Point cannot give." Entry for August 17, 1862, in Gienapp and Gienapp, *Civil War Diary of Gideon Welles,* 10.

10. In multiple letters over the first six months of the war, William Sherman explained to his brother why he believed the war had to be managed by professional soldiers and not by the volunteers that Republicans cherished. The officer's words seemed to have little effect, though John Sherman told his older brother that he expected William to attain a high rank during the war and to "play a high part in the tragedy." See John Sherman to William Sherman, April 14, 1861, in Thorndike, *Sherman Letters,* 114. The series of letters concerned with William T. Sherman's advocacy for professional troops began on May 20, 1861, in which the officer affirmed that "paper soldiers won't do" (121), particularly in a war that required the invasion and occupation of the South. See also the letter of May 24, 1861. In his memoirs, John Sherman admitted that, looking back at the war's earliest days from the vantage point of 1895, he could see that his brother "had a better conception of the magnitude and necessities of war than civilians like myself." Sherman, *Recollections,* 1:245.

3. The Republican War within the War, 1861–1865

1. Lincoln, *Collected Works,* 4:354.

2. *Congressional Globe,* 37th Cong., 1st Sess. (July 11, 1861), 72.

3. Ibid., 73.

4. Grant, Papers of Ulysses S. Grant, 8:385; hereafter PUSG.

5. Indeed, even for statistical purposes the numbers of regular troops were always separated from the numbers of volunteer soldiers enlisted in Union armies. The regular army increased to thirty regiments during the war (nineteen infantry, six cavalry, and five artillery) but never numbered more than 25,463 troops. See Phisterer, *Statistical Record of the Armies of the United States,* 21, 62.

6. Kreidberg and Henry, *History of Military Mobilization,* 109.

7. Rafuse, "United States' Experience with Volunteer and Conscript Forces," 19.

8. Though significant in the legislative history of the war, the Joint Committee has received relatively little attention from scholars. When looking for opposition to the Lincoln administration, historians have typically investigated the activities of Democratic Copperheads rather than the Radicals within the president's own party. One notable exception is Bruce Tap, who has offered two excellent studies dealing with the committee. See Tap, *Over Lincoln's Shoulder;* and Tap, "Inevitability, Masculinity, and the American Military Tradition," 19–46.

9. For a markedly negative view of the Radicals' behavior in this regard, see Williams, *Lincoln and the Radicals.* A more measured view can be found in Trefousse, *Radical Republicans.*

10. See Skelton, *American Profession of Arms,* 356, table 18.2.

11. Notable exceptions were western battles often ignored by legislators, foreign observers, and the press. Victories at Forts Henry and Donelson, as well as at Shiloh, in addition to Union success in turning around Braxton Bragg's invasion of Kentucky, paled in comparison to the

failure to take Richmond and the debacles at the Second Battle of Bull Run and Fredericksburg. Lack of attention to western successes proved agonizing for Lincoln. "It seems unreasonable," the president wrote, "that a series of successes, extending through half-a-year, and clearing more than one hundred thousand miles of territory, should help us so little, while a single half-defeat [the Seven Days] should hurt us so much." Lincoln, *Collected Works,* 5:355–356.

12. *Congressional Globe,* 37th Cong., 2nd Sess. (January 7, 1862), 201.

13. Heather Cox Richardson, in a popular history of the Republican Party, explains that, prodded by the needs of the Union cause, Republicans "created a new, strong, national government that worked to develop the economy from the bottom, educating young men and giving them land to farm." Richardson, *To Make Men Free,* xiv.

14. Limerick, *Legacy of Conquest.*

15. Dean, *Agrarian Republic,* 82.

16. Richardson, *To Make Men Free,* 18–20.

17. Dean, *Agrarian Republic,* 99.

18. Richardson, *To Make Men Free,* 18–20.

19. *Congressional Globe,* 37th Cong., 2nd Sess., 910.

20. William Seward, quoted in F. Seward, *Seward at Washington,* 359.

21. *New York Tribune,* May 7, 1862.

22. John Sherman to William T. Sherman, May 30, 1861, in Thorndike, *Sherman Letters,* 116–117. John Sherman deemed the desertion "treachery."

23. *Congressional Globe,* 37th Cong., 2nd Sess., 165.

24. "Annual Report of the Secretary of War," 37th Cong., 1st Sess., 27–28.

25. T. Harry Williams investigated the anti–West Point feeling of Radicals. Williams, "Attack on West Point during the Civil War," 491–504.

26. *Congressional Globe,* 37th Cong., 2nd Sess., 328.

27. Abraham Lincoln's Indian policy, meanwhile, promoted the colonization of Native land as necessary for the advancement of the Republican Party's free labor vision. As historian David Nichols writes, "[Lincoln's] sympathies for Indians, however genuine, never altered his priorities for the development he deemed essential to the prosecution of the Civil War and the nation's destiny. . . . Thus, he ordered the continued removal and concentration of Indian tribes while espousing reform of the Indian System. Lincoln never really faced the contradiction inherent in his desire for the West, 'to render it secure for the advancing settler, and to provide for the welfare of the Indian.'" Nichols, *Lincoln and the Indians,* 119. Maynard's rhetoric suggests that Republicans were so blinded by their reputation as reformers that they failed to see the limits of their efforts—or they cast the blame onto their political opponents.

28. *Congressional Globe,* 37th Cong., 2nd Sess., 328.

29. This argument could be seen as an extension of that in O'Brien, *Firsting and Lasting,* which explored how the earliest white Americans erased the existence of Native nations to lay claims to their land and deny them legal, political, and social rights. The Republican Party's public obfuscation of their reliance on the army allowed them to deny culpability in the most egregious elements of settler-colonial policy while benefiting from its results. As Boyd Cothran has shown in his work on the Modoc War, which is also an extension of O'Brien's arguments,

nineteenth-century Americans created political, social, cultural, and memorial frameworks to justify their territorial acquisitions, conquest, violence, and colonialism as inevitable and even redemptive. Cothran, *Remembering the Modoc War.*

30. *Congressional Globe,* 37th Cong., 2nd Sess., 328.

31. Smith, *Civil War in America,* 52.

32. *Cincinnati Gazette,* July 11. 1861.

33. *Hydraulic Press,* July 27, 1861.

34. *New York Tribune,* December 14, 1861.

35. Ellet, *Military Incapacity and What It Costs the Country,* 10. Ellet was a professional engineer who wrote numerous treatises on military science. He received his military education in France, at the École nationale des ponts et chaussées. He volunteered for Civil War service and was wounded in the First Battle of Memphis in 1862. The only Union casualty in the fight, he died from his wounds in late June.

36. *Congressional Globe,* 37th Cong., 2nd Sess. (December 23, 1861), 164.

37. Julian, "The Rebellion," 202, 204.

38. Jonathan W. White shows that Republican politicans made abolition a test of orthodoxy in the army and used army discipline to force out officers who disagreed—many of them professional soldiers who were reassigned or removed. White, *Emancipation.*

39. Fry, *Republic in the Ranks.*

40. As early as the war of 1812, militias demonstrated that they brought little of military value when called upon to respond to national threats. In the antebellum United States, militia meetings were gatherings of social and political importance that put little emphasis on training or military education. By the 1820s, compulsory militias (as required by the militia act of 1792) had given way to volunteer militias, which were more fraternal organization than military company and reflected the failure of many states to compel men to serve as mandated by federal law. Dickson D. Bruce Jr. explains that in southern states, where militias were more popular, many units were little more than half full by the 1850s. Bruce, *Violence and Culture in the Antebellum South,* 167.

41. *Congressional Globe,* 37th Cong., 2nd Sess. (December 23, 1861), 164.

42. Anonymous to Zachariah Chandler (December 1861), James W. Newton to Chandler (January 9, 1862), and William E. Doubleday to Chandler (December 6, 1861), Chandler Papers, Library of Congress; F. M. Finan to Julian, January 26, 1862, Giddings-Julian Papers, Library of Congress.

43. *Congressional Globe,* 37th Cong., 2nd Sess., 1184.

44. *Congressional Globe,* 37th Cong., 2nd Sess., 1190.

45. *Congressional Globe,* 37th Cong., 2nd Sess. (December 23, 1861), 165.

46. *Congressional Globe,* 37th Cong., 2nd Sess., 135.

47. *Congressional Globe,* 37th Cong., 2nd Sess. (December 23, 1861), 165.

48. Indeed, most histories of education entirely neglect the military provision of the Morrill Acts. Rudolph, *American College and University,* for instance, omits, without even any ellipses, the clause "and including military tactics," even when quoting the key paragraph of the act (252).

49. Quoted in Pollard, *Military Training in the Land-Grant Colleges and Universities,* 57–58.

50. *Congressional Globe,* 38th Cong., 1st Sess., 1058.

51. *Congressional Globe,* 37th Cong., 3rd Sess., 165, 324–327.

52. *Congressional Globe,* 37th Cong., 3rd Sess., 328–329. One editorialist in the *New York Journal of Commerce* wrote in support of West Point: "The aim is to force the resignation or procure the removal of these patriotic generals of conservative instincts and put in their place a lot of rabid politicians, who are guiltless of a West Point education." Quoted in *Detroit Free Press,* January 29, 1863.

53. Heitman, *Historical Register,* 2:285.

54. *Congressional Globe,* 38th Cong., 2nd Sess. (February 20, 1865), 920. Lyman Trumball, an Illinois Republican, informed senators that they should not be scared into preferring the regulars just because West Point had produced capable officers. "[General Sherman's] name is used to frighten us from doing a just and proper act."

55. *Philadelphia Age,* March 24, 1865.

56. George B. McClellan to the Democratic National Committee, September 8, 1864, in Sears, *Civil War Papers,* 595.

57. Sears, *Civil War Papers,* 135.

58. From almost the first moments of contact between Union armies and enslaved people in the Confederacy, it became clear to all observers that the war would significantly disrupt the institution of slavery. This fact should not have come as a surprise. The same patterns had played out in the American Revolution and the War of 1812 as enslaved people sought their freedom during the chaos caused by war—some through military service, others by making their way to enemy lines and demanding freedom, others by refusing to perform the work required to support the cause of their enslavers. Regardless of whether white Union soldiers supported the actions of enslaved Black Americans to seek their freedom, they could not escape confronting the mass movement of self-emancipation undergirded by the war. Politicians in Washington, likewise, sought solutions that would empower Union troops to take legal action against slavery in a way that would be defensible as part of the war effort—by dismantling the instruments of war vital to the Confederacy, which included a population of nearly 4 million enslaved people. See James M. McPherson, "Who Freed the Slaves?," 1–10, for an overview of the scholarly debate on wartime emancipation. See also Ayers, *Thin Light of Freedom;* Reidy, *Illusions of Emancipation;* Manning, *What This Cruel War Was Over.*

59. Though few Americans today question the maintenance of the country's vast military bureaucracy, Americans in the eighteenth and nineteenth centuries had a great deal of uneasiness about the nation's military forces, because large armies were antithetical to democratic republics. As Richard H. Kohn explains, wariness of large bodies of armed men was "central to the Revolutionary tradition, deeply interwoven with the language of independence and the birth of the United States as a nation." Kohn, *Eagle and Sword,* 6.

60. T. Harry Williams, "The Committee on the Conduct of the War: A Study of Civil War Politics" (PhD diss., University of Wisconsin, Madison, 1937), 43. Williams judged the Radical response "a concomitant of American war-time history," and he mustered little affection for

the Radicals in his work on the faction, *Lincoln and the Radicals,* frequently referring to them as "Jacobins."

61. *Congressional Globe,* 37th Cong., 2nd Sess., 83.

62. Joseph Medill to Edwin McMasters Stanton, January 21, 1862, Edwin McMasters Stanton Papers, 1818 to 1921, Correspondence, 1831–1870, folder January 14–February 2, 1862, Library of Congress, http://hdl.loc.gov/loc.mss/ms010150.mss41202.002.

63. Lincoln's reasoning for countermanding Frémont probably had more to do with the president's concern over alienating the border states of Missouri and Kentucky, where the federal government had to tread lightly to avoid provoking proslavery partisans to agitate for secession. See Lincoln's letter to Frémont in September 1861, which warned the general not to take any action that might "ruin our rather fair prospect for Kentucky." John C. Frémont, "Proclamation" (August 30, 1861), in *OR,* ser. 1, 3:466–467; Lincoln to Frémont, September 2, 1861, in Lincoln, *Collected Works,* 4:506–507.

64. Tap, *Over Lincoln's Shoulder,* 17.

65. As William A. Blair notes, the precedents and guidance of international law provided essential direction for understanding how the federal government could legally deal with Confederates and how they ought to define the conflict—whether as a war between two nations or an act of domestic insurrection. Confiscation could only be legal if the United States insisted it was waging war on a foreign power. As Blair puts it, the government had to manage "running a war against a domestic traitor who acted like a belligerent foreigner." Blair, *With Malice toward Some,* 80.

66. Letter from Abraham Lincoln to Orville H. Browning, September 22, 1861.

67. In his first message to Congress, Lincoln continued to promote colonization as the best possible outcome should emancipation become a widespread result of the war. Lincoln maintained a steady focus on the preservation of the Union as the war's paramount (and solitary) goal, saying he "thought it proper to keep the integrity of the Union prominent as the primary objective of the contest." Lincoln, *Collected Works,* 5:49.

68. White, *Trumbull,* 171–172.

69. Williams, *Lincoln and the Radicals,* 60.

70. "The Second Confiscation Act," Freedmen and Southern Society Project, http://www.freedmen.umd.edu/conact2.htm.

71. Marvel, *Radical Sacrifice,* 96.

72. In January 1864, the Democratic membership of the committee changed to Benjamin Harding of Ohio, Charles Buckalew of Pennsylvania, and Unconditional Unionist Benjamin F. Loan of Missouri, from the House. Wade and Chandler carefully designed the joint committee to ensure that its Democratic members would not impede their political objectives. The sole Democrat from the House, Odell, was an obscure first-term congressman who lacked a reputation that would have justified taking an outspoken role. Andrew Johnson, at the time of his appointment, was widely considered trustworthy by the Republican Party because of his strong denunciations of secession. The Democratic committee members, in other words, were less likely to frustrate Republicans than were the Democrats who were leading Union armies.

73. C. H. Nay to L. Trumbull, December 6, 1861, Lyman Trumbull Papers, Library of Congress; A. Denny to B. Wade, November 28, 1861, Wade Papers, Library of Congress; B. R. Wood to Charles Sumner, November 12, 1861, Charles Sumner Papers, Houghton Library, Harvard University; Edgar George to Zachariah Chandler, December 14, 1861, and J. J. Bagley to Chandler, December 6, 1861, Chandler Papers, Library of Congress.

74. Beale, *Diary of Edward Bates*, 229.

75. *Congressional Globe,* 37th Cong., 2nd Sess., 16–17.

76. *New York Herald,* April 10, 1863.

77. W. E. Doubleday to Chandler, December 6, 1861, Chandler Papers, Library of Congress.

78. Tap, "Inevitability, Masculinity, and the American Military Tradition," 21. Tap writes that committee members regarded "an educated professional officer corps as unnecessary and unrepublican, [and] Committee investigations often blamed military defeat on lackluster military professionals and recommended that right-thinking volunteer officers replace such officers" (21).

79. George B. to Mary Ellen McClellan, February 28, 1863, in Sears, *Civil War Papers,* 540.

80. Pfanz, "Surrender Negotiations," 66; Catton, *This Hallowed Ground,* 99; Commager et al., *Growth of the American Republic,* 1:713–714.

81. Tap, *Over Lincoln's Shoulder.*

82. Neely, *Union Divided,* 71.

83. Gideon Welles wrote in his diary on August 17, 1862, that the federal government had tried for too long to "adapt and reconcile the theory and instruction of West Point to the war that was being prosecuted." Welles, concurring with the judgments of the joint committee, observed that "our generals act on the defensive. It is not and has not been the policy of the country to be aggressive." Gienapp and Gienapp, *Civil War Diary of Gideon Welles,* 10.

84. The committee's investigation into George McClellan underscored its impatience with generals who were not pursuing a "hard war" that targeted Confederate property—including property in slaves. Tap, *Over Lincoln's Shoulder,* 101–102. Mark Grimsley notes that some Republican generals openly courted the favor of the joint committee by emphasizing their hard war bona fides. Grimsley, *Hard Hand of War,* 127.

85. Cunliffe, "Soldiers and Politicians in the American Civil War," 10.

86. Diary entry of July 21, 1862, in Chase, *Inside Lincoln's Cabinet,* 94–95.

87. *New York Daily Tribune,* June 26, 1862.

88. "Report of the Joint Committee on the Conduct of the War," 37th Cong., 3rd Sess., Rep. Com. No. 106, 279, 282.

89. *New York Tribune,* July 23, 1862.

90. Scott quoted in Sears, *Lincoln's Lieutenants,* 14.

91. Upton, *Military Policy of the United States from 1775,* 316. Upton also presciently observed that relying on a general whose views were at odds with the policy of the administration in a civil war created intractable problems, and he noted that for as long as George McClellan refused to accept emancipation as a war aim, his time in command of any Union forces would necessarily be limited. Upton did acknowledge that many soldiers and civilians agreed with

McClellan's views on emancipation, but according to Upton this did not matter when it was not in line with the policy of either the executive or the legislative branch of the government.

92. *Congressional Globe,* 37th Cong., 2nd Sess., 32. Wilson also affirmed that the committee would reveal to the American people the failures of professional soldiers. Wilson wanted the investigations into the conduct of the war to show "military men" that they could not advocate for "the preservation of the old Army" when confronted with "the responsibility of the errors of the past." In their early biography of Abraham Lincoln, John Nicolay and John Hay noted that Wade and Chandler had faith in the omnipotence of the legislature. They represented "the more ardent and eager spirits" of the legislative branch and wanted aggressive military action. When operations were not active enough, "they felt themselves formally entrusted with a mandate from the people to that effect." Nicolay and Hay, *Abraham Lincoln,* 5:150–151.

Interlude: The Parade

1. The canteen bears the trefoil insignia of the First Division of the Second Corps. During the war, Homer traveled with this division (in the Sixty-First New York Infantry regiment) as a war correspondent.

2. For an argument that this subversion also occurred during the Grand Review, see Zander, "Victory's Long Review," 45–77.

3. *Frank Leslie's Illustrated Newspaper,* July 13, 1867.

4. *New York Times,* May 7, 1865.

5. McClay, *The Masterless,* 11.

6. *Boston Post,* May 23, 1865.

7. Albert Harrison to his parents, June 3, 1865, DL1503.159, Nau Civil War Collection, Houston, Texas.

8. *New Haven Daily Palladium,* May 20, 1865; *Frank Leslie's Illustrated Newspaper,* June 10, 1865.

9. At the close of the Civil War, the United States still could claim never to have lost a war. The men (most of them southerners) who had served in the Confederate armies could no longer make this claim. The tradition of victory that the United States could claim only added to its sense of prestige and superiority. For a discussion of the effects of Confederate defeat and Union victory on the divergent sectional character of the North and the South, see Woodward, "Irony of Southern History."

10. *New York Times,* May 25, 1865.

11. *North American and United States Gazette,* May 23, 1865.

12. Adams, *Letter from Washington, 1863–1865,* 265–266.

13. Frank M. Guernsey to Fannie, May 26, 1865, DL301.089, Nau Civil War Collection, Houston, Texas.

14. *Caledonian,* May 26, 1865.

15. Mulholland, *Story of the 116th Regiment Pennsylvania Volunteers,* 401.

16. Beath, *History of the Grand Army of the Republic,* 9.

17. *OR,* ser. 3, 5:126.

18. Sherman to William Conant Church, July 18, 1874, William C. Church Papers, Library of Congress.

19. *Congressional Globe,* 39th Cong., 2nd Sess. (February 13, 1867), 1208.

4. The Republican Army, 1865–1872

1. One historian has recently identified Logan as "the most influential critic of the regulars." Wooster, *United States Army and the Making of America,* 234.

2. Logan, *Volunteer Soldier,* 411, 417, 419, 422.

3. In his work on the postbellum army, for example, Robert M. Utley writes that Congress "came close to spawning two armies—the forces occupying the South, beholden largely to Congress; and the army on the frontier . . . serving the Executive." Utley, *Cavalier in Buckskin,* 41. Harold Hyman, "Stanton, and Grant: A Reconsideration of the Army's Role in the Events Leading to Impeachment," makes the same argument, saying that "the first 'army' was assigned to relatively traditional duties," such as border patrols, Indian wars, and training troops. The second army, meanwhile, engaged in "the military government of large numbers of their countrymen," and was a "political issue" (85–100 at 86).

4. *Congressional Globe,* 41st Cong., 2nd Sess. (May 10, 1870), 3317.

5. The Republican Party's postwar treatment of the army underscored the uneven expansion of federal power across the country in the wake of the Civil War. The classic study of postbellum federal power is Bensel, *Yankee Leviathan.* See also Skocpol, *Protecting Soldiers and Mothers;* and Skowronek, *Building a New American State.*

6. Carter et al., *Historical Statistics of the United States.*

7. *Congressional Globe,* 39th Cong., 1st Sess. (May 4, 1866), 2383.

8. *Congressional Globe,* 39th Cong., 1st Sess. (January 16, 1866), 258.

9. *Congressional Globe,* 39th Cong., 1st Sess. (March 10, 1866), 1309.

10. Stevens, "Reconstruction—Speech in Lancaster, PA, September 6, 1865," in Palmer and Ochoa, *Selected Papers of Thaddeus Stevens,* 2:23.

11. Foner, *Reconstruction,* 241.

12. Ibid., 238.

13. *Congressional Globe,* 39th Cong., 1st Sess. (January 11, 1866), 193.

14. Foner, *Reconstruction,* 23.

15. Tariffs were the other strategy adopted by Republicans to decrease the national debt. The Civil War debt of $2.8 billion was erased during the 1880s by a $2.1 billion income from protective tariffs. These tariffs helped to support the Republican push for infrastructure construction—particularly railroads. Irwin, *Clashing over Commerce,* 221, 255.

16. Summers, *Ordeal,* 276.

17. Downs, *After Appomattox,* 203; Sefton, *United States Army and Reconstruction,* 202.

18. By the presidential election of 1872, conservative resistance to martial law in the former Confederacy had found its way into the Democratic Party's platform. "The public welfare requires the supremacy of the civil over the military authority," the platform declared, advocating "a return to the methods of peace and the constitutional limitations of power." "Democratic

Party Platforms: 1872 Democratic Party Platform," July 9, 1872, American Presidency Project, http://www.presidency.ucsb.edu/node/273178.

19. Wooster, *Military and United States Indian Policy,* 85.

20. "An Act to provide for the more efficient Government of the Rebel States," *United States Statutes at Large,* 14 Stat. 39, chap. 428, section 3.

21. According to *Civil War Times* 40, no. 6 (112), the Twenty-First New York Cavalry was the final unit to muster out, at Denver, on June 26, 1866. However, a check of the NPS Soldiers and Sailors Database shows the Fifty-Seventh United States Colored Troops mustering out on December 31, 1866, with a total of 189 units that completed their service in 1866. Some of the veteran reserve companies remained in service until August 1866, when the army reorganization bill ended their service terms.

22. Only five senators voted against the bill: Republicans James Grimes, Ira Harris, and Samuel J. Kirkwood; Democrat George Read Riddle; and Unionist Garrett Davis. *Congressional Globe,* 39th Cong., 1st Sess. (March 14, 1866), 1386.

23. The substitute bill passed 95–30. *Congressional Globe,* 39th Cong., 1st Sess. (July 9, 1866), 3684.

24. White, *Republic for Which It Stands,* 116.

25. Dobak and Phillips, *Black Regulars,* xiv.

26. "An Act to increase and fix the Military Peace Establishment of the United States," *United States Statutes at Large,* chap. 299, 14 Stat. 39 (July 28, 1866), 333.

27. *PUSG,* 16:21; Utley, *Frontier Regulars,* 11.

28. William T. Sherman to John Sherman, January 8, 1867, in Thorndike, *Correspondence,* 288.

29. Sefton, *United States Army and Reconstruction,* 66.

30. William T. Sherman to John Sherman, February 23, 1866, in Thorndike, *Sherman Letters,* 264–265.

31. Sefton, *United States Army and Reconstruction,* 65.

32. The opening of the Powder River route to the Montana goldfields required the army to deploy to the Great Plains, a region to which they had never devoted a substantial military presence in the decades before the Civil War. Between 1865 and 1870, for example, soldiers built seven military installations in what is now Wyoming: Phil Reno (1865), Kearny (1866), Sanders (1866), D. A. Russell (1867), Fetterman (1867), Fred Steele (1868), and Augur (1869). Though many were temporary or abandoned pursuant to the 1868 Treaty of Fort Laramie, they represented the need to provide some protection to overland traffic on the central and northern Plains.

33. "Proposed Reduction of the Military Establishment, Sea-Coast Fortifications, and National Foundries and Arsenals," 43rd Cong., 1st Sess., 12.

34. Leckie, *Buffalo Soldiers,* 11.

35. Lang, *In the Wake of War,* 206–209; Grant quoted in Nash, *Andrew Johnson,* 59.

36. *Congressional Globe,* 39th Cong., 1st Sess. (June 5, 1866), 2973–2974. Apparently names like Grant, Sheridan, Sherman, and Thomas meant little to the first-term congressman.

37. Rosseau served one year in the territory known better as "Seward's Folly" before returning to the continental United States to command the perpetually unruly Department of Louisiana until his death in 1869. See "Rosseau, Lovell Harrison (1818–1869)," *Biographical Directory of the United States Congress,* https://bioguide.congress.gov/search/bio/R000468.

38. *Congressional Globe,* 39th Cong., 1st Sess. (June 19, 1866), 3271.

39. Ibid., 3272. Le Blond fundamentally disagreed with Woodbridge, insisting that the people of the South were "crippled" and posed no military threat to the reconstruction processes then under way.

40. This was likely just a personal quirk of Woodbridge. Congress had demonstrated intense interest in the Southwest immediately after the Civil War ended. It sent an official congressional delegation, headed by James R. Doolittle, a Republican senator from Wisconsin, to inquire into the condition of the Native nations in the region, and it set aside $15,000 from the treasury to fund the survey. See White, *Chronicle of a Congressional Journey.*

41. "Annual Report of the Secretary of War," 39th Cong., 2nd Sess., 22. A few years later, Sherman referred to New Mexico as "a damned ugly elephant," claiming that the United States was saddled with feeding and maintaining "its mongrel population forever," in a ready indication of the racism that pervaded his judgments. See Athearn, *William Tecumseh Sherman,* 206.

42. *New York Tribune,* June 6, 1866.

43. *New York Herald,* April 22, 1866

44. *Vermont Chronicle,* May 12, 1866.

45. *North American,* May 10, 1866.

46. *North American,* March 21, 1866.

47. The paper's editor, Henry Jarvis Raymond, was a Republican. He supported Andrew Johnson in the aftermath of the Civil War, however, until the Swing Around the Circle campaign put him firmly back in the Republican ranks. The editorials appeared in February 1866, five months prior to the Swing Around the Circle and during Raymond's pro-Johnson period. Raymond also opposed Johnson's impeachment. See Holzer, *Lincoln and the Power of the Press,* 555.

48. *New York Times,* February 15, 1866.

49. Simpson, *Reconstruction Presidents.* By 1867 "most congressional Republicans were no longer willing to work with Johnson" (112).

50. Summers, *Ordeal of the Reunion,* chap. 5. Summers notes that the New Orleans massacre in the summer of 1866 also helped to convince Republicans of the need for further intervention in the South (95–97).

51. *Congressional Globe,* 39th Cong., 2nd Sess. (February 15, 1867), 1367.

52. Ibid., 1368.

53. The Bureau of Indian Affairs had been transferred from the War Department to the Interior Department in 1849.

54. *Congressional Globe,* 39th Cong., 2nd Sess. (February 22, 1867), 1717.

55. Ibid., 1718. California Democrat James A. McDougall concurred with Howard, despite his status as a western representative, proclaiming that "a lieutenant or captain commanding a post thinks his business is, if he sees a band of Indians, to order out his men booted and saddled;

and as soon as he can approach them to draw and strike and slay and slaughter" (1719). Historian Gregory Downs has noted that in the late 1860s, "wariness of the military was stronger in the West." Downs, *After Appomattox*, 131–133.

56. As Banks's biographer James G. Hollandsworth points out, many professional soldiers loathed Banks because he received a high rank in the volunteer service due to his political connections but refused to cooperate with professional soldiers to improve his own abilities. See Hollandsworth, *Pretense of Glory*, 51–52.

57. *Appendix to the Congressional Globe*, 39th Cong., 2nd Sess., 175.

58. See Trefousse, *Andrew Johnson*, 289–290.

59. Sheridan, *Personal Memoirs of P. H. Sheridan*, 2:279–280; Grant letter at 277.

60. "If it be asked whether the creation of such a tribunal within a State is warranted as a measure of war, the question immediately presents itself, whether we are still engaged in war," Johnson wrote in his veto message. "The country has entered or is returning to a state of peace and industry, and the rebellion is in fact at an end. The measure, therefore, seems to be as inconsistent with the actual condition of the country as it is at variance with the Constitution of the United States." Andrew Johnson, "Veto of the Freedman's Bureau Bill," in McPherson, *Political History*, 68.

61. Throughout 1866 and 1867, Grant became "uncomfortable with the trend of Johnson's Reconstruction policy" and committed himself to helping congressional Republicans pursue their strategies for bringing order to the defeated South. See Waugh, *U. S. Grant*, 115.

62. Bensel, *Yankee Leviathan*, 345.

63. For two recent studies of the political and social impetus for the formation of postbellum paramilitary organizations in the white South, see Parsons, *Ku-Klux*, and Broomall, *Private Confederacies*.

64. Singletary, *Negro Militia and Reconstruction*, 617.

65. Bradley, *Army and Reconstruction*, 31.

66. *Congressional Globe*, 39th Cong., 2nd Sess. (February 26, 1867), 1849.

67. Doolittle, quoted by Carl Schurz to Mrs. Schurz, September 4, 1867, in Bancroft, *Speeches, Correspondence and Political Papers of Carl Schurz*, 1:437.

68. Doolittle's geographic sense, meanwhile, indicated that he did not consider the army in the West to be the same as the army of occupation in the South.

69. *Congressional Globe*, 40th Cong., 2nd Sess. (February 21, 1868), 1316; 2nd Sess. (May 25, 1868), 2561. Johnson signed the bill on June 6; 2nd Sess., 2901.

70. *Congressional Globe*, 40th Cong., 2nd Sess. (March 21, 1868), 2032.

71. Ibid., 2030.

72. Croushore and Potter, *Union Officer in the Reconstruction*, 6.

73. Alvord, Semi-annual Report on Schools for Freedmen, 8.

74. Howell C. Flournoy to C. C. Sibley, October 5, 1868, in Records of the Assistant Commissioner for the State of Georgia, Bureau of Refugees, Freedmen, and Abandoned Lands, 1865–1869, transcribed by the Smithsonian, https://transcription.si.edu/view/47544/NMAAHC-007676431_00100.

75. See West, *Contested Plains,* for a narrative of the consequences of the Colorado gold rush for Native communities and the environment of the Great Plains.

76. Sherman, quoted in Athearn, "Montana Volunteers of 1867," 128.

77. "Annual Report of the Secretary of War," 40th Cong., 3rd Sess., 1.

78. *Congressional Globe,* 40th Cong., 2nd Sess. (April 8, 1868), 2269, and (March 21, 1868), 2033.

79. See 40th Cong., 2nd Sess. (March 21, 1868), 2037 (Charles R. Buckalew), and 2034 (Thomas A. Hendricks).

80. Downs, *After Appomattox,* 242. By the 1880s, the professional army realized that a public campaign for greater support would likely fail. In response, the institution looked inward and developed a series of professional schools for army officers, such as the Cavalry School at Fort Leavenworth. If average Americans did not understand or appreciate what soldiers did, they would have little interest in supporting the institution. By placing an emphasis on formal military training and joining a multitude of other professions in advocating higher education and career training, officers launched a movement for professionalization within the army. Leading military officers aimed to use the movement to raise the reputation of the military in the public's mind. See Reardon, *Soldiers and Scholars.*

81. *Appendix to the Congressional Globe,* 42nd Cong., 2nd Sess., 720–722.

82. Richmond, Virginia's, *Daily Dispatch* of February 23, 1870, offered a southern perspective. In a brief note, the editors speculated that the reductions would need to be far greater to please the most ardent Republican economizers. "The military are below par with the philanthropists," the editors explained, noting that the federal government had "sung a different song with their 'On to Richmond!'" The comment suggested that some in the South felt that the federal government used the army differently in their region than it did elsewhere in the country.

83. For a more detailed discussion of Logan's theories, see Weigley, *Towards an American Army,* 127–136.

84. *Appendix to the Congressional Globe,* 41st Cong., 2nd Sess., 147–148, 154.

85. For both Logan and Shanks, see *Congressional Globe,* 41st Cong., 2nd Sess. (March 10, 1870), 1849.

86. *Appendix to the Congressional Globe,* 41st Cong., 2nd Sess., 154.

87. *Congressional Globe,* 41st Cong., 2nd Sess. (March 10, 1870), 1851.

88. Ulysses S. Grant to Henry Wilson, January 12, 1866, *PUSG,* 16:21.

89. By 1903, 212 West Point graduates had become presidents, superintendents, or chief engineers of railroads across the country. United States Military Academy, *Centennial of the United States Military Academy at West Point,* 847. Many former Confederates, such as Edward Porter Alexander and Thomas Rosser, who had been trained at West Point but could not return to the postbellum army, also pursued railroad careers.

90. *Congressional Globe,* 41st Cong., 2nd Sess. (March 10, 1870), 1850–1851.

91. *Chicago Tribune,* March 20, 1870; *Advocate of Peace,* April 1870.

92. *Congressional Globe,* 41st Cong., 2nd Sess. (March 10, 1870), 1851.

93. Williams, "Readiness for War," 239.

Interlude: The General

1. From 1819 to 1879 the War Department was housed in what came to be called the Northwest Executive Building, a two-story brick office with an Ionic portico facing Pennsylvania Avenue. Edwin Stanton added two additional stories during the Civil War. When Sherman returned to Washington after his Saint Louis sojourn, in 1876, he helped to oversee the transition from the original War Department offices to the new State, War, and Navy department building commissioned by Congress in 1870. The War and Navy departments moved into a portion of the new building in 1879. By the end of World War I, the army had again outgrown its home. In 1938, the department moved its headquarters from the State, War, and Navy Building next to the White House to the Munitions Building next to the Reflecting Pool, and then divided its workforce between the Munitions Building and the present-day Harry S. Truman Building in Foggy Bottom, now home to the State Department. Growing pains struck again and the federal government, realizing it owned large tracts along the Potomac River waterfront, acquired during the Civil War when the Union Army seized the Custis–Lee mansion and Arlington estate of the family of Confederate general Robert E. Lee, began construction on the Pentagon, which was designated the headquarters for the consolidated Department of Defense in 1947. In other words, save for rebuilding in the aftermath of the burning of Washington during the War of 1812, the United States Army grew so little in the nineteenth century that only one new office building was required, while the well-supported and -funded twentieth-century national fighting force got three upgrades.

2. See Cushman, *General's Civil War*, 20.

3. Marszalek, *Sherman*, 423–428.

4. Sherman also appeared before the Joint Committee on the Conduct of the War to discuss his handling of the surrender. Stanton publicly criticized Sherman in the *New York Times*. See Fellman, *Citizen Sherman*, 248–250.

5. Sherman, *Memoirs*, 2:454.

6. Proceedings of the Senate Sitting for the Trial of William W. Belknap.

7. White, *American Ulysses*, 566–570.

8. Sherman to Pope, April 24, 1876, William Tecumseh Sherman Papers, Library of Congress.

5. Western Military Challenges, 1865–1872

1. *Omaha Weekly Herald*, November 10, 1865.

2. Athearn, *William Tecumseh Sherman*, 43; Pueblo incident, 78.

3. Downs and Masur, *World the Civil War Made*, 1.

4. Scholars making broader claims about the Civil War's relationship to the West complain of a tendency to view the war "from vantage points along the Eastern seaboard." Arenson, "Introduction," in *Civil War Wests*, ed. Arenson and Graybill, 2. See also West, "Reconstructing Race," 6–26, which has proposed the idea of "Greater Reconstruction." Hämäläinen, "Reconstructing the Great Plains," 481–509, also links the ideals regarding freedom and citizenship at the center of Reconstruction to the postbellum West, as has Smith, *Freedom's Frontier*.

5. "Annual Report of the Secretary of War," 40th Cong., 2nd Sess., 36–37.

6. Wooster, *United States Army and the Making of America,* 207.

7. Downs and Masur, *World the Civil War Made,* 6–7.

8. "Annual Report of the Secretary of War," 40th Cong., 2nd Sess., 36.

9. See Silver, *Our Savage Neighbors,* for an explanation of how Europeans powers identified Indian nations as their common enemy during the Seven Years' War, laying a foundation for the religious, racial, and ethnic intolerance that would define the Indian wars that followed the creation of the United States. See also Grenier, *First Way of War;* Starkey, *European and Native American Warfare.*

10. Monnett, *Eyewitness to the Fetterman Fight,* 32, 35.

11. Coffman, *Old Army,* 171.

12. By the end of 1865, the army had managed to return 801,000 (77 percent) of the 1,034,064 soldiers present at the war's end to the pursuits of peace.

13. Algernon Badger to Dear Father, September 8, 1865, Algernon Badger Family Papers, 1813–1900, box 1, Louisiana Research Collection, Howard–Tilton Library, Tulane University, New Orleans.

14. For the better part of 1865 to 1866, however, volunteer troops were used to garrison many installations across the former Confederacy while they awaited their opportunity to muster out of service. Based on what was occurring in the South, western officers had some reason to expect they could use volunteer troops in their geographic departments.

15. Monnett, *Where a Hundred Soldiers Were Killed,* 9.

16. Instead of the projected 4,500 men, Dodge received 2,500, which he could only muster by stripping soldiers from their duty protecting overland travelers along the Platte River route. Hafen and Hafen, *Powder River Campaigns and Sawyer Expedition of 1865,* 22.

17. In Texas, Brigadier General James W. Forsyth reported that when he arrived in camp at Alexandria, robbery, plundering, and murder were daily occurrences and that almost the entire division of volunteers retained in service was in open mutiny. The enlisted men did almost as they pleased. Some deserted, took their horses, and formed guerilla bands, while others rode around the area dressed, Forsyth reported, inappropriately for the time and place. "Annual Report of the Secretary of War," 39th Cong., 2nd Sess., H. Ex. Doc. No. 1, 46.

18. *Powder River Campaigns and Sawyer Expedition of 1865,* 38–39.

19. Ibid., 55.

20. Transcript of the diary of Isaac B. Pennick, typed, bound, and owned by E. A. Brininstool, 69–70.

21. "Annual Report of the Secretary of War," 39th Cong., 2nd Sess., 19.

22. *PUSG,* 16:581–582 notes.

23. Ibid., 16:580–581 note. Sherman was correct about the white population of New Mexico, which declined from 93,516 in 1860 to 91,874 in 1870.

24. Sherman's assumptions drew on a long-established pattern of rhetoric that portrayed Indigenous communities as incapable of creating, building, or sustaining societies that rivaled, in influence or importance, those created by Europeans. Thomas Jefferson, for example, rejected "any notion that Indian cultures might have created 'monuments' worthy of comparison to those of Greek and Roman antiquity." Jefferson, "Notes on the State of Virginia," in *Thomas*

Jefferson: Writings, ed. Peterson, 218–232. Nineteenth-century Americans believed strongly in the idea that the Indigenous nations they encountered were not capable of constructing structures such as the burial mounds of the Ohio River valley or the cliff dwellings of the American Southwest. The societies that possessed those skills, they believed, had vanished and been replaced by the culturally inferior Natives with whom they had greater familiarity. In William Cullen Bryant's 1832 poem, "The Prairies," for example, the poet described the earthworks encountered by white settlers who moved into the Trans-Allegheny West in the late eighteenth century. Bryant wrote of "the mighty mounds / That overlook the rivers, or that rise / In the dim forest crowded with old oaks, / Answer. A race, that long has passed away, / Built them." In Bryant's telling, the vanished race was a peaceful farming people that was wiped out by "the red man . . . The roaming hunter tribes." Sayre, "Mound Builders," 226; Bryant, "The Prairies," in *American Poetry: The Nineteenth Century,* ed. Hollander, 1:163.

25. Nieto-Phillips, *Language of Blood,* 16–17.

26. "Reduction of the Military Establishment," 43rd Cong., 1st Sess., H. Rep. 384, 5.

27. See, for example, Dippie, *Vanishing American.* This is the pervasive myth-making that scholars such as Cothran, *Remembering the Modoc War,* argue helped to facilitate a nonviolent narrative of Western progress that allowed nineteenth-century Americans to maintain a fiction of innocence and excuse their culpability in the violence that accompanied white settlement of sovereign Native land. See also Jacoby, *Shadows at Dawn;* and, for the founding era, Taylor, *William Cooper's Town,* especially Taylor's discussion of the works of James Fenimore Cooper.

28. *PUSG,* 16:413.

29. *Army and Navy Journal,* January 6 and January 20, 1866.

30. "Annual Report of the Secretary of War," 39th Cong., 2nd Sess., 20; William T. Sherman to John Sherman, February 23, 1866, in *Sherman Letters,* ed. Thorndike, 264–265.

31. "Annual Report of the Secretary of War," 40th Cong., 2nd Sess., 60.

32. "Annual Report of the Secretary of War, 40th Cong., 3rd Sess., x (Grant), 1 (Sherman), 17 (Sheridan), 34 (Terry).

33. "Annual Report of the Secretary of War," 39th Cong., 2nd Sess., 43.

34. McAlexander, *History of the Thirteenth Regiment,* 74.

35. A. L. Hough to U. G. McAlexander, n.d., in *History of the Thirteenth Regiment,* ed. McAlexander, 73. "Conversation was apt to run," Hough further recalled, "rather upon the marches and battles of the Civil War, with men from the Western armies comparing notes with those who had fought on the Potomac, than upon the details of daily garrison life" (76).

36. Much of the difference between the two conflicts had to do with the size and mobility of the military forces. More critically, however, as Robert Utley explains, "The Army as an institution never evolved a doctrine of Indian warfare." Because no course of instruction to distinguish between conventional and unconventional warfare was ever instituted at West Point, Utley concluded that "lacking a formal doctrine of unconventional war, the Army waged conventional war." Utley, *Indian Frontier,* 166–167. While the army implemented some consistent strategies in its Indian war campaigning, as detailed by Jamieson, *Crossing the Deadly Ground,* the training of recruits in terms of drilling and of officers in terms of tactics did not evolve drastically from the antebellum manuals. Because so many of the army's leading officers

viewed the Indians wars as a temporary duty, they did not value the development of a doctrine to fight them, nor did they invest heavily in training their troops to do so. Wooster, *Military and United States Indian Policy,* 213.

37. Grandstaff, "Preserving the Habits and Usages of War," 521–545.

38. "Annual Report of the Secretary of War," 42nd Cong., 1st Sess., 4, 16–17, 22, 24, 27, 29–33, 41, 43–44.

39. "Annual Report of the Secretary of War," 42nd Cong., 2nd Sess., 44.

40. McChristian, *Regular Army O!,* 400.

41. Oliva, *Fort Union.*

42. "Annual Report of the Secretary of War," 42nd Cong., 2nd Sess., 7.

43. *Army and Navy Journal,* February 19, 1870.

44. "Annual Report of the Secretary of War," 39th Cong., 2nd Sess., 23, 30.

45. Monnett, *Where a Hundred Soldiers Were Killed.* Carrington's first wife, Margaret Irvin Carrington, recalled the controversy over the battle in her memoir, *Absaraka: Home of the Crows.* According to historian Robert A. Murray, Colonel Carrington edited and rewrote large portions of *Absaraka* to improve his own image and defend his conduct in the aftermath of the 1866 Fetterman Fight. See Murray, *Army on the Powder River.* Carrington spent much of his retirement defending his failure to send troops to Fetterman's aid or to better protect his post against Indian attacks, often citing lack of resources—when he was not working on maligning Fetterman's character.

46. Utley, *Frontier Regulars,* 128.

47. "Annual Report of the Secretary of War," 39th Cong., 2nd Sess., 23.

48. Hämäläinen, *Lakota America,* 293.

49. A little more than six months after the treaty at Fort Laramie, troops under the command of George Custer attacked Black Kettle's Southern Cheyenne camp on the Washita River in present-day Oklahoma, killing perhaps as many as 150 men, women, and children. Though Red Cloud had achieved a notable victory earlier that year, it is important to note that the vast geography occupied by the army could mean defeat in one sector and military dominance in another. The unevenness of military operations is a reminder of the uncoordinated ways in which federal power could be expressed in the West. For more on the events at Washita, see Brill, *Custer, Black Kettle, and the Fight on the Washita;* and Greene, *Washita.* Paul Andrew Hutton uses the Washita campaign to illustrate the ethos of total war pursued by Phil Sheridan in postbellum Indian campaigns.

50. Sherman to C. C. Augur, May 6, 1867, Adjutant General's Office, folder no. 286W.1867, RG 94, National Archives, Washington, DC.

51. Simpson, "Lincoln and His Political Generals," 63–77.

52. Athearn, "Montana Volunteers of 1867," 136.

53. John R. Pulliam to Governor J. W. Throckmorton, September 13, 1866, copied in Walter Prescott Webb Papers, 1857–1966, box 2M277, folder Research Notes: Indians, Briscoe Center for American History, University of Texas, Austin.

54. Scott, "'Whiskey Is the Enemy Most Formidable,'" 36.

55. "House Journal of the Legislative Assembly of the Territory of Colorado," 38–39.

56. For the report of the Sand Creek Commission, see 39th Cong., 2nd Sess., S. Ex. Doc. No. 96.

57. W. T. Sherman to G. P. Ihrie, June 8, 1867, in House Journal of the Legislative Assembly of the Territory of Colorado, Seventh Session, 39.

58. *Army and Navy Journal,* June 15, 1867.

59. *PUSG,* 17:147.

60. *Ibid.,* 16:579.

61. See, for example, *Montana Post,* May 11, 1867.

62. See the report of Alfred Terry, "Annual Report of the Secretary of War," 40th Cong., 2nd Sess., 49–53.

63. *Montana Post,* November 9, 1867.

64. "Annual Report of the Secretary of War," 40th Cong., 2nd Sess., 33.

65. Leforge, *Memoirs of a White Crow Indian,* 19. Leforge, also known as Thomas Marquis, lived among the Crow Indians for much of his adult life and served as an Indian scout through the 1870s. He was with Alfred Terry's column during the campaign that ended at the Battle of the Little Bighorn.

66. Athearn, "General Sherman and the Montana Frontier," 56.

67. "Montana War Claims," 43rd Cong., 2nd Sess., H. Ex. Doc. No. 9.

68. Athearn, "Montana Volunteers of 1867," 128, 133–134.

69. Thane, "The Montana 'Indian War' of 1867," 153.

70. *PUSG,* 16:321.

71. Special Order No. 105, July 30, 1867, reprinted in *Congressional Record,* 51st Cong., 1st Sess. (June 28, 1890), 6718.

72. Colonel Charles Griffin to Governor E. M. Pease, September 12, 1867, copied in Walter Prescott Webb Papers, 1857–1966, box 2M277, folder Research Notes: Indians, Briscoe Center for American History, University of Texas, Austin.

73. "Annual Report of the Secretary of War," 39th Cong., 2nd Sess., 48.

74. *PUSG,* 16:326, 461.

75. Quasi Rangers had patrolled most of West Texas during the Civil War, helping to provide some protection to the remote region. When Confederate forces surrendered, however, these units were disbanded along with other Confederate home guards and militias. See Smith, *Frontier Defense in the Civil War.*

76. *Daily Journal,* July 26 and August 12, 1870.

77. *Galveston News,* March 18, 1873.

78. McConnell, *Five Years a Cavalryman,* 212–213.

79. Richter, *Army in Texas during Reconstruction,* 26.

80. "Annual Report of the Secretary of War," 42nd Cong., 2nd Sess., 3–5.

81. Ibid., 9.

82. Wooster, *Fort Davis.* From Fort Buford in Dakota Territory in 1874, an infantry soldier described his fellow recruits living predictable and mundane lives. Soldiers visited the post

library, three to six men undertook guard duty, mule teams were sent to bring in the mail, hunting parties left to pursue supplemental food for the post, others milled flour or cleaned the post corral. On an especially disagreeable day, some enlisted men were assigned to clean the garden of an officer, but they ended the day playing a game of baseball. The soldier even received a copy of George Armstrong Custer's *My Life on the Plains* and eagerly read the volume. "Fort Buford Diary of Private Sanford, 1876–1877," ed. Hill and Innis, 2–39. See also Hedren, *Fort Laramie in 1876;* and Buecker, *Fort Robinson and the American West.*

83. Rickey, *Forty Miles a Day on Beans and Hay,* 88.

84. Ibid., 24.

85. "Annual Report of the Secretary of War," 39th Cong., 2nd Sess., 959.

Conclusion: Custer's Last Beer

1. Maclean, *Norman Maclean Reader,* 56.

2. The question of disobedience centers on whether General Alfred Terry's orders specifically required Custer and Colonel John Gibbon to link forces on June 26, 1876. If there is any consensus in Little Bighorn historiography, it is in the belief that the two commands were to unite, as Terry explained in his report following the campaign: "Lieutenant-Colonel Custer should keep still further to the south before turning toward that river [the Little Bighorn] . . . in order, by a longer march, to give time for Colonel Gibbon's column to come up." See copy of Alfred Terry's November 21, 1876, report to the Secretary of War in Brady, *Indian Fights and Fighters,* 225. Athearn, *High Country Empire,* affirms that because of "his [Custer's] supreme eagerness to win additional military fame he neglected to consider the magnitude of the enemy's forces" (118–119). Utley, *Cavalier in Buckskin,* contends that Custer, suffering from his recent humiliation at the hands of President Grant, rushed into battle, disobeying orders and losing to a superior Indian force.

3. Warren, *Buffalo Bill's America,* 137.

4. Matheson, *Westerns and War Films of John Ford,* 147.

5. On July 1, the cover of *Harper's* carried a Thomas Nast cartoon complaining of the corruption of Boss Tweed and the Tammany Hall politicians running Samuel Tilden as the Democratic nominee for president. July 8 featured a cover depicting Rutherford Hayes and the Republican platform. Both issues featured multipage supplements with illustrations of the Centennial International Exhibition at Fairmount Park in Philadelphia, as well as portraits of the signers of the Declaration of Independence. The cover for July 15 depicted a somber patriot draped in an early American flag, accompanied by an extensive editorial recounting the nation's first century.

6. Wooster, *Military and United States Indian Policy,* 86.

7. *Congressional Record,* 44th Cong., 1st Sess. (July 15, 1876), 4628.

8. *Congressional Record,* 44th Cong., 1st Sess. (July 8, 1876), 4477.

9. Janney, *Remembering the Civil War,* 6.

10. *Congressional Record,* 44th Cong., 1st Sess. (July 8, 1876), 4477.

11. Roosevelt, *Winning of the West,* 3:233.

12. See Bederman, *Manliness and Civilization,* esp. chap. 5.

13. Federal coffers experienced minimal strain as the national treasury began to pay out benefits for the regular army veterans of the nation's Indian wars. From 1893 to 1916, the federal government paid $13,790,298 in Indian war pensions. Of this total, $4,918,870 went to survivors and $8,871,428 to widows. The number of pensioners peaked in 1896, with nearly seven thousand widows and veterans on the rolls. By 1916, the number fell to 2,500. In comparison, in 1896 there were nearly 1 million Civil War pensions, for survivors and dependents, being paid at a total cost of $142,212,080. The number decreased only slightly by 1916, to 709,000 pensions at a greater cost than in 1896, $160,811,812, due to an increase in the rates for Civil War survivors. In 1866, just one year after the Civil War's conclusion, pensions paid to veterans and widows totaled $15,857,714—more than the amount paid to Indian wars veterans over a period of nearly twenty-five years. Glasson, *Federal Military Pensions,* 114–115.

14. George Baird, "Winter Campaign in Montana and its Results," 22:437.

BIBLIOGRAPHY

Manuscript Materials

Briscoe Center for American History (Austin, Texas)

    Earl Alonzo Brininstool Collection, 1850–1945

    Fort Duncan Records, 1857–1861

    James Webb Throckmorton Papers, 1838–1888

    Journal of Ebenezer Hanna, February 10 to March 27, 1862

    Robert Simpson Neighbors Papers, 1838–1935

    Walter Prescott Webb Papers, 1857–1966

The Filson Historical Society (Louisville, Kentucky)

    Don Carlos Buell Papers

    Edward R. S. Canby Papers, 1837–1873

    James W. Earl Collection

Henry E. Huntington Library (San Marino, California)

    The Alice Blackwood Baldwin Letter Collection, 1869–1885

    George H. Derby Correspondence, 1850–1859

    George H. Pettis Collection

    H. W. M. Merrill Collection, 1833–1897

    Kinzie Bates Papers, 1863–1929

Library of Congress

    DeButts-Ely Collection of Lee Family Papers

    Edwin McMasters Stanton Papers

    Lyman Trumbull Papers

    Phillip H. Sheridan Papers

    William C. Church Papers

    William Tecumseh Sherman Papers

    Zachariah Chandler Papers

Small Special Collections Library (Charlottesville, Virginia)
  Nau Civil War Collection
  Thomas L. Rosser Collection
Southern Methodist University–DeGolyer Library (Dallas, Texas)
  Captain Nathaniel S. Wheeler Papers
  Celeste Willard and Charlotte Willard Correspondence
  Letters of William Jackson Palmer
  Pamphlet Collection
  Robert Bruce Papers
State Historical Society of North Dakota (Bismarck)
  John Victor Bean Papers
Western History Collections, University of Oklahoma (Norman, Oklahoma)
  Alan Farley Collection of Kansas and Oklahoma History, and the US Civil War
  Diary of Isaac B. Pennick, Company I, 11th Kansas Cavalry on the Wind River
    Expedition of 1865
  Edward Everett Dale Collection of Western History and Oklahoma History
  James B. Denver Collection
  Norman Brillhart Collection on Indian Wars in the Trans-Mississippi West and
    General George Armstrong Custer

Newspapers

Advocate of Peace
The Army and Navy Journal
The Baltimore Sun
The Boston Globe
The Boston Post
The Buffalo Daily Republic
The Burlington Free Press
The Caledonian
The Carolina Spartan
The Cavalry Journal
Charleston Standard
Chicago Democratic Press
The Chicago Tribune
The Cincinnati Commercial Advertiser
The Cincinnati Gazette
The Cincinnati Inquirer
The Continental Monthly

Daily American Organ

The Daily Journal

Daily National Intelligencer

The Dearborn Independent

Detroit Free Press

The Detroit Post

The Emporia News

Frank Leslie's Illustrated Newspaper

Galveston News

The Garland Globe

Harper's Weekly

The Hillsdale Standard

The Hydraulic Press

Indianapolis Daily Sentinel

Journal of the Military Service Institution of the United States

Knoxville Chronicle

Milwaukee Daily Sentinel

Mobile Commercial Register

Montana Post

The Morning Oregonian

National Anti-Slavery Standard

New Haven Daily Palladium

New York Herald

The New York Times

North American

Rocky Mountain News

St. Paul Press

San Antonio Weekly Herald

Texas State Gazette

The Union

Vermont Chronicle

Watertown Republican

The Weekly Arizonian

Western Democrat

Winners of the West

The Woods County Reporter

Yankton Dakotan

Government Documents
Appendix to the Congressional Globe
Asher C. Hinds, Hinds' Precedents of the House of Representatives of the United States
Biographical Directory of the United States Congress
Congressional Globe
Congressional Record

Serial Set
"Annual Report of Board of Indian Commissioners," 41st Cong., 3rd Sess., S. Exec. Doc. No. 39.

"Annual Report of Captain A. A. Humphreys, Topographical Engineers, in Charge of Office of Explorations and Surveys, War Department, December 1858." Washington, DC, 1859.

"Annual Report of the Secretary of War," 31st Cong., 1st Sess., H. Exec. Doc. No. 1.

"Annual Report of the Secretary of War," 36th Cong., 2nd Sess., H. Exec. Doc. No. 1.

"Annual Report of the Secretary of War," 37th Cong., 1st Sess., S. Exec. Doc. No. 1.

"Annual Report of the Secretary of War," 39th Cong., 2nd Sess., H. Exec. Doc. No. 1.

"Annual Report of the Secretary of War," 40th Cong., 2nd Sess., H. Exec. Doc. No. 1.

"Annual Report of the Secretary of War," 40th Cong., 3rd Sess., H. Exec. Doc. No. 1.

"Annual Report of the Secretary of War," 42nd Cong., 1st Sess., H. Exec. Doc. No. 1.

"Annual Report of the Secretary of War," 42nd Cong., 2nd Sess., H. Exec. Doc. No. 1, Pt. 2.

"Bill to Pension Survivors of Certain Indian Wars," 59th Cong., 1st Sess., H. Rep. No. 4104.

"Documents from War Department," 27th Cong., 1st Sess., H. Doc. No. 2.

"Franklin Pierce to the Senate of the United States, August 4, 1856," 34th Cong., 1st sess., Sen. Exec. Doc. 97.

"Increase and Better Organization of the Army," 33rd Cong., 2nd Sess., H. Rep. No. 40.

"Indians in the Northwest," 37th Congress, 3rd Session, Exec. Doc. No. 68.

"Military Roads—Kansas," 33rd Cong., 2nd Sess., H. Rep. No. 36.

"New Mexico and California," 30th Cong. 1st Sess. H. Exec. Doc. No. 76.

"Notes of a military reconnaissance . . ." 30th Cong., 1st Sess., H. Exec. Doc. 41.

"Pensions for Indian War Veterans," 62nd Cong., 3rd Sess., H. Rep. No. 1417.

"Pensions for Survivors of Certain Indian Wars," 63rd Cong., 2nd Sess., H. Exec. Doc. No. 973.

"Pensions—Indian Wars," 72nd Cong., 1st Sess., H. Rep. No. 8976.

"Proposed Reduction of the Military Establishment, Sea-Coast Fortifications, and National Foundries and Arsenals," 43rd Cong., 1st Sess.

"Reduction of the Military Establishment," 43rd Cong., 1st Sess., H. Rep. 384.

"Reorganization of the Army," 45th Cong., 2nd Sess., H. Misc. Doc. No. 56.

"Report of the Joint Committee on the Conduct of the War," 37th Cong., 3rd Sess., Rep. Comm. No. 106.

"Report of the Peace Commission," 40th Cong., 2nd Sess., H. Exec. Doc. No. 97.

"Report of the Sand Creek Commission," 38th Cong., 2nd Sess., S. Exec. Doc. No. 96.

"Report of the Select Committee on the Pacific Railroad and Telegraph," 34th Cong., 1st Sess., H. Rep. No. 358.

"Route from Fort Smith to Santa Fe," 31st Cong., 1st sess., H. Exec. Doc. 45, ser. 577.

"Slavery in the Territory of New Mexico," 36th Cong., 1st Sess., H. Rep. No. 508.

"Transfer of the Indian Bureau," 39th Cong., 2nd Sess., H. Exec. Doc., No. 23.

Primary Sources

Adams, Lois Bryan. *Letter from Washington, 1863–1865*. Detroit, MI: Wayne State University Press, 1999.

Adjutant General's Office. *Chronological List of Actions, &c with Indians from January 15, 1837, to January 1891*. Fort Collins, CO: Old Army Press, 1977.

Alexander, Edward Porter. *Fighting for the Confederacy: The Personal Recollections of General Edward Porter Alexander*. Ed. Gary W. Gallagher. Chapel Hill: University of North Carolina Press, 1989.

Alvord, J. W. *Semi-annual Report on Schools for Freedmen*. Washington, DC: U.S. Government Printing Office, 1867.

Baird, George. "A Winter Campaign in Montana and its Results," in *Personal Narratives of Events in the War of the Rebellion: Addresses Delivered Before the Commandery of the State of New York*. 4 vols. Rhode Island Soldiers and Sailors Historical Society, 1891–1912. Reprinted in *Military Order of the Loyal Legion of the United States*. 66 vols. Wilmington, NC: Broadfoot, 1991–1997.

Baldwin, Alice Blackwood. *An Army Wife on the Frontier: The Memoirs of Alice Blackwood Baldwin*. Ed. Robert C. Carriker and Eleanor Carriker. Salt Lake City: University of Utah Library, 1975.

Bancroft, Frederic, ed. *Speeches, Correspondence and Political Papers of Carl Schurz*. 6 vols. New York: G. P. Putnam's Sons, 1913.

Barnes, Thurlow Weed, ed. *Memoir of Thurlow Weed*. 2 vols. Boston: Houghton, Mifflin, 1884.

Beale, Howard K, ed. *The Diary of Edward Bates, 1859–1866*. Washington, DC: U.S. Government Printing Office, 1933.

The Boston Slave Riot, and Trial of Anthony Burns. Boston: Fetridge, 1854.

Brill, Charles J. *Custer, Black Kettle, and the Fight on the Washita*. 1938; repr. Norman, OK: Red River Books, 2002.

Byrne, P. E. *Soldiers of the Plains*. New York: J. J. Little and Ives Company, 1926.

Cairnes, John E. *The Slave Power: Its Character, Career, and Probable Designs.* 1862; repr., Columbia: University of South Carolina Press, 2003.

Carrington, Margaret Irvin. *Absaraka: Home of the Crows.* 1879; repr., Lincoln: University of Nebraska Press, 1983.

Carter, Susan B., Scott Sigmund Gartner, Michael R. Haines, Alan L. Olmstead, Richard Sutch, and Gavin Wright, eds. *Historical Statistics of the United States: Millennial Edition.* New York: Cambridge University Press, 2006.

Chase, Salmon P. *Inside Lincoln's Cabinet: The Civil War Diaries of Salmon P. Chase.* New York: Longmans, Green, 1954.

Channing, William E. *Slavery.* Boston: James Munroe, 1835.

Cogley, Thomas S. *History of the Seventh Indiana Cavalry Volunteers.* Dayton, OH: Morningside Press, 1991.

Croushore, James H., and David M. Potter, eds. *A Union Officer in the Reconstruction.* New Haven, CT: Yale University Press, 1948.

Custer, Elizabeth Bacon. *Boots and Saddles, or Life in Dakota with General Custer.* New York: Harper Brothers, 1885.

———. *Following the Guidon.* 1890; repr., University of Oklahoma Press, 1966.

———. *Tenting on the Plains, Or General Custer in Kansas and Texas.* New York: Webster's, 1887.

Custer, George Armstrong. *My Life on the Plains.* 1952; repr., Lincoln, NE: Bison Books, 1966.

Davis, Jefferson. *Jefferson Davis, Constitutionalist: His Letters, Papers, and Speeches.* 10 vols. Ed. Dunbar Roland. New York: J. J. Little and Ives, 1923.

———. *The Papers of Jefferson Davis.* 14 vols. Ed. Haskell M. Monroe and others. Baton Rouge: Louisiana State University Press, 1971–2015.

Doubleday, Abner. *My Life in the Old Army: The Reminiscences of Abner Doubleday.* Ed. Joseph E. Chance. Fort Worth: Texas Christian University Press, 1998.

Douglass, Frederick. *The Frederick Douglass Papers. Series One: Speeches, Debates, and Interviews.* 5 vols. Ed. John Blassingame. New Haven, CT: Yale University Press, 1979–1992.

———. *My Bondage and My Freedom.* New York: Penguin, 2003.

Eckert, Edward K., and Nicholas J. Amato, eds. *Ten Years in the Saddle: The Memoir of William Woods Averell, 1851–1862.* San Rafael, CA: Presidio Press, 1978.

Elder, Jane Lenz, and David J. Weber, eds. *Trading in Santa Fe: John M. Kingsbury's Correspondence with James Josiah Webb, 1853–1861.* Dallas, TX: Southern Methodist University Press, 1996.

Ellet, Charles. *Military Incapacity and What It Costs the Country.* New York: Ross and Tousey, 1862.

Ewell, Richard Stoddert. *The Letters of General Richard S. Ewell: Stonewall's Succes-sor.* Ed. Donald C. Pfanz. Knoxville: University of Tennessee Press, 2012.

———. *The Making of a Soldier: Letters of General R. S. Ewell.* Ed. Percy Gatling Hamlin. Richmond, VA: Whittet and Shepperson, 1935.

Frazer, Robert W., ed. *Mansfield on the Condition of Western Forts, 1853–54.* Norman: University of Oklahoma Press, 1963.

Giddings, Joshua R. *The Exiles of Florida: Or, the Crimes Committed By Our Government Against the Maroons, Who Fled from South Carolina, and Other Slave States, Seeking Protection under Spanish Laws.* Columbus, OH: Follett, Foster, 1858.

Gienapp, William E., and Erica L. Gienapp, eds. *The Civil War Diary of Gideon Welles: Lincoln's Secretary of the Navy.* Urbana: University of Illinois Press, 2014.

Glasson, William Henry. *Federal Military Pensions in the United States.* New York: Oxford University Press, 1918.

Grant, Ulysses S. *The Papers of Ulysses S. Grant.* 32 vols. Ed. John Y. Simon and others. Carbondale: Southern Illinois University Press, 1967–2012.

———. *Personal Memoirs of U. S. Grant.* 2 vols. New York: C.L. Webster, 1886.

Grimké, Charlotte Forten. *The Journals of Charlotte Forten Grimké.* Ed. Brenda Stevenson. New York: Oxford University Press, 1988.

Hafen, LeRoy R., and Ann W. Hafen, eds. *Powder River Campaigns and Sawyer Expedition of 1865: A Documentary Account Comprising Official Reports, Diaries, Contemporary Newspaper Accounts, and Personal Narratives.* Glendale, CA: Arthur H. Clark, 1961.

Halleck, H. Wager. *Elements of Military Art and Science: or, Course of Instruction in Strategy, Fortification, Tactics of Battles, &c.; Embracing the Duties of Staff, Infantry, Cavalry, Artillery, and Engineers. Adapted to the Use of Volunteers and Militia.* New York: D. Appleton, 1846.

Hancock, Almira Russell. *Reminiscences of Winfield Scott Hancock.* New York: Charles L. Webster, 1887.

Heitman, Francis P. *Historical Register and Dictionary of the United States Army: From Its Organization, September 29, 1789, to March 2, 1903.* 2 vols. Washington, DC: U.S. Government Printing Office, 1903.

Higginson, Thomas Wentworth. "Massachusetts in Mourning: A Sermon, Preached in Worcester, on Sunday, June 4, 1854." Boston: James Munroe, 1854.

Holloway, John N. *History of Kansas: From the First Exploration of the Mississippi Valley, to Its Admission into the Union: Embracing a Concise Sketch of Louisiana; American Slavery, and Its Onward March; the Conflict of Free and Slave Labor in the Settlement of Kansas, and the Overthrow of the Latter, with All Other Items of General Interest.* Lafayette, IN: James, Emmons, 1868.

Hood, John Bell. *Advance and Retreat: Personal Experiences in the United States and Confederate Armies.* New Orleans: G. T. Beauregard, 1880.

House Journal of the Legislative Assembly of the Territory of Colorado: Seventh Session. Central City, CO: David C. Collier, Register Office, 1868.

Howard, William A., John Sherman, and Mordecai Oliver. *Committee of Three, Appointed by the House of Representatives to Investigate Troubles in Territory of Kansas.* Washington, DC: U.S. Government Printing Office, 1856.

Johnson, Robert Underwood, and Clarence Clough Buell, eds. *Battles and Leaders of the Civil War.* 4 vols. Edison, NJ: Castle, 1995.

Johnson, R. W. *A Soldier's Reminiscences in Peace and War.* Philadelphia: J. B. Lippincott, 1886.

Johnston, William Preston. *The Life of General Albert Sidney Johnston: His Service in the Armies of the United States, the Republic of Texas, and the Confederate States.* New York: D. Appleton and Company, 1879.

Julian, George Washington. *Speeches on Political Questions, 1850–1868.* New York: Hurd and Houghton, 1872.

Leforge, Thomas H. *Memoirs of a White Crow Indian (Thomas H. Leforge) as Told by Thomas B. Marquis.* 1928; repr. Lincoln: University of Nebraska Press, 1974.

Lesley, Lewis Burt, ed. *Uncle Sam's Camels: The Journey of May Humphreys Stacey Supplemented by the Report of Edward Fitzgerald Beale, 1857–1858.* Cambridge, MA: Harvard University Press, 1929.

Lincoln, Abraham. *The Collected Works of Abraham Lincoln.* 9 vols. Ed. Roy P. Basler and others. New Brunswick, NJ: Rutgers University Press, 1953.

Logan, John A. *The Volunteer Soldier of America.* Chicago: R. S. Peale and Company, 1887.

"Madison Debates, June 29." Avalon Project, Lillian Goldman Law Library, Yale Law School. https://avalon.law.yale.edu/subject_menus/debcont.asp.

McAlexander, U. G. *History of the Thirteenth Regiment, United States Infantry.* Regimental Press, 13th Infantry, 1905.

McConnell, H. H. *Five Years a Cavalryman: Or, Sketches of Regular Army Life on the Texas Frontier, Twenty Odd Years Ago.* Jacksboro, TX: J. N. Rogers, 1889.

McPherson, Edward. *The Political History of the United States of America, during the Period of Reconstruction.* Washington, DC: Philp and Solomons, 1871.

Military Order of the Loyal Legion of the United States. 66 vols. Wilmington, NC: Broadfoot, 1992.

Mormoniad. Boston: A. Williams, 1858.

Nicolay, John G., and John Hay. *Abraham Lincoln: A History.* 10 vols. New York: Century, 1890.

OR [US War Department]. *The War of the Rebellion: A Compilation of the Official Records of the Union and Confederate Armies*. 127 vols., index and atlas. Washington, DC: U.S. Government Printing Office, 1880–1901.

Palmer, Beverly Wilson, and Holly Byers Ochoa, eds. *The Selected Papers of Thaddeus Stevens*. 2 vols. Pittsburgh: University of Pittsburgh Press, 1998.

Peterson, Merrill. *Thomas Jefferson: Writings*. New York: Library of America, 1984.

Phisterer, Frederick. *Statistical Record of the Armies of the United States*. New York: Charles Scribner's Sons, 1883.

Price, George F. *Across the Continent with the Fifth Cavalry*. New York: D. Van Nostrand, 1883.

Proceedings of the Senate Sitting for the Trial of William W. Belknap, Late Secretary of War, on the Articles of Impeachment Exhibited by the House of Representatives. Washington, DC: U.S. Government Printing Office, 1876.

Report of the Joint Committee on the Conduct of the War. Washington, DC: U.S. Government Printing Office, 1865.

Roosevelt, Theodore. *The Winning of the West*. Vol. 3. New York: G. P. Putnam's Sons, 1894.

Sears, Stephen W., ed. *The Civil War Papers of George B. McClellan: Selected Correspondence, 1860–1865*. New York: Ticknor and Fields, 1989.

Sedgwick, John. *Correspondence of John Sedgwick: Major-General*. 2 vols. 1902–3; repr., Baltimore: Butternut and Blue, 1999.

Seward, Frederick W. *Seward at Washington as Senator and Secretary of State*. New York: Derby and Miller, 1891.

Seward, William H. *The Slaveholding Class Dominant in the Republic: Speech of William H. Seward at Detroit, October 2, 1856*. Washington, DC: Republican Association of Washington, 1857.

———. *Speech of Hon. William H. Seward for the Immediate Admission of Kansas into the Union; Delivered in the Senate of the United States, April 9, 1856*. Washington: Congressional Globe Printing Office, 1856.

Sherman, John. *Recollections of Forty Years in the House, Senate and Cabinet*. 2 vols. Chicago: Werner, 1895.

Sherman, William Tecumseh. *Memoirs of General W. T. Sherman*. 2 vols. New York: D. Appleton, 1889.

———. *The Sherman Letters*. Ed. Rachel Sherman Thorndike. New York: Charles Scribner's Sons, 1894.

Stevenson, Brenda, ed. *The Journals of Charlotte Forten Grimké*. New York: Oxford University Press, 1988.

Sumner, Charles. *The Crime against Kansas*. Boston: John P. Jewett, 1856.

Thoreau, Henry David. *Essays: A Fully Annotated Edition*. Ed. Jeffrey S. Cramer. New Haven, CT: Yale University Press, 2013.

Transactions of the Kansas State Historical Society, Embracing the Fifth and Sixth Biennial Reports, 1886–1888. Vol. 4. Comp. F. G. Adams. Topeka: Kansas Publishing House, 1890.

United States Statutes at Large, Treaties, and Proclamations of the United States of America. Boston: Little, Brown, 1866.

Upton, Emory. *The Military Policy of the United States*. Washington, DC: U.S. Government Printing Office, 1904.

Young, Joshua. *God Greater than Man: A Sermon Preached June 11 after the Rendition of Anthony Burns*. Burlington, VT: Samuel B. Nichols, 1854.

Secondary Sources

Articles

Athearn, Robert G. "General Sherman and the Montana Frontier." *Montana Magazine of History* 3, no. 1 (January 1953): 55–64.

———."The Montana Volunteers of 1867." *Pacific Historical Review* 19, no. 2 (May 1950): 127–136.

Blair, William. "The Use of Military Force to Protect the Gains of Reconstruction." *Civil War History* 51, no. 4 (December 2005): 388–402.

Breeden, James O. "Health of Early Texas: The Military Frontier." *Southwestern Historical Quarterly* 80, no. 4 (April 1977): 357–398.

Cotterill, R. S. "Memphis Railroad Convention, 1849." *Tennessee Historical Magazine* 4, no. 2 (June 1918): 83–94.

Cunliffe, Marcus. "Soldiers and Politicians in the American Civil War." *American Studies in Scandinavia* 2, no. 1 (March 1969): 1–10.

Ericson, David F. "The United States Military, State Development, and Slavery in the Early Republic." *Studies in American Political Development* 31 (April 2017): 130–148.

Hämäläinen, Pekka. "Reconstructing the Great Plains: The Long Struggle for Sovereignty and Dominance in the Heart of the Continent." *Journal of the Civil War Era* 6, no. 4 (2016): 481–509.

Hill, Michael D., and Ben Innis, eds. "The Fort Buford Diary of Private Sanford, 1876–1877." *North Dakota History* 52 (Summer 1985): 12–13.

Isenberg, Andrew C., and Thomas Richards Jr. "Alternative Wests: Rethinking Manifest Destiny." *Pacific Historical Review* 86, no. 1 (2017): 4–17.

Jacobs, Margaret D. "Genocide or Ethnic Cleansing? Are These Our Only Choices?" *Western Historical Quarterly* 47, no. 4 (Winter 2016): 444–448.

Kelly, Patrick J. "The North American Crisis of the 1860s." *Journal of the Civil War Era* 2, no. 3 (September 2012): 337–368.

Lurie, Shira. "Liberty Poles and the Fight for Popular Politics in the Early Republic." *Journal of the Early Republic* 28, no. 4 (Winter 2018): 673–697.

Murray, Robert A. "The Hazen Inspections." *Montana: The Magazine of Western History* 18, no. 1 (Winter 1968): 24–33.

Ostler, Jeffrey, and Karl Jacoby. "After 1776: Native Nations, Settler Colonialism, and the Meaning of America." *Journal of Genocide Research* 24, no. 2: 321–336.

Paine, Sarah C. M. "Centuries of Security: Chinese, Russian and U.S. Continental versus Maritime Approaches." *Journal of Military History* 86, no. 4 (October 2022): 813–836.

Pfanz, Harry W. "The Surrender Negotiations Between General Johnston and General Sherman, April 1865." *Military Affairs* 16, no. 2 (Summer 1952): 61–70.

Rafuse, John L. "United States' Experience with Volunteer and Conscript Forces." In *Studies Prepared for the President's Commission on an All-Volunteer Armed Force*. Vol. 2. Washington, DC: U.S. Government Printing Office, 1970.

Ramsdell, Charles. "The Natural Limits of Slavery Expansion." *Southwestern Historical Quarterly* 33, no. 2 (October 1929): 151–171.

Rao, Gauthum. "The Federal 'Posse Comitatus' Doctrine: Slavery, Compulsion, and Statecraft in Mid-Nineteenth-Century America." *Law and History Review* 26, no. 1 (Spring 2008): 1–56.

Robinson, W. Stitt, ed. "The Kiowa and Comanche Campaign of 1860 as Recorded in the Personal Diary of Lt. J. E. B. Stuart." *Kansas History* 23, no. 4 (Winter 1957): 382–400.

Roland, Charles P., Richard C. Robbins, and Eliza Johnston. "The Diary of Eliza (Mrs. Albert Sidney) Johnston: The Second Cavalry Comes to Texas." *Southwestern Historical Quarterly* 60, no. 4 (1957): 463–500.

Sayre, Gordon M. "The Mound Builders and the Imagination of American Antiquity in Jefferson, Bartram, and Chateaubriand." *Early American Literature* 33, no. 3 (1998): 225–249.

Scott, Kim Allen. "'Whiskey Is the Enemy Most Formidable in This Campaign': Capt. Gustavus Cheyney Doane's Fight with Boredom and Vice during the Geronimo Pursuit." *Journal of Arizona History* 48, no. 1 (2007): 31–52.

Simpson, Brooks D. "Lincoln and His Political Generals." *Journal of the Abraham Lincoln Association* 21, no. 1 (Winter 2000): 63–77.

Smith, Thomas T. "US Army Combat Operations in the Indian Wars of Texas, 1849–1881." *Southwestern Historical Quarterly* 99, no. 4 (April 1996): 501–531.

St. John, Rachel. "The Unpredictable America of William Gwin: Expansion, Secession, and the Unstable Borders of Nineteenth-Century North America." *Journal of the Civil War Era* 6, no. 1 (March 2016): 56–84.

Tap, Bruce. "Inevitability, Masculinity, and the American Military Tradition: The Committee on the Conduct of the War Investigates the American Civil War." *American Nineteenth Century History* 5, no. 2 (January 2004): 19–46.

Teigrob, Robert. "Empire and Cultures of Militarism in Canada and the United States." *American Review of Canadian Studies* 43, no. 1 (Spring 2013): 30–48.

Thane, James L., Jr. "The Montana 'Indian War' of 1867." *Arizona and the West* 10, no. 2 (Summer 1968): 153–170.

Trauschweizer, Ingo. "On Militarism." *Journal of Military History* 76, no. 2 (April 2012): 507–543.

Williams, T. Harry. "The Attack on West Point during the Civil War." *Mississippi Valley Historical Review* 25, no. 4 (March 1939): 491–504.

Wolfe, Patrick. "Land, Labor, and Difference: Elementary Structures of Race." *American Historical Review* 106, no. 3 (June 2001): 466–905.

———. "Settler Colonialism and the Elimination of the Native." *Journal of Genocide Research* 8, no. 4 (December 2006): 387–409.

Wooster, Robert. "Fort Davis and the Antebellum Military Frontiers." *Montana: The Magazine of Western History* 56 (Spring 2006): 50–59.

Zander, Cecily N. "'Victory's Long Review': The Grand Review of Union Armies and the Meaning of the Civil War." *Civil War History* 66, no. 1 (March 2020): 45–77.

Monographs

Adams, Kevin. *Class and Race in the Frontier Army: Military Life in the West, 1870–1890.* Norman: University of Oklahoma Press, 2012.

Anderson, Gary Clayton. *Ethnic Cleansing and the Indian: The Crime That Should Haunt America.* Norman: University of Oklahoma Press, 2014.

Andrews, Thomas G. *Killing for Coal: America's Deadliest Labor War.* Cambridge, MA: Harvard University Press, 2010.

Arenson, Adam, and Andrew R. Graybill, eds. *Civil War Wests: Testing the Limits of the United States.* Berkeley: University of California Press, 2015.

Athearn, Robert G. *High Country Empire.* Lincoln: University of Nebraska Press, 1960.

———. *William Tecumseh Sherman and the Settlement of the West.* Norman: University of Oklahoma Press, 1956.

Ayers, Edward L. *The Thin Light of Freedom: The Civil War and Emancipation in the Heart of America.* New York: W. W. Norton, 2017.

Ayers, Edward L., Gary W. Gallagher, and Andrew J. Torget, eds. *Crucible of the Civil War: Virginia from Secession to Commemoration.* Charlottesville: University of Virginia Press, 2008.

Bacevich, Andrew J. *The New American Militarism: How Americans Are Seduced by War.* New York: Oxford University Press, 2013.

Barker, Gordon S. *The Imperfect Revolution: Anthony Burns and the Landscape of Race in America.* Kent, OH: Kent State University Press, 2010.

Bederman, Gail. *Manliness and Civilization: A Cultural History of Gender and Race in the United States, 1880–1917.* Chicago: University of Chicago Press, 1995.

Bensel, Richard. *Yankee Leviathan: The Origins of Central State Authority in America, 1859–1877.* Cambridge: Cambridge University Press, 1991.

Black, Megan. *The Global Interior: Mineral Frontiers and American Power.* Cambridge, MA: Harvard University Press, 2018.

Blackhawk, Ned. *Violence over the Land: Indians and Empires in the Early American West.* Cambridge, MA: Harvard University Press, 2008.

Blair, William A. *With Malice Toward Some: Treason and Loyalty in the Civil War Era.* Chapel Hill: University of North Carolina Press, 2014.

Bowes, John P. *Land Too Good for Indians: Northern Indian Removal.* Norman: University of Oklahoma Press, 2016.

Brady, Cyrus Townsend. *Indian Fights and Fighters.* 1903; repr. Lincoln: University of Nebraska Press, 1971.

Bradley, Mark L. *The Army and Reconstruction, 1865–1877.* Washington, DC: Center of Military History, 2015.

Brettle, Adrian. *Colossal Ambitions: Confederate Planning for a Post–Civil War World.* Charlottesville: University of Virginia Press, 2020.

Brooks, James F. *Captives and Cousins: Slavery, Kinship, and Community in the Southwest Borderlands.* Chapel Hill: University of North Carolina Press, 2002.

Bruce, Dickson D., Jr. *Violence and Culture in the Antebellum South.* Austin: University of Texas Press, 2013.

Bryan, William D. *The Price of Permanence: Nature and Business in the New South.* Athens: University of Georgia Press, 2018.

Buecker, Thomas R. *Fort Robinson and the American West, 1874–1899.* Lincoln: Nebraska State Historical Society, c1999.

Burge, Daniel. *A Failed Vision of Empire: The Collapse of Manifest Destiny, 1845–1872.* Lincoln: University of Nebraska Press, 2022.

Campbell, Stanley W. *The Slave Catchers: Enforcement of the Fugitive Slave Law, 1859–1860.* Chapel Hill: University of North Carolina Press, 1968.

Catton, Bruce. *This Hallowed Ground: The Story of the Union Side of the Civil War.* New York: Doubleday, 1956.

Coffman, Edward M. *The Old Army: A Portrait of the American Army in Peacetime, 1784–1898*. New York: Oxford University Press, 1986.

Commager, Henry Steele, Samuel Eliot Morison, and William Edward Leuchtenburg. *The Growth of the American Republic*. Vol. 1. New York: Oxford University Press, 1930.

Cothran, Boyd. *Remembering the Modoc War: Redemptive Violence and the Making of American Innocence*. Chapel Hill: University of North Carolina Press, 2014.

Cummings, Bruce. *Dominion from Sea to Sea: Pacific Ascendancy and American Power*. New Haven, CT: Yale University Press, 2009.

Cushman, Stephen. *The General's Civil War: What Their Memoirs Can Teach Us Today*. Chapel Hill: University of North Carolina Press, 2021.

Dawson, Joseph G. III. *Army Generals and Reconstruction Louisiana, 1862–1877*. Baton Rouge: Louisiana State University Press, 1982.

Dean, Adam Wesley. *An Agrarian Republic: Farming, Antislavery Politics, and Nature Parks in the Civil War Era*. Chapel Hill: University of North Carolina Press, 2015.

Deloria, Vine, Jr. *We Talk, You Listen: New Tribes, New Turf*. Lincoln, NE: Bison Books, 2007.

Dippie, Brian W. *The Vanishing American: White Attitudes and US Indian Policy*. Lawrence: University Press of Kansas, 1991.

Dobak, William A., and Thomas D. Phillips. *The Black Regulars, 1866–1898*. Norman: University of Oklahoma Press, 2001.

Downs, Gregory P. *After Appomattox: Military Occupation and the Ends of War*. Cambridge, MA: Harvard University Press, 2015.

Downs, Gregory P., and Kate Masur, eds. *The World the Civil War Made*. Chapel Hill: The University of North Carolina Press, 2015.

Elder, Robert. *Calhoun: American Heretic*. New York: Basic Books, 2021.

Faragher, John Mack, ed. *Rereading Frederick Jackson Turner "The Significance of the Frontier in American History," and Other Essays*. New Haven, CT: Yale University Press, 1998.

Fellman, Michael. *Citizen Sherman: A Life of William Tecumseh Sherman*. Lawrence: University Press of Kansas, 1995.

Foner, Eric. *Free Soil, Free Labor, Free Men: The Ideology of the Republican Party Before the Civil War*. New York: Oxford University Press, 1970.

——. *Reconstruction: America's Unfinished Revolution, 1863–1887*. New York: Harper and Row, 1988.

Ford, Lisa. *Settler Sovereignty: Jurisdiction and Indigenous People in America and Australia, 1788–1836*. Cambridge, MA: Harvard University Press, 2010.

Frazer, Robert W. *Forts of the West*. Norman: University of Oklahoma Press, 1965.

Freeman, Joanne B. *The Field of Blood: Congressional Violence in Antebellum America.* New York: Farrar, Straus and Giroux, 2018.

Fry, Zachary. *A Republic in the Ranks: Loyalty and Dissent in the Army of the Potomac.* Chapel Hill: University of North Carolina Press, 2020.

Furniss, Norman F. *Mormon Conflict: 1850–1859.* New Haven, CT: Yale University Press, 2005.

Gallagher, Gary W. *The Union War.* Cambridge, MA: Harvard University Press, 2011.

Gallagher, Gary W., and Stephen Cushman, eds. *Civil War Witnesses and Their Books: New Perspectives on Iconic Works.* Baton Rouge: Louisiana State University Press, 2021.

Genetin-Pilawa, Joseph C. *Crooked Paths to Allotment: The Fight over Federal Indian Policy after the Civil War.* Chapel Hill: University of North Carolina Press, 2012.

Gienapp, William E. *The Origins of the Republican Party, 1852–1856.* New York: Oxford University Press, 1987.

Gillette, William. *Retreat from Reconstruction, 1869–1879.* Baton Rouge: Louisiana State University Press, 1982.

Goetzmann, William H. *Army Exploration in the American West, 1803–1863.* New Haven, CT: Yale University Press, 1959.

González-Quiroga, and Miguel Ángel. *War and Peace on the Rio Grande Frontier, 1830–1880.* Norman: University of Oklahoma Press, 2020.

Gould, Eliga H. *The Persistence of Empire: British Political Culture in the Age of the American Revolution.* Chapel Hill: University of North Carolina Press, 2000.

Graybill, Andrew R. *Policing the Great Plains: Rangers, Mounties, and the North American Frontier, 1875–1910.* Lincoln: University of Nebraska Press, 2007.

Greenberg, Amy S. *Manifest Manhood and the Antebellum American Empire.* New York: Cambridge University Press, 2006.

Greene, Jerome A. *Washita: The US Army and the Southern Cheyennes, 1867–1869.* Norman: University of Oklahoma Press, 2004.

Grenier, John. *The First Way of War: American War Making on the Frontier, 1607–1814.* New York: Cambridge University Press, 2008.

Grimsley, Mark. *The Hard Hand of War: Union Military Policy toward Southern Civilians, 1861–1865.* New York: Cambridge University Press, 1995.

Grimsley, Mark, and Clifford J. Rodgers, eds. *Civilians in the Path of War.* Lincoln: University of Nebraska Press, 2002.

Hämäläinen, Pekka. *Lakota America: A New History of Indigenous Power.* New Haven, CT: Yale University Press, 2019.

Hedren, Paul L. *Fort Laramie in 1876: Chronicle of a Frontier Post at War.* Lincoln: University of Nebraska Press, 1988.

Hess, Earl J. *Civil War Infantry Tactics: Training, Combat, and Small-Unit Effectiveness*. Baton Rouge: Louisiana State University Press, 2015.

Hixson, Walter L. *American Settler Colonialism: A History*. New York: Palgrave Macmillan, 2013.

Hollander, John, ed. *American Poetry: The Nineteenth Century*. Vol. 1: *Philip Freneau to Walt Whitman*. New York: Library of America, 1993.

Hollandsworth, James G. *Pretense of Glory: The Life of General Nathaniel P. Banks*. Baton Rouge: Louisiana State University Press, 1998.

Holt, Michael. *The Rise and Fall of the American Whig Party: Jacksonian Politics and the Onset of the Civil War*. New York: Oxford University Press, 1999.

Holzer, Harold. *Lincoln and the Power of the Press: The War for Public Opinion*. New York: Simon and Schuster, 2014.

Hope, Ian C. *A Scientific Way of War: Antebellum Military Science, West Point, and the Origins of American Military Thought*. Lincoln: University of Nebraska Press, 2015.

Hsieh, Wayne Wei-siang. *West Pointers and the Civil War: The Old Army in War and Peace*. Chapel Hill: University of North Carolina Press, 2009.

Huntington, Samuel P. *The Soldier and the State: The Theory and Politics of Civil–Military Relations*. Cambridge, MA: Harvard University Press, 1952.

Hutton, Paul Andrew. *Philip Sheridan and His Army*. Lincoln: University of Nebraska Press, 1985.

Jacoby, Karl. *Shadows at Dawn: A Borderlands Massacre and the Violence of History*. New York: Penguin Press, 2008.

Jamieson, Perry D. *Crossing the Deadly Ground: United States Army Tactics, 1865–1899*. Tuscaloosa: University of Alabama Press, 2004.

Janney, Caroline E. *Remembering the Civil War: Reunion and the Limits of Reconciliation*. Chapel Hill: University of North Carolina Press, 2013.

Johnson, Walter. *River of Dark Dreams: Slavery and Empire in the Cotton Kingdom*. Cambridge, MA: Harvard University Press, 2013.

Karp, Matthew. *This Vast Southern Empire: Slaveholders at the Helm of American Foreign Policy*. Cambridge, MA: Harvard University Press, 2016.

Kelman, Ari. *A Misplaced Massacre: Struggling over the Memory of Sand Creek*. Cambridge, MA: Harvard University Press, 2013.

Kiser, William S. *Borderlands of Slavery: The Struggle over Captivity and Debt Peonage in the American Southwest*. Philadelphia: University of Pennsylvania Press, 2017.

Kohn, Richard H. *Eagle and Sword the Federalists and the Creation of the Military Establishment in America, 1783–1802*. New York: Macmillan, 1975.

Kohout, Amy. *Taking the Field: Soldiers, Nature, and Empire on American Frontiers.* Lincoln: University of Nebraska Press, 2023.

Krug, Mark K. *Lyman Trumbull: Conservative Radical.* New York: A. S. Branes, 1956.

LaFeber, Walter. *The New Empire: An Interpretation of American Expansion, 1860–1898.* Ithaca, NY: Cornell University Press, 1963.

Lahti, Janne. *Cultural Construction of Empire: The US Army in Arizona and New Mexico.* Lincoln: University of Nebraska Press, 2012.

Lang, Andrew F. *A Contest of Civilizations: Exposing the Crisis of American Exceptionalism in the Civil War Era.* Chapel Hill: University of North Carolina Press, 2021.

——. *In the Wake of War: Military Occupation, Emancipation, and Civil War America.* Baton Rouge: Louisiana State University Press, 2017.

Leckie, William H. *The Buffalo Soldiers: A Narrative of the Negro Cavalry in the West.* Norman: University of Oklahoma Press, 1967.

Limerick, Patricia Nelson. *The Legacy of Conquest: The Unbroken Past of the American West.* New York: Norton, 1987.

Lindsay, Brendan C. *Murder State: California's Native American Genocide, 1846–1873.* Lincoln: University of Nebraska Press, 2012.

Maclean, Norman. *The Norman Maclean Reader.* Ed. O. Alan Weltzein. Chicago: University of Chicago Press, 2008.

Madley, Benjamin. *An American Genocide: The United States and the California Indian Catastrophe, 1846–1873.* New Haven, CT: Yale University Press, 2016.

Matheson, Sue. *The Westerns and War Films of John Ford.* Lanham, MD: Rowman and Littlefield, 2016.

May, Robert E. *Manifest Destiny's Underworld: Filibustering in Antebellum America.* Chapel Hill: University of North Carolina Press, 2004.

Marvel, William. *Radical Sacrifice: The Rise and Ruin of Fitz John Porter.* Chapel Hill: University of North Carolina Press, 2021.

Marzsalek, John F. *Sherman: A Soldier's Passion for Order.* New York: Free Press, 1993.

McChristian, Douglas C. *Regular Army O!: Soldiering on the Western Frontier, 1865–1891.* Norman: University of Oklahoma Press, 2017.

McClay, Wilfred M. *The Masterless: Self and Society in Modern America.* Chapel Hill: University of North Carolina Press, 1994.

McPherson, James. *Battle Cry of Freedom: The Civil War Era.* New York: Oxford University Press 1988.

Millett, Allan R., Peter Maslowski, and William B. Feis. *For the Common Defense: A Military History of the United States from 1607 to 2012.* New York: Free Press, 2012.

Monnett, John H., ed. *Eyewitness to the Fetterman Fight: Indian Views*. Norman: University of Oklahoma Press 2017.

——. *Where a Hundred Soldiers Were Killed: The Struggle for the Powder River Country in 1866 and the Making of the Fetterman Myth*. Albuquerque: University of New Mexico Press, 2010.

Mullis, Troy R. *Peacekeeping on the Plains: Army Operations in Bleeding Kansas*. Columbus: University of Missouri Press, 2004.

Murray, Robert A. *The Army on the Powder River*. Bellevue, NE: Old Army Press, 1969.

Nash, Howard P., Jr. *Andrew Johnson: Congress and Reconstruction*. Rutherford, NJ: Farleigh Dickinson University Press, 1972.

Neely, Mark E., Jr. *The Civil War and the Limits of Destruction*. Cambridge, MA: Harvard University Press, 2007.

——. *The Union Divided: Party Conflict in the Civil War North*. Cambridge, MA: Harvard University Press, 2002.

Ness, George T., Jr. *The Regular Army on the Eve of the Civil War*. Baltimore, MD: Toomey Press, 1990.

Nevins, Allan. *Ordeal of the Union: Fruits of Manifest Destiny, 1847–1852*. New York: Charles Scribner's Sons, 1947.

Nichols, David A. *Lincoln and the Indians: Civil War Policy and Politics*. Columbia: University of Missouri Press, 1978.

Nieto-Phillips, John M. *The Language of Blood: The Making of Spanish-American Identity in New Mexico, 1880s–1930s*. Albuquerque: University of New Mexico Press, 2004.

O'Brien, Jean M. *Firsting and Lasting: Writing Indians Out of Existence in New England*. Minneapolis: University of Minnesota Press, 2010.

Oliva, Leo E. *Fort Union and the Frontier Army in the Southwest*. Santa Fe, NM: Division of History, National Park Service, 1993.

Onuf, Peter. *Jefferson's Empire: The Language of American Nationhood*. Charlottesville: University of Virginia Press, 2000.

Ostler, Jeffrey. *The Plains Sioux and US Colonialism from Lewis and Clark to Wounded Knee*. New York: Cambridge University Press, 2004.

——. *Surviving Genocide: Native Nations and the United States from the American Revolution to Bleeding Kansas*. New Haven, CT: Yale University Press, 2019.

Parks, Joseph H. *General Edmund Kirby Smith, CSA*. Baton Rouge: Louisiana State University Press, 1954.

Parsons, Elaine Frantz. *Ku-Klux: The Birth of the Klan during Reconstruction*. Chapel Hill: University of North Carolina Press, 2016.

Porte, Joel. *Emerson in His Journals*. Cambridge, MA: Belknap Press of Harvard University Press, 1982.

Potter, David. *The Impending Crisis, 1848–1861*. New York: Harper and Row, 1976.

Quigley, Paul. *Shifting Grounds: Nationalism and the American South, 1848–1865*. New York: Oxford University Press, 2010.

Reidy, Joseph P. *Illusions of Emancipation: The Pursuit of Freedom and Equality in the Twilight of Slavery*. Chapel Hill: University of North Carolina Press, 2019.

Reséndez, Andrés. *The Other Slavery: The Uncovered Story of Indian Enslavement in America*. Boston: Houghton Mifflin Harcourt, 2016.

Richards, Leonard L. *The Slave Power: The Free North and Southern Domination, 1780–1860*. Baton Rouge: Louisiana State University Press, 2000.

Richards, Thomas, Jr. *Breakaway Americas: The Unmanifest Future of the Jacksonian United States*. Baltimore: Johns Hopkins University Press, 2020.

Richardson, Heather Cox. *To Make Men Free: A History of the Republican Party*. New York: Basic Books, 2014.

Richter, William L. *The Army in Texas during Reconstruction, 1865–1870*. College Station: Texas A&M University Press, 1987.

Rickey, Don, Jr. *Forty Miles a Day on Beans and Hay: The Enlisted Soldier Fighting the Indian Wars*. Norman: University of Oklahoma Press, 1963.

Rister, Carl Coke. *Robert E. Lee in Texas*. 1946; repr., Norman: University of Oklahoma Press, 2004.

Robbins, William G. *Colony and Empire: The Capitalist Transformation of the American West*. Lawrence: University Press of Kansas, 1994.

Rudolph, Frederick. *The American College and University: A History*. Athens: University of Georgia Press, 1990.

Scharff, Virginia, ed. *Empire and Liberty: The Civil War and the West*. Berkeley: University of California Press, 2015.

Sears, Stephen W. *Lincoln's Lieutenants: The High Command of the Army of the Potomac*. New York: HarperCollins, 2017.

Sefton, James E. *The United States Army and Reconstruction, 1865–1877*. Baton Rouge: Louisiana State University Press, 1967.

Shannon, Fred Albert. *The Organization and Administration of the Union Army, 1861–1865*. Gloucester, MA: Peter Smith, 1965.

Simpson, Harold B. *Cry Comanche: The 2nd US Cavalry in Texas*. Hillsboro, TX: Hill Junior College Press, 1979.

Singletary, Otis. *Negro Militia and Reconstruction*. Austin: University of Texas Press, 1957.

Skelton, William B. *An American Profession of Arms: The Army Officer Corps, 1784–1861*. Lawrence: University Press of Kansas, 1982.

Skocpol, Theda. *Protecting Soldiers and Mothers: The Political Origins of Social Policy in the United States*. Cambridge, MA: Harvard University Press, 1992.

Skowronek, Stephen. *Building a New American State: The Expansion of National Administrative Capacities, 1877–1920.* New York: Cambridge University Press, 1982.

Slap, Andrew L. *The Doom of Reconstruction: The Liberal Republicans in the Civil War Era.* New York: Fordham University Press, 2010.

Slaughter, Thomas P. *The Whiskey Rebellion: Frontier Epilogue to the American Revolution.* New York: Oxford University Press, 1988.

Smith, Adam I. P. *No Party Now: Politics in the Civil War North.* New York: Oxford University Press, 2006.

Smith, David Paul. *Frontier Defense in the Civil War: Texas' Rangers and Rebels.* College Station: Texas A&M University Press, 1992.

Smith, Sherry L. *The View from Officers Row: Army Perceptions of Western Indians.* Tucson: University of Arizona Press, 1990.

Smith, Stacey L. *Freedom's Frontier: California and the Struggle over Unfree Labor, Emancipation, and Reconstruction.* Chapel Hill: University of North Carolina Press, 2015.

Stampp, Kenneth M. *The Imperiled Union: Essays on the Background of the Civil War.* New York: Oxford University Press, 1980.

Stanley, F. E. V. *Sumner: Major-General United States Army, 1897–1863.* Author, 1969.

Starkey, Armstrong. *European and Native American Warfare.* Norman: University of Oklahoma Press, 1998.

Summers, Mark Wahlgren. *The Ordeal of the Reunion: A New History of Reconstruction.* Chapel Hill: University of North Carolina Press, 2014.

Tap, Bruce. *Over Lincoln's Shoulder: The Committee on the Conduct of the War.* Lawrence: University Press of Kansas, 1998.

Taylor, Alan. *William Cooper's Town: Power and Persuasion on the Frontier of the Early American Republic.* New York: Knopf, 1995.

Trefousse, Hans L. *Andrew Johnson: A Biography.* New York: Norton, 1989.

——. *The Radical Republicans: Lincoln's Vanguard for Racial Justice.* New York: Alfred A. Knopf, 1969.

United States Military Academy. *The Centennial of the United States Military Academy at West Point, New York, 1802–1902.* Washington, DC: US Government Printing Office, 1904.

Utley, Robert M. *Cavalier in Buckskin: George Armstrong Custer and the Western Military Frontier.* Norman: University of Oklahoma Press, 1988.

——. *Custer and the Great Controversy: The Origin and Development of a Legend.* Los Angeles: Westernlore Press, 1962.

——. *Frontier Regulars: The United States Army and the Indian, 1866–1890.* New York: Macmillan, 1973.

———. *Frontiersmen in Blue: The United States Army and the Indian, 1848–1865.* New York: Macmillan, 1967.

———. *The Indian Frontier of the American West, 1846–1890.* Albuquerque: University of New Mexico Press, 1984.

Varon, Elizabeth R. *Disunion!: The Coming of the American Civil War, 1789–1859.* Chapel Hill: University of North Carolina Press, 2010.

Veracini, Lorenzo. *Settler Colonialism: A Theoretical Overview.* New York: Palgrave Macmillan, 2010.

Waite, Kevin. *West of Slavery: The Southern Dream of a Transcontinental Empire.* Chapel Hill: University of North Carolina Press, 2021.

Warren, Louis. *Buffalo Bill's America: William Cody and the Wild West Show.* New York: Knopf, 2005.

Waugh, Joan. *U. S. Grant: American Hero, American Myth.* Chapel Hill: University of North Carolina Press, 2009.

Webb, Walter Prescott. *The Great Plains.* 2nd ed. Lincoln: University of Nebraska Press, 2022.

Weigley, Russell F. *History of the United States Army.* New York: Macmillan, 1967.

———. *Towards an American Army: Military Thought from Washington to Marshall.* New York: Columbia University Press, 1962.

West, Elliott. *The Contested Plains: Indians, Goldseekers, and the Rush to Colorado.* Lawrence: University Press of Kansas, 1998.

White, Jonathan W. *Emancipation, the Union Army, and the Reelection of Abraham Lincoln.* Baton Rouge: Louisiana State University Press, 2014.

White, Lonnie J., ed. *Chronicle of a Congressional Journey: The Doolittle Committee in the Southwest, 1865.* Boulder, CO: Pruett, 1975.

White, Richard. *It's Your Misfortune and None of My Own: A New History of the American West.* Norman: University of Oklahoma Press, 1991.

———. *Railroaded: The Transcontinentals and the Making of Modern America.* New York: W. W. Norton, 2012.

———. *The Republic for Which It Stands: The United States during Reconstruction and the Gilded Age, 1865–1896.* New York: Oxford University Press, 2017.

White, Ronald C. *American Ulysses: A Life of Ulysses S. Grant.* New York: Random House, 2017.

Williams, T. Harry. *Lincoln and the Radicals.* 1969; repr., Madison: University of Wisconsin Press, 1941.

Wilson, Mark R. *The Business of Civil War: Military Mobilization and the State, 1861–1865.* Baltimore, MD: Johns Hopkins University Press, 2006.

Winders, Richard Bruce. *Mr. Polk's Army: The American Military Experience in the Mexican War.* College Station: Texas A&M University Press, 1997.

Wolnisty, Claire M. *A Different Manifest Destiny: US Southern Identity and Citizenship in Nineteenth-Century South America*. Lincoln: University of Nebraska Press, 2020.

Woods, Michael E. *Arguing until Doomsday: Stephen Douglas, Jefferson Davis, and the Struggle for American Democracy*. Chapel Hill: University of North Carolina Press, 2021.

Wooster, Robert. *Fort Davis: Outpost on the Texas Frontier*. Austin: Texas State Historical Association, 1994.

———. *The Military and United States Indian Policy, 1865–1903*. New Haven, CT: Yale University Press, 1988.

———. *The United States Army and the Making of America: From Confederation to Empire, 1775–1883*. Lawrence: University Press of Kansas, 2021.

Zvengrowski, Jeffrey. *Jefferson Davis, Napoleonic France, and the Nature of Confederate Ideology, 1815–1870*. Baton Rouge: Louisiana State University Press, 2020.

Dissertations

Adams, Francis Raymond, Jr. "An Annotated Edition of the Personal Letters of Robert E. Lee, April 1855–April 1861." PhD diss., University of Maryland, 1955.

Ammann, Lillian. "Jefferson Davis: Secretary of War." Master's thesis, University of Texas, Austin, 1935.

Inbody, Donald Stephen. "Grand Army of the Republic or Grand Army of the Republicans?: Political Party and Ideological Preferences of American Enlisted Personnel." PhD diss., University of Texas, Austin, 2009.

Pfanz, Harry W. "Soldiering in the South during the Reconstruction Period, 1865–1877." PhD diss., Ohio State University, 1958.

Williams, T. Harry. "The Committee on the Conduct of the War: A Study of Civil War Politics." PhD diss., University of Wisconsin, Madison, 1937.

INDEX

Maynard, Horace, 80–81, 192n27

McClellan, George B., 83–84, 87–89, 91–92, 95–97, 170; and the Joint Committee, 93–94, 196n84, 196n91

McClernand, John Alexander, 75–76

McConnell, H. H., 164

McDougall, James A., 85, 200n55

McPherson, James B., 85

Meade, George G., 119

Meagher, Thomas F., 159–61

Meigs, Montgomery C., 5, 22

Military Reconstruction Act, 116, 123

Merrill, H. W., 36–37

Mitchell, Robert B., 148

Montana (territory), 52, 118, 120, 130, 141, 145, 150, 159–61, 163, 170, 172, 199n32

Mormon War (1857–58), 64–67

Morrill, Justin S., 86

Morrill, Lot M., 123, 128–29, 131

Morrill Land Grant Act, 78, 117; as antiarmy legislation, 86–87, 193n48

National Capitol Building, 5–6, 69, 75, 77, 95, 101, 120, 172; renovations of, 22

Nebraska (territory), 19, 45, 52, 130, 142, 145, 161

Nebraska military units: First Cavalry, 146

Negley, James S., 134–35

Nelson, William, 83

New Mexico (territory), 19, 25, 27–29, 31–32, 36–38, 78, 118, 120, 127, 130, 147–48, 151–52, 158–59, 161, 187n4, 204n23; slaveholding and, 32–33, 34; and the regular army, 33–34

Oak Grove (battle), 95

Odell, Moses, 91, 195n72

Oregon, 19, 23, 28, 96, 118, 120; annexation of, 23; Oregon Trail, 55

Pacific Railway Act, 78–79

Paramilitary organizations, 127–28, 201n63

Pease, E. M., 162

Phillips, Wendell, 55

Pierce, Franklin, 14–15, 17–18, 24, 38–39, 41–43, 59–60, 62–64, 67; presidency of, 21–23, 183n17; and Kansas, 41, 53–85; comparisons to Oliver Cromwell, 62–63

Pomeroy, Samuel C., 108

Pope, John, 35, 94–96, 141, 146–47, 153, 160, 186n60; artesian well expedition, 36–38, 186n63

Porter, Fitz John, 83, 87

Pulliam, John R., 156

Reagan, Ronald, 169

Reconstruction, 1, 9–10, 35, 61–62, 64, 97, 105–6, 108, 114–19, 123–33, 135, 140–41, 143, 153, 170, 174; failure of, 4–5; use of the army in, 3, 104–5, 114, 116–17; Texas and, 161–66

Red Cloud (Oglala Lakota), 154–55

Remington, Frederick, 169, 173

Republican Party, 23, 38, 54, 57, 59, 62, 66–68, 72, 74–75, 104, 139, 162, 173–74, 180n25; as antislavery party, 3–4, 11, 45–46, 56, 192n27; origins of, 9, 23–24, 45; antimilitarism and, 5, 9–10, 17, 41, 43, 52, 58, 60–61, 64–65, 71, 129–30, 134–35, 141, 149, 174; and the regular army, 76–97, 119, 123–24, 149–50, 191n10; Radical wing of, 39, 69, 84, 71, 76, 94–95, 114–15, 117–18, 128–29, 131, 140, 142, 170; newspapers, 55, 63–64, 121–22 influence in the Union Army, 83, 193n38; and Lincoln, 90; and Reconstruction, 105–6, 107–8, 120, 123–24, 125–26, 129–30, 133–34, 143, 163; alliance with Democrats, 116–17, 120; and the American West, 123–24, 127, 144, 148, 170, 174

Roosevelt, Theodore, 173

Rousseau, Lovell H., 119–20

Runnels, H. R., 32

Sackett, D. B., 154

San Antonio, Texas, 28, 30–32, 163, 167

www.ingramcontent.com/pod-product-compliance
Lightning Source LLC
Chambersburg PA
CBHW020443100426

42812CB00036B/3438/J